See Malta
& Gozo

Inge Severin

a complete guide
with maps and
gazetteer

FORMAT

Acknowledgments

The author, who lives in Malta, would like to thank the following for their generous help in the preparation of this book:

Dr V. A. Depasquale, Librarian of the National Library; Fr. M. J. Zerafa, O.P., Curator of the National Museum of Fine Arts; Mr John Bezzina of the National Library; Chevalier Joseph Galea, Archivist

A special message of thanks is offered to Canon A. Zammit Gabarretta, Research Officer and Cataloguer of the National Library, for his personal interest and invaluable advice.

The author would also like to express her appreciation for all the practical assistance given by Mr Joseph Vassallo of the Malta Government Tourist Board.

Finally, a grateful acknowledgment to Mr Stewart Perowne, for his scrutiny of the manuscript.

Front cover photo: Grand Harbour, by Feature-Pix (Van Phillips)
Back cover: Gozo landscape
Front endpapers: Country scene near Rabat
Back endpapers: Liesse Hill, Valletta
Frontispiece: Tal Hlas church, near Zebbug

Photographs are by Paul Watkins with the following exceptions:
Malta Government Tourist Board: 15, 34, 99, 105, 106, 108, 110, 116/117; Malta Government Department of Information: 38/39, 86, 100/101, 127, 128, 137, 142 (top); Peter Baker: 71, 135; John Bethell: 11, 40 (top), 42; Mansell/Alinari: 41; David Wrightson (from 'Fortress' published by Lund Humphries): 60, 61, 82, 83, 92 (top), 118, 120, 141

Edited and with additional material by Paul Watkins

First published 1978
Revised editions 1979, 1984
© Paul Watkins 1978, 1979, 1984
Published by Format Books
23 Jeffreys Street London NW1

ISBN 0 903372 08 8 (hardback)
ISBN 0 903372 09 6 (paperback)

Filmsetting by Oliver Burridge & Co. Ltd. Crawley, Sussex
Printing by Artes Graficas Grijelmo s.a., Bilbao

In the same series

See Cyprus
by Paul Watkins

See Sicily
by Paul Watkins

See Madeira & the Canaries
by Annette Pink

Contents

6 Introduction
The island · The economy · The people

12 Malta in history

19 Practical information
Travel to Malta · Travel in Malta
Inclusive holidays · Accommodation
Food and Drink · Folk Art and Crafts
Festivals · Language · Climate · Beaches
Sports, Museums and Monuments
Currency and Banks · Shopping · Health
Police · Tourist information

30 Archaeology
Temples · Dolmens · Cart ruts · Rock tombs
Catacombs

34 Art and architecture
Churches · Fortifications · Watch towers
Villages · Domestic architecture
Decorative features · Artists

42 The Knights of St John

46 Plants and flowers Trees Cultivation
Wild life Maltese curiosities

50 Exploring Malta

56 Road map and itineraries

58 Gazetteer

133 Gozo

144 Bibliography

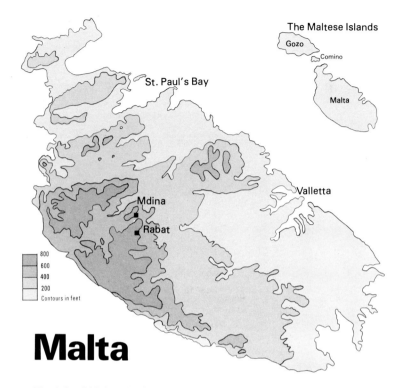

The Maltese Islands

Gozo

Comino

Malta

St. Paul's Bay

Valletta

Mdina

Rabat

800
600
400
200
Contours in feet

Malta

The island Malta, the largest island of the Maltese archipelago, lies in the heart of the Mediterranean. It has an area of only 95 square miles. The longest distance from north-west to south-east is about 17 miles, and the widest distance 9 miles. Yet for its size Malta has as rich a cultural heritage as any of its Mediterranean neighbours, dramatized by its unique megalithic temples, its complex fortifications—built largely by the Knights of St John—and its historic palaces and churches.

The correct origin of the island's name is debatable, the most likely contenders being *malat*, the Phoenician word for port of refuge, or *meli*, the Greek word for the honey for which the island was renowned (seen later in the Roman name for the island and its capital, *Melita*).

The island tilts from the sheer cliffs in the west to the bays and inlets— the drowned valleys—of the north and east. In the north, geological upheavals have created a number of fault lines, resulting in steep rocky ridges and fertile valleys. The major fault, which runs across the northern breadth of the island, forms the escarpment chosen as a natural line of defence by the British—the Victoria Lines. South of here the country rises and falls gently, always with a downward slope to the east.

The geological structure of the island is of great importance. It is roughly in the form of a sandwich with coralline limestone the 'bread' and the 'filling' a layer of golden globigerina limestone topped with blue clay and a thin layer of greensand. It was the availability of this coralline limestone, which can be fissured naturally into megalithic slabs, that enabled the Stone Age inhabitants to build their great temples. The soft globigerina, easy to quarry and carve (but hardening on exposure to the elements) was also used. It is this stone that has served as the island's principal building material since prehistoric times.

The blue clay is highly fertile. It is also impervious to water, and where the upper coralline limestone has eroded—notably in the northern valleys—there is plentiful grain, fruit and vegetable cultivation. Vines are also grown, mainly in the north, and flowering shrubs are found throughout the island. Except for the tenacious carob, however, Malta has very few trees: the result of wholesale felling in ancient times. An intensive afforestation programme is currently under way (see *Economy*).

Despite a rapid increase in population in the last hundred years, four-fifths of Malta is still rural. In the past the main settlements have been round Grand Harbour and in the little fortified city of Mdina, with lesser concentrations towards the centre of the island of inhabitants seeking protection from raiding corsairs in close-knit communities away from the coast. The larger settlements are now towns and the 19th century fishing villages have become tourist resorts, but the countryside has retained its essential character.

Low stone walls stretch endlessly across a gently rolling terrain: little terraced fields rise to the ridges in shallow steps, creating a pattern of white, ochre and brown. These are the bare colours of the summer months: the autumn rains change the patchwork to greens and richer browns and the spring brings the vivid hues of wild flowers. But always, winter and summer, the lasting impression is of bright blue, dark green and soft yellow—the sky, the carob tree and the building stone.

Scattered across the countryside are the cubic shapes of farmhouses, some isolated, some gathered into hamlets, and the small rustic churches built before the time of the Knights. This is the indigenous architecture of Malta, little changed since the time of the Phoenicians.

The Maltese landscape sets man against nature with dramatic effect. Magnificent Baroque churches tower over villages on a rural skyline, the forts and watch-towers of the Knights stand guard over the now peaceful coves, and their great fortifications encircle the deep waters of Grand Harbour. That so much of man's work is contained in so small an area increases its visual impact. Yet there is a unity, a feeling of continuity, for what is man-made is part of the island itself—stone laid on stone.

Cream or honey-coloured, deep yellow or glowing pink, the colour of the stone changes with the light. But its quality endures, and with it the image of Malta.

Dockyard, Grand Harbour, Valletta

The economy Since the merchant adventurers of ancient times first beached their craft on her shores, Malta's geographical position has been the most important factor in her economic progress. The Knights of St John held it as an outpost of Christendom, and endowed it lavishly with their wealth and fine architecture. The British in turn, having secured their base, supported the island's economy.

Grand Harbour, developed as a naval headquarters by the Knights, has become Malta's biggest commercial asset. It enabled the island to enjoy a boom period in the 19th century, first in entrepôt trade and then as a coaling station on the Imperial route to India. But strategic considerations shifted the emphasis to naval shipping, followed by the establishment of an air base. This had a distorting effect on the Maltese economy. By the late 1950's approximately two-thirds of all employees were working for the Government, the services or supporting industries. After the service run-down in 1958 energies had to be re-directed to new industries and the expansion of agriculture and tourism.

With the closure of the British military base in 1979, the loss of economic returns from the island's defence arrangements had to be balanced by an increase in her productive activities. Efforts have been concentrated on export-oriented goods and services, in particular manufactured goods, ship repair and shipbuilding, food production, tourism and freight services.

Dockyard With a labour force of 5000, the Malta Drydocks is the largest single employer in Malta. The five drydocks, Tanker Cleaning Installation, engineering shops and Yacht Yard make this former Royal Navy base one of the major shipyards in the Mediterranean. The yard's building range includes tankers, cargo vessels and floating docks, and docking facilities are available for the largest vessels in transit in the Mediterranean. A new ship-building yard at Marsa, in which a partnership with Libya has been secured, is also being constructed. All this is a long way from the first galley port of the Knights: but their presence remains in the great fortifications which tower over the modern yard.

Industry With State aid, industrial development is expanding. There are now over 200 enterprises covering a wide range of products, and a diversity of export markets is being explored.

The local handicraft industry is also flourishing. Craftware, including silver, brass, polished stone, glassware, lace and weaving, is of a very high standard and the visitor can be assured of getting value for money.

Tourism has a major role to play in Malta's economy. At present the island has more than 300,000 visitors every year, and resort development has been rapid, but without too many of the architectural abuses that typify similar developments elsewhere. Historical associations, and the use of English as a second language by the Maltese, offer obvious attractions to the British, who form the majority of visitors. Additionally, however, one should not forget the attractions of the Maltese people themselves, who with their charm and hospitality are the island's greatest asset.

Agriculture Industries born of the 20th century have inevitably reduced the significance of farming, a preoccupation of the islanders since the arrival of the first settlers. The farming community, however, still comprises one sixth of the population and agricultural development has a high priority. The problems for the Maltese farmer are in the climate, with its meagre rainfall and strong seasonal winds, and in the terrain, whose limitations will be obvious to the visitor who drives into the countryside and sees the small rocky fields terraced with laboriously built stone walls to conserve the thin covering of soil. Other problems are more of the farmers' own making: the small farming units, inherited through the generations, and the inevitable reluctance to abandon traditional methods.

Food production is now insufficient to meet the demands of both the home consumer and the expanding tourist trade. Only onions and potatoes can be exported in quantity, and many items such as fruit which could be grown in the island in greater quantity are being imported. The Government has plans for raising production with land reclamation and water collection projects, and by offering grants to farmers for improvements.

Afforestation Malta's lack of trees is almost proverbial, but the Government has recently undertaken a considerable afforestation programme. Thousands of semi-tropical trees and shrubs from Africa, Australia and southern Europe are being planted all over the island. The main object is to plant more trees for shade, to colonize bare rocky areas, and check soil erosion. The latter is a particularly serious problem in Malta. Rain, when it comes, is often of tropical intensity and the soil covering the sloping terrain is washed down into the sea. In the hot dry months, in a treeless environment, the precious field soil is swirled away by the summer winds.

Tree planting is being carried out on waste land, roadsides and public grounds. In particular the ditches and moats around the Knights' fortifications are being converted into sheltered citrus groves and leased to farmers. Given average rainfall Malta, deprived of tree cover since the Bronze Age, should within a decade be as green as other Mediterranean islands.

Water remains Malta's most precious resource. Rainfall averages 20 in. a year, and much of this is lost, running off the surface of the thick limestone crust which covers most of the island. The Department of Agriculture is trying to overcome the problem of water shortage by building covered tanks to collect rainwater off the streets, constructing dams and reservoirs in the valleys, repairing old communal village wells out of use for many years, and tapping underground water sources.

The people The population of Malta is approximately 300,000. The Maltese are a mixed Caucasian race stemming from the Phoenicians who colonized the islands in the 1st millenium BC. Their ancient language is mainly Semitic (a legacy from the Arabs who ruled Malta from 870–1090 AD) but with Phoenician origins. Later ingredients were from the Latin languages of the Middle Ages (Romance) and a sprinkling of English and Italian words.

Malta is one of the most devoutly Roman Catholic countries in the world. The many churches, often built with village funds and voluntary labour, are a matter for intense pride. Devoutly cared for and seldom empty, they are beautifully decorated for the festivals held in every town and village to celebrate the local Saint's day. This is an occasion for the renewal and strengthening of family ties, a time of devotional processions, and a time of festivity—of newly painted houses and illuminated streets, of bands, flags and fireworks.

For the Maltese the most venerated event in their history was the shipwreck of St Paul on their island in 60 AD. 'And when we had escaped, then we knew that the island was called Melita, but the barbarians showed us no small courtesy.'

Thus wrote St Luke, nearly two thousand years ago. What was true then is still true today, for generosity and friendliness are the keynotes of the Maltese character. And although essentially peace-loving, their courage and fortitude in two historic sieges four hundred years apart was a vital factor, at first in the successful defence of Christendom and subsequently in the defeat of the dark forces enslaving the free world.

The valour of the fighting men, and the steadfastness of the women during the Great Siege of 1565 is commemorated in the Archives of the Knights of St John. A recent parallel was the second great siege of the island, from 1940–42. On the outer wall of the great palace of the Grand Masters of the Order in Valletta are inscribed these words:

The Governor
Malta   Buckingham Palace

To honour her brave people I award the George Cross to the Island Fortress of Malta to bear witness to a Heroism and Devotion that will long be famous in History.

George R.I.

April 15th 1942

The emblem of the George Cross is now emblazoned on the red and white national flag of Malta.

Night procession on the feast of St Paul Shipwrecked, Valletta   11

Malta in history

Neolithic period (c. 3800–3200 BC) The first known inhabitants of the Maltese Islands probably came from Sicily. Their pottery found at *Ghar Dalam* (the type site from which the first Neolithic phase takes its name) bears a distinct resemblance to that of the Impressed ware from the Stentinello site near Syracuse in Sicily. Bones of domestic animals and carbonized grains of wheat and barley found at Skorba show that these people were farmers. The second Neolithic phase, *Grey Skorba* (c. 3600 BC) produced little change: the pottery, however, is of a grey colour and less decorated. The final, or *Red Skorba* phase (c. 3400 BC) is marked by a change in pottery colour to red with a monochrome finish. The foundations of a shrine of this period found at Skorba is the first indication of religion in the islands.

Temple Culture period (c. 3200–2000 BC) This is contemporary with the Copper Age in neighbouring Sicily, but so far no trace of copper has been found on the prehistoric sites in the Maltese Islands. Stone implements were used in the construction of the megalithic temples with obsidian imported from Lipari and Pantelleria.

Reaching its climax with the great temple complex at Tarxien, the Temple Culture period has been divided into phases (see table on p. 32) relating to the development of pottery and temple construction. The temple builders were a mysterious people. Their religious customs can only be surmised from their tombs and temples and the only hard evidence of their crafts lies in their pottery and the representation of woven material on their cult statues. Of their dwellings, only the traces of huts at Skorba have so far been discovered. That they were peaceable is shown by the absence of weapons.

The reason for the collapse of this civilization after more than a thousand years is unknown. There is no record of any invasion or new immigration during the period.

Bronze Age period (c. 2000–800 BC) Following the decline of the Temple Culture, Malta was colonized in turn by three groups of immigrants, probably from Italy, who brought with them implements of bronze. The first, the **Tarxien Cemetery** people, adapted the abandoned Tarxien temples to crematoria, levelling the floors with sand and enclosing the burnt remains of their dead together with funerary offerings in urns. The fate of this culture is unknown.

The second group was a warlike tribe, the *Borg-in-Nadur* people, who reached the island c. 1400 BC and lived in fortified villages on hill-tops. The bell-shaped storage chambers and the 'cart ruts' found all over the island probably date from the Borg-in-Nadur phase. A third group, the *Bahrija* people, settled on the uplands at Bahrija on the western coast c. 900 BC.

Phoenician and Carthaginian periods (c. 800–218 BC) The only material evidence of Phoenician settlement in Malta comes from their many tombs. By the 6th c. BC the Maltese Islands had passed into the hands of Carthage, and Punic culture was to last for many centuries. The Greek historian Diodorus Siculus, writing of Melita (Malta) in the 1st c. BC, refers to the skill of those 'who make linen webs, remarkable for their fineness and softness' and concludes 'it is a colony of the Phoenicians who, extending their commercial operations as far as the western ocean, found this a place of refuge, from the excellence of its harbours and its situation in the middle of the sea.'

Although the central Mediterranean was of vital interest to both the Carthaginians and the Greeks, there is no evidence of any Greek domination of the island. In 257 BC, during the First Punic War, the Romans captured Malta, then a Carthaginian naval base, devastating the countryside. Two years later the Carthaginians regained possession, but in 218 BC, in the Second Punic War, the Romans under the consul Tiberius Sempronius gained undisputed control.

Roman period (218 BC–318 AD) Vestiges of their occupation—the villa sites and the records of their city of Melita (Mdina) are evidence of the prosperity of the island's Roman overlords. It is doubtful, however, that this prosperity extended to the common people. Under the Romans the Maltese had the status of *socii*, which though allowing them to keep their own laws and elect their own magistrates maintained the overall authority of the Roman *propraetor* who held the highest civil offices, and the *quaestor* who had charge of the revenue.

Malta, part of the province of Sicily, suffered the same oppressive taxation by unscrupulous Roman officials. The most corrupt of these was the *praetor* Verres (73–71 BC) who, among his lesser crimes, pillaged the island of Malta. 'I do not ask now', said Cicero in his impeachment of Verres, 'whence you got those 400 jars of honey, or such quantities of Maltese cloth, or 50 cushions for sofas, or so many candelabra. What could you want with so many Maltese garments, as if you were going to dress all your friends' wives?'

Reforms carried out by Julius Caesar (d. 44 BC) and Augustus (27 BC–14 AD) did much to relieve suffering in the Roman provinces. Under Caesar there was a limited relief from taxation, and Augustus checked the abuses of the provincial governors' powers. Malta entered a period of prosperity and the island became famous for its honey, textile weaving (a skill of the Phoenicians) and sailcloth. The condition of the Maltese Islands was further improved under the Emperor Hadrian (117–138 AD) when Malta and Gozo were raised separately to the status of a Roman *municipium*. This entitled them to full Roman franchise and permitted them to send an ambassador to Rome.

In spite of 600 years of Roman rule, Malta was not Romanized. Roman manners and customs were undoubtedly adopted, but there was no ethnographical change and the language remained Punic. For the Maltese, the most important event was the shipwreck of St Paul on the island in 60 AD, described in the Acts as follows:

'And when they were escaped, then they knew that the island was called Melita.'

'And the barbarous people shewed us no little kindness: for they kindled a fire, and received us every one . . .'

The account goes on to relate how the Roman governor Publius gave the Apostle hospitality, and how Paul responded by curing his father of an illness. This miraculous cure was enough to secure Publius' conversion and with it the foundation of Christianity in Malta.

After three months St Paul sailed on to Rome, and Publius became the island's first bishop.

Byzantine period (318–870 AD) With the death of Constantine the Maltese Islands came into the possession of the Eastern Roman Empire and remained, as in Roman times, part of the province of Sicily. Little is known of this shadowy period. It is doubtful if the islands were ever occupied by the Vandals, then challenging the waning power of the Roman Empire in the Western Mediterranean.

Arab period (870–1090) Malta was taken from the Byzantines by the Arabs. Although little material evidence of their occupation remains, it was a period marked by cultural and economic changes. The language and place names of Malta are basically Arabic. The Arabs, expert farmers, brought their system of agriculture to the island and introduced cotton and citrus fruits.

It was a time of prosperity. A contemporary Arabic description of the islands, called by the names Malitah, Ghawdex and Chemmuna (by which the two last named are still known) describes the magnificence of the harbours, the abundance and excellence of the produce: 'It is an island rich in all the good things of God—a veritable land of blessings.' The Maltese had their own assembly or Gemgha, composed of Christians and Muslims under an Arab Hakem or governor. That the Arabs were tolerant rulers is shown by the survival of the Christian religion and the peaceful co-existence of former masters and subjects under the succeeding Normans.

Norman period (1090–1194) In 1090 Roger the Norman, following his conquest of Sicily, occupied Malta without bloodshed. Under his son Roger II, the first Norman king of Sicily, it became part of the Kingdom of Sicily.

The Christian religion was restored to the island and new churches built, including a cathedral at Mdina (since destroyed). As the conquered race, the Arabs were in no way persecuted and were allowed to remain in the island.

The chief effect of the Norman conquest was the union of Malta with Sicily. Up to the time of the Knights its history would be dictated by its relationship to the larger island.

Swabian period (1194–1268) A dispute in the Norman succession was exploited by the Holy Roman Emperor Henry VI, who claimed the throne of Sicily through his marriage to the daughter of Roger II. Henry (the head of the Swabian house of Hohenstaufen) was succeeded by his son Frederick (1197–1250), who became King Frederick I of Sicily. As the Holy Roman Emperor, Frederick's powers extended far beyond his own kingdom. The conflicts in Italy resulting from the contest between Emperor and Pope were hardly felt in Malta, although a man of Frederick's power was capable, when the need arose, of radical action. In 1224 the entire population of Celano in Italy was deported to Malta following the destruction of that city by Frederick to punish the feudal lord for high treason. In the same year, the king finally expelled all the Arabs from the island.

Angevin period (1268–84) On the death of Manfred, last of the Swabian kings, Malta passed into the hands of Charles of Anjou, who had seized the throne of Sicily. Under his despotic rule Malta fared no better than Sicily, where the extreme hardships suffered by the people finally drove them to the armed revolt known as the Sicilian Vespers (1282). Profiting by the defeat of the French in the uprising, Peter of Aragon (a Spanish prince related by marriage to the Swabians) landed in Sicily and was proclaimed king. The following year his fleet, under Admiral Roger Loria, defeated that of the Angevins, commanded by the Englishman William Corner, off Grand Harbour. The stronghold of Fort St Angelo, garrisoned by the French, was subsequently reduced by Loria, thus bringing Malta under Aragonese rule.

Aragonese and Castilian periods (1284–1530) After an initial prosperity, the renewal of tyrannical government (with the Maltese islands enfeoffed to a succession of Sicilian overlords) brought a period of great hardship. At this time, too, the people suffered frequent incursions by African corsairs.

Università It is difficult to trace the development of local government in the islands during the Middle Ages, but by the time of the Aragonese domination the Commune or Università existed in Malta and Gozo to administer local affairs.

Its authority resided in an elected council, the Consiglio Popolare, which had no legislative power but had the right to represent to the sovereign the needs of the people, to appoint officials and impose taxes. Its head was the Hakem or Captain of the Rod, appointed by the sovereign.

The main concern of the Università was to maintain the favour of the sovereign in order that Malta should remain a royal domain and not become a feudal estate at the mercy of the barons. To this end the Maltese raised taxes and made gifts to the sovereign.

In 1410 the Aragonese king Martin II died without issue and the Kingdom of Sicily (including Malta) passed to Ferdinand of Castile. Sicily and Malta were now ruled jointly from Spain.

Corsair raids on Malta became such a menace that in 1419 the Università petitioned Alfonso V 'The Magnificent' (1416–38), son of Ferdinand, for permission to levy an import duty on wine for the purpose of erecting a fortified tower on Comino, 'the nest of the Saracens'. The duty was levied and the sum collected, but the money was appropriated by the Crown and Comino remained without a tower for another 200 years.

In 1420 Alfonso mortgaged the islands to Don Antonio Cardona for 30,000 gold florins and forced the Maltese to transfer their allegiance to the new feudal lord. Cardona had absolute control: he appropriated all revenue and appointed all officials. Later the rights granted to Cardona were transferred to another noble, and the pattern of exploitation continued.

In 1427 the people were able to raise the sum for which the islands had been mortgaged, thus re-uniting them with the Crown. The charter of 'perpetual reunion' granted by Alfonso (broken when the islands were handed over to the Knights) authorized the Maltese to vindicate their rights if necessary by force of arms without incurring punishment.

The frequency of piratical raids and pestilence during this period was such that in 1431 the Maltese people were compelled to ask the sovereign to exempt them from the payment of customs dues on provisions imported from Sicily. Ensuing years brought further calamities: a disastrous famine in 1471 and the first concerted attack by the Turks in 1488. These troops, under the command of the Ottoman Sultan Bajazet II, landed at Marsascirocco (Marsaxlokk) and attacked Birgu before going on to raid Gozo. In 1526 the Barbary corsairs ravaged the island, carrying off 400 inhabitants.

This was the impoverished and desolate land that the Emperor Charles V offered the Order of St John in 1530. Since their expulsion from Rhodes in 1522, the Knights had been searching unsuccessfully for a new base in the Mediterranean. A Commission of Knights visited Malta, and their report on conditions in the island was daunting. Nevertheless the Grand Master, de L'Isle Adam, with no other option open to him, was obliged to accept the Emperor's offer.

At first Malta was seen merely as a temporary refuge, the Knights' intention being to return to Rhodes and recapture their former stronghold. In 1530, when the Great Carrack sailed into Grand Harbour, few of those on board would have seen the island as the home of the Order for the next 270 years. And few watching their arrival would have dared hope for the protection and prosperity their rule would ultimately bring to a defenceless and exploited people.

Knights of St John (1530–1798) The Order set up its Convent in the fishing village of Birgu, beneath the walls of Fort St Angelo. In recognition of the authority of the Knights, The Jurats of the Università handed the key of Mdina to Grand Master de L'Isle Adam. In August 1534 the revered leader of the Order died in Rabat.

Before the accession of Grand Master **Juan de Homedes** (1536–53) little had been done to fortify the island. On the advice of the Italian engineer Ferramolino, de Homedes improved the defences of Birgu and St Angelo. The engineer also advised the building of a fortified town on Mt Sceberras, but the Order's funds were inadequate for such a vast project. At the suggestion of another engineer, Pedro Pardo, the small fort of St Elmo at the tip of the Sceberras peninsula was enlarged, and Fort St Michael constructed on the landward side of the Isola peninsula—fortifications which were to prove their worth in the Great Siege.

The reign of Grand Master **Jean de la Vallette** (1557–68) proved to be the most critical for the Order. He too recognized the importance of the Sceberras peninsula in the defence of the harbour, but faced with the threat of an imminent Turkish attack decided that work should be concentrated on existing fortifications. A major Turkish raid had already taken place with the landing of a party led by the corsair, Dragut in 1551. After an unsuccessful siege of Mdina, Dragut had invaded Gozo, carrying off 5000 of its inhabitants.

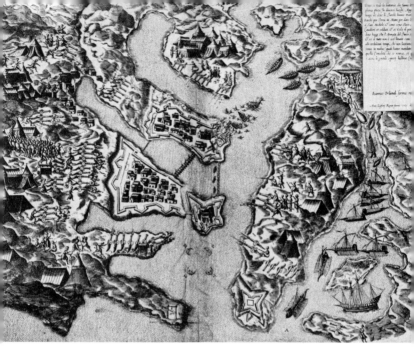

Recovering from the reversal of Rhodes, the Order's navy was once more harassing and plundering Moslem shipping. In 1564 Suleiman the Magnificent—the same Sultan who had expelled them from Rhodes—resolved to finally rid himself of the Knights by attacking them in their new home, a stronghold considerably less powerful than Rhodes.

When news reached La Vallette of the preparation of a Turkish invasion fleet he summoned his Knights from the Commanderies to the defence of their Convent. He also appealed for help to Philip II of Spain through Don Garcia, Viceroy of Sicily: when this was not immediately forthcoming he realized the Knights must rely on their own resources. All that winter the Knights toiled to strengthen the defences, and with the coming of spring food and ammunition were brought over from Sicily.

On 16 May 1565 the Turkish fleet appeared on the horizon and the Knights, led by the 70-year-old La Vallette, prepared to put their new stronghold to the test.

The Great Siege The Turkish force numbered 200 vessels carrying about 40,000 fighting men. Opposing them were 540 Knights and servants-at-arms, 1000 Spanish foot soldiers and about 4000 Maltese militia. Despite their numerical advantage the Turks suffered a serious weakness—a command divided between the head of the army,

Mustapha Pasha, and the commander of the fleet, Piali Pasha. (The two rivals were temporarily united under the command of the great corsair Dragut, but he was soon to be killed in the assault on St Elmo.)

The main body of the Turkish army came ashore at Marsascirocco (Marsaxlokk) and camped at Marsa. Piali, anxious for the safety of the Sultan's fleet, insisted on berthing in Marsamuscetto (Marsamxett Harbour). To achieve this, Fort St Elmo had to be subdued.

Turkish guns, sited on the heights of Mt Sceberras, poured a rain of fire on the small fort. With little hope of survival, the defenders put up a heroic resistance, aided by the supplies and men ferried across Grand Harbour from Fort St Angelo. For 31 days the Turkish guns battered the walls of the fort before it finally succumbed.

With the destruction of St Elmo, Mustapha was able to turn his attention to the Knights' other fortifications on the peninsulas of L'Isola and Birgu. These were sealed off with troops on the landward side and dominated by guns on the Sceberras, Corradino, Margherita and Salvatore heights. La Vallette's defence was to seal off Galley Creek with a heavy chain strung across the entrance between the two peninsulas, and to build a bridge of boats midway down the creek to connect the two fortifications.

The first major assault was launched on

Contemporary engraving showing the climax of the Great Siege, August 1565

L'Isola. This was both by bombardment from the land batteries and by a seaborne attack. The latter operation presented special problems. Exposed to the Knights' guns on Fort St Angelo, the Turkish ships were unable to enter Grand Harbour from the sea. The only way in was by conveying them across the neck of the Sceberras peninsula and launching them on the waters of Grand Harbour. The Knights, however, had prepared for this by erecting a palisade along the western side of L'Isola wherever it was shallow enough to run a boat ashore. Maltese swimmers armed with knives were then ready to attack the Turks as they attempted to breach the obstruction. At the same time a concealed battery on the water's edge at Fort St Angelo decimated a force of Janissaries attempting to land on the tip of the peninsula.

Repeated attacks were launched against Birgu and L'Isola. In August the walls of Fort St Michael were breached, and the Turks were poised to capture the peninsula. Then came the incident which was to prove a turning point in the siege. Hearing news of a force of cavalry attacking his base camp at Marsa, Mustapha ordered a retreat, imagining a relief force had arrived on the island. When the Turks reached Marsa, however, they discovered that the enemy force was merely 200 horsemen from Mdina who, fearing their comrades were on the point of defeat, had created a diversion by striking at the base camp.

Through the blistering heat of August the siege dragged on, the two citadels suffering shattering cannonades from the guns on the heights. In growing concern, the Council proposed to the Grand Master that all able-bodied fighting men should retreat into Fort St Angelo and there hold out until help arrived. La Vallette refused. He would not abandon the Maltese people who had fought alongside the soldiers, nor did he think it wise to concentrate the enemy's fire on one point. To make certain that there would be no retreat he blew up the bridge between Birgu and the fort.

On 18 August part of the main bastion of the Post of Castile was mined. As the Turks poured into the breach, La Vallette rallied the defenders and led a counter-charge. The Grand Master was wounded but refused to leave his post until the Turks were thrown back and the breach secured.

On 6 September Don Garcia's long promised help arrived as 8000 troops disembarked at Mellieha Bay. By now the Turks were demoralized by casualties, sickness and food shortage. As news of the relief force reached them Piali and Mustapha were at last in agreement. On 8 September the remnants of proud Suleiman's army embarked at St Paul's Bay after a last bloody battle on its shores.

When it was all over the surviving defenders looked out over their crumbling fortifications at a countryside in ruins. Their recovery, however, would be assured by a grateful Europe, saved by their valour from the embrace of the mighty Suleiman. The first priority was the fulfillment of the vision of the fortress city on Mt Sceberras, and there was no shortage of funds for its construction.

In 1566 Grand Master La Vallette laid the foundation stone of the city which was to bear his name. The street plan and the fortifications were the work of the Italian military engineer Francesco Laparelli and his assistant Gerolamo Cassar (see p. 37). In 1568 the indomitable La Vallette died, loved and respected by his Brotherhood and the people of Malta.

The new city rapidly took shape and three years later Grand Master **Pietro del Monte** (1568–72) moved the Convent across from Birgu. Unfortunately the recent ordeal had left its mark on the Order, which had now lost much of its solidarity. New knights filled the places of those killed in the siege, and disorders and rivalry broke out between the different Langues.

Del Monte's successor, Grand Master **Jean de la Cassière** (1572–81), a proud and arrogant man, offended the Maltese people by quarrelling with their Bishop. This led to the installation of an Inquisitor in the island, whose role was to arbitrate between the Church and the Order. Although disliked by his knights, La Cassière was a great benefactor of the Order, and it was through his munificence that the Conventual Church of St John was built.

In 1592 plague struck the island, followed by famine. Out of a population of 30,000, deaths from plague numbered 4000; a further 3000 died from starvation. Relations between the Order and the people deteriorated under the rule of the pleasure-loving and despotic Grand Master **Hugues de Verdalle** (1581–95). Verdalle deprived the Università of many of its hard-won privileges, and indulged himself with the building of the luxury Verdala Palace. A very different ruler was his successor, Grand Master **Martin Garzes** (1595–1601). A compassionate man, he instituted the *Monte di Pietà*, whose object was to free the poor from the clutches of usurers.

Another enlightened ruler with the welfare of the Maltese people at heart was Grand Master **Alof de Wignacourt** (1601–22). He respected the rights of the Università, instituted the *Monte di Redenzione* for the redemption of Christian slaves, and built an aqueduct to bring water to the new city of Valletta, which by 1632 had a Maltese population of nearly 9000. Frequent incursions by Turks and corsairs at this time persuaded the Grand Master to construct the Forts of St Lucian, St Thomas and the Wignacourt Tower at St Paul's Bay.

For the next century a succession of Grand Masters continued the process of building the island's defences. They included **Antoine de Paule** (1623-26) who commissioned the building of the new land front at Floriana, **Jean Paul de Lascaris** (1636-57) the Margherita Lines; **Martin de Redin** (1657-60) the coastal watch towers and bastions at Mdina; **Nicolas Cotoner** (1663-80) the Cottonera Lines and **Manoel de Vilhena** (1722-36) Fort Manoel and improvements to Mdina and Vittoriosa.

The building of coastal defences in the 17th c. encouraged the growth of rural communities, while improvement in trade created flourishing settlements round Grand Harbour, protected by the guns of Valletta and the fortifications of the Cottonera Lines. Although the Knights had little contact with the people, the wealth from their Commanderies and their maritime successes against the Turks and Barbary corsairs now brought prosperity to the island. The building of churches, palaces and houses gave work to the Maltese, patronized by masters who could afford lavish sums for their construction and embellishment.

The 18th c. saw a change in the moral standards of the Order. The Knights became less monastic, more worldly. With piracy and Turkish naval activity on the decline, the Brotherhood which had dedicated itself to the fighting of the infidel lost much of its motivation. The vows of poverty, chastity and obedience were flouted, and the Convent vied with the courts of Europe in its observance of pomp and ceremony.

Grand Master **Manoel Pinto** (1741-73) assumed all the prerogatives of sovereignty. Although he encouraged learning and ennobled Maltese families he was not a popular ruler. In spite of their prosperity the people were becoming increasingly resentful of the arrogance of the Knights. Pinto's successor, Grand Master **Francisco Ximenes** (1773-75), was a tyrant, a much hated man. In 1775 the priests rose against him, but the rebellion was crushed and the ringleaders executed.

The next Grand Master, **Emmanuel de Rohan** (1775-97), was an able man who did his best to uphold the law and follow the tenets of the Brotherhood. But his rule came too late to reverse the decline of the Order.

In 1792, following the French Revolution, the Knights' extensive possessions in France were confiscated, leaving them in severe financial straits. Their weakness was exploited by the Russians, anxious for a naval base in the Mediterranean, offered the Knights 72 Commanderies in Russia for the establishment of a Russian Langue. In exchange, the Russian Tsar would be given the title of Protector of the Order, which would give the Russians control of the island. This move created considerable anxiety for

the British, who at that time, in the struggle with France, had their own designs on the island.

Once more Malta was at the centre of the stage but without the leadership that had served her so well in past crises. After the death of de Rohan the knights elected their first German Grand Master, **Ferdinand von Hompesch** (1797-98). A weak and simple man, von Hompesch accepted the Tsar's offer. This was a provocation to the French, who under Napoleon had just conquered Italy. To maintain their position in the Mediterranean, and to keep out Britain and Russia, a French annexation of Malta was essential.

On 9 June 1798 Napoleon, *en route* to Egypt, asked permission to water his ships in Grand Harbour. The Knights refused, whereupon Napoleon landed his troops and served Hompesch with a surrender ultimatum. On 11 June the Order, in the person of the Grand Master, capitulated. Von Hompesch and the knights remaining loyal to him embarked a few days later, leaving behind them the accumulated treasures of three centuries and a people who, having served the Order for so long, were now abandoned to their fate.

French period (1798-1800) Betrayed by the Knights, the Maltese were ready to welcome the French. The new masters, however, had little benign feeling for their subjects, and the harshness of their rule was reminiscent of the feudal past. With determination the French set out to erase all evidence of the Knights' rule, looting and despoiling their churches and defacing their escutcheons.

The long-suffering tolerance which had helped the Maltese endure past oppression deserted them now. A spontaneous uprising in Mdina, provoked by the sale of tapestries from the Carmelite church, spread throughout the countryside. The French commander was forced to withdraw his troops to the security of Valletta.

Ill-equipped for an assault on the city, the Maltese appealed to the King of Naples, and through him his allies the British. The British response was to blockade the island with ships of the Royal Navy under the command of Captain Alexander Ball. After 18 months, the French were starved into surrender.

British period (1800-1974) In 1802 the Treaty of Amiens returned the Maltese Islands to the Knights. This however proved to be impracticable, as the Order was divided (many of the Knights being French) and incapable of resuming effective government. In the meantime the British under Captain Ball were administering the islands. This was agreeable to the Maltese, who had expressed a wish to remain under the British Crown.

17

Aware of the strategic value of Malta, Captain Ball (later Rear-Admiral Sir Alexander Ball, Bart) urged the British Government to retain the islands. The renewed war with France increased their importance, particularly to the British fleet under Nelson during his Mediterranean manoeuvres. At the Treaty of Paris in 1814 following the abdication of Napoleon, British possession of the islands was formally recognized and Sir Thomas Maitland became their first Governor.

The story of Malta under the British is of a succession of constitutions introduced, suspended or revoked, and of a fluctuating economy at first dependent on the changing pattern of Mediterranean trade and then on the demands of a military and naval presence. The importance of the latter is seen today in the surviving fortifications of the British period (Victoria Lines and coastal defences) and in the dockyard in Grand Harbour created for the Royal Navy.

As a Crown Colony, Malta was ruled by a Governor responsible only to the British Government. Various constitutions gave the Maltese a measure of internal self-government, but this was always through councils answerable to the Governor. Demands for autonomy increased and in 1921, after serious rioting, the Maltese were given independent responsibility for their own affairs. (The British Government, through the Governor, retained responsibility for all matters of Imperial concern.) The constitution setting this up was later suspended (1930 and 1933) following further dissension. The war intervened, and internal self-government was not restored until 1947. In 1955 proposals for the integration of Malta with Britain were considered, but the idea received little support. Following a further suspension of the constitution (1959-61) the island was finally given independence in September 1964, becoming a Republic on 13 December 1974.

The Second Siege (1940-42) When Italy entered World War 2 in June 1940 no adequate defences had been prepared in Malta. The island was considered too close to the enemy airfields in Sicily, and the supply problem insurmountable.

There were, however, strong arguments for holding on to the island, recognizing its strategic importance on the convoy route between Gibraltar and Alexandria. (Axis occupation of Malta would certainly have prevented any supplies reaching the British Army in North Africa.)

Unfortunately the defence of Britain's Mediterranean stronghold depended on aircraft which at the time of Dunkirk and the Battle of Britain could not be spared. To meet the Italians' first bombing raid on 11 June 1940 there were just three obsolete Gloster Gladiators, found packed in crates in an R.N. store. Named 'Faith', 'Hope' and 'Charity' they took on the full weight of the Italian air attack, succeeding miraculously in holding the ring until the arrival three weeks later of the first Hurricanes sent to reinforce the island's air defences.

By the end of 1940 Malta showed every sign of containing the threat from Italy. The convoys were getting through, a good Hurricane force was assembled at Luqa and a submarine fleet in the harbour. In January 1941, however, the battle entered a grimmer phase with the arrival of the Luftwaffe on Sicilian airfields. With German participation the bombing raids increased in ferocity, the main targets being the airfields, harbour area and the convoys on which the island was totally dependent for survival.

With the build-up of a bomber force in the island in mid-1941 the British were able to hit back at the Axis for the first time, bombing Naples and Sicily and destroying enemy shipping en route to Libya. The effect of this was for the Germans to redouble their efforts to crush the island.

Malta's heroic resistance, the unbroken morale of her people, has become a part of history. It was a heroism matched only by that of the sailors manning the convoys and of the pilots of the heavily outnumbered British aircraft.

Perhaps the most legendary story of the siege is that of the American tanker Ohio, whose precious cargo saved the island at the eleventh hour.

By the summer of 1942, the Axis grip on Malta had become a stranglehold. Ammunition and food stocks were virtually exhausted and the island had only two or three weeks' supplies left. The only hope was a convoy of 14 merchant ships under heavy escort, heading for the island in an attempt to break the Axis blockade. Dive-bombed and torpedoed, many of the ships were either sunk or forced to turn back, and only four of the merchantmen got through. Singled out for attack, the Ohio was set on fire and her engines and steering smashed. But by some miracle she reached Malta and was towed into harbour, her cargo of aircraft fuel still intact. Malta was saved.

With the invasion of Sicily in 1943 pressure on Malta eased. But for more than two years the tiny island had suffered an incessant aerial bombardment. Thousands of her people were killed or injured: thousands more lived in catacomb shelters tunnelled out of the rock, their homes destroyed. All were brought close to starvation. In April 1942 (the worst month) 6,700 tons of bombs were dropped in an average of eight raids a day and over 10,000 buildings destroyed or damaged. In that month King George VI awarded the George Cross to the island in recognition of her fortitude—and sacrifice.

Practical information MALTA & GOZO

TRAVEL TO MALTA

Air

Regular flights to Malta (Luqa airport) are operated by **Air Malta** and **British Airways** throughout the year.

From London (Heathrow)
Both airlines offer daily flights from Nov–Mar, increasing the frequency during the Apr–Oct period to twice-daily flights at the peak of the season (Jul–Sep).

Economy flights Both airlines offer Purchase Excursion Fares (PEX) on services from the UK. These apply to return tickets purchased in full for a stay in Malta of at least one Sat night and a maximum of three months.
'Super PEX' fares operate for direct flights London-Malta departing Mon-Thur, minimum stay six days, maximum one month.
Late Hop This is an economy one-way fare on direct services between London and Malta. Reservations are only accepted from the day before travel and seats allocated on a 'first come first served' basis.

For further information apply to:

Air Malta St James' House, 13 Kensington Square, London W8
British Airways Air Terminal, Victoria SW1

Sea/Car ferry

For those travelling by car through Italy who wish to put their vehicle on a boat to Malta, **Tirrenia Lines** offer the following services:

From Naples
Once weekly, arr. 24 hrs later in Malta

From Reggio di Calabria (Sicily) via Catania and Syracuse
Three times weekly, arr. 15 hrs later in Malta

For further details apply to:
Serena Holidays (agents) 40/42 Kenway Rd, London SW5

TRAVEL IN MALTA

Roads

There are three types of road in Malta:

Main roads connecting the principal towns and villages. These are signposted. As there is a current road expansion programme they are not always marked as major roads on the latest maps.
Secondary roads to villages. These are surfaced, but poorly signposted.
Country lanes to remoter villages, and often dead ends. These lanes are unsurfaced, narrow and winding. The low stone walls on either side block the view of the countryside and one can easily get lost.

Motorists are advised to keep to the sign-posted roads. It should be remembered that signs usually direct only to the next town or village ahead.

Road maps

The most useful maps for motorists are:
Malta Survey Map Ordnance Survey, scale 1:32,000
Malta and Gozo Fairey Leisure Series, scale 1:50,000

Both these maps are available from Edward Stanford Ltd, 12/14 Long Acre, London WC2 or from other good mapsellers. In Malta the Ordnance Survey map is available from the Government Information Dept, Castile Place, Valletta

Driving formalities

The only requirement for motorists from the UK is a current driving licence. This should be taken on arrival to the former Customs House on Lascaris Wharf for endorsement. Driving is on the left. There is a speed limit of 40mph (in built-up areas 25mph).

Self-drive cars

Most car-hire firms in Malta and Gozo offer the following as part of their service:

1. Full insurance (this can exclude the first £M40 of any damage sustained)
2. Delivery to airport or hotel to meet the visitor on arrival
3. Unlimited mileage, i.e. no additional charge per mile driven
4. Oil and maintenance

The average charges are £M6 for one day and £M42 for one week, inclusive of insurance etc. (cheaper in winter). Details of local agents may be obtained from the Malta Government Tourist Office, 18 Kensington Square, London W8 or the tourist office in City Gate Arcade, Valletta.

Car hire firms represented in London:

Avis Rent A Car (International Reservations) Trident House, Station Rd, Hayes, Middlesex
Godfrey Davis Europcar Bushey House, High St, Bushey, Herts
Hertz Rent A Car (UK & International Reservations) Radnor House, London Rd, Norbury, London SW16

Petrol stations

These open early in the morning and close at 20.00 daily. They are closed on Sundays and holidays.

Bus services

MALTA

With a few exceptions buses start from and return to Valletta. Most villages and towns are connected to the capital. Village buses stop at or near the parish church square. Most services are frequent (a few are hourly). Enquiries about times should be made at the police post or despatcher's kiosk at the Valletta terminus (City Gate). Buses should be signalled to stop at a bus stop, the bell rung to alight. The driver and fellow passengers are always helpful, and the fares cheap.

Circular Tour of Valletta From its starting point at the City Gate the No **98** bus offers a perimeter tour of Valletta

No. Route

Cottonera

1 Valletta to Vittoriosa (Terminus)
2 Valletta to Vittoriosa (Victory Square)
3 Valletta to Senglea
4 Valletta to Kalkara
5 Valletta to Paola

Gudja/Ghaxaq

8 Valletta to Gudja (via Ghaxaq)
9 Gudja to Cospicua (via Ghaxaq)

Kalafrana

11 Valletta to Birzebbuga
12 Valletta to Kalafrana
13 Valletta to Hal-Far
14 Valletta to Birzebbuga (via Qajjenza)
15 Valletta to Sta. Lucia

Zabbar

18 Valletta to Zabbar
19 Valletta to Marsaskala
20 Zabbar to Cospicua
21 Valletta to Xghajra
22 Cospicua to Marsaskala
23 Cospicua to Xghajra

Zejtun

26 Valletta to Zejtun
27 Valletta to Marsaxlokk
28 Marsaxlokk to Cospicua (via Zejtun and Bulebel)
29 Valletta to Zejtun (via Bulebel)

Zurrieq

32 Valletta to Zurrieq (via Luqa village)
33 Valletta to Zurrieq (via Luqa village, Karwija and Safi)
34 Valletta to Zurrieq (via Luqa village, Kirkop—Safi)
35 Valletta to Qrendi (via Guardroom—Mqabba)
36 Valletta to Luqa village
37 Valletta to Mghieret
38 Valletta to Wied iz-Zurrieq

Attard/Lija

40 Valletta to Attard

Birkirkara/St Julian's

42 Birkirkara to St Julian's (Mrabat Street)

Mellieha

43 Valletta to Mellieha
44 Valletta to Ghadira
45 Valletta to Marfa
   Valletta to Cirkewwa
46 Valletta to Mgarr (via Mosta)
47 Valletta to Ghajn Tuffieha (via Mgarr)
48 Valletta to Marfa (via Sliema)
49 Valletta to Bugibba
50 Valletta to Armier
51 Valletta to Armier (via Hamrun)
52 Valletta to Ghajn Tuffieha (via St Paul's Bay)

Mosta/Naxxar

3 Valletta to Mosta
54 Valletta to Naxxar
55 Valletta to Gharghur
56 Mosta to Naxxar
57 Naxxar to St Julian's

Sliema

60 Valletta to Savoy
61 Valletta to Ferry (Sliema)
62 Valletta to Spinola and St Andrews
63 Valletta to Sliema 'C' (via Ta'Xbiex)
64 Valletta to Sliema 'D' (via Ta'Xbiex)
65 Valletta to San Gwann (via tal-Qroqq)
66 Valletta to Ta'Giorni
67 Ferry (Sliema) to Ta'Giorni (via Dingli Street)

Birkirkara

71 Valletta to Birkirkara
72 Valletta to Birkirkara (Brared)
73 Valletta to Hamrun
74 Valletta to Balzan (Corinthia Palace Hotel)
75 Valletta to G'Mangia (St Luke's)
76 Msida to G'Mangia (St Luke's)
77 Birkirkara (Brared) to G'Mangia (St Luke's)
78 Valletta to Birkirkara (via Sta. Venera)

Rabat

80 Valletta to Rabat
81 Valletta to Dingli
82 Rabat to Birkirkara
83 Rabat to St Paul's Bay
84 Rabat to Mtarfa
85 Rabat to St Vincent de Paul Hospital

Zebbug/Siggiewi

88 Valletta to Zebbug
89 Valletta to Siggiewi
90 Valletta to Qormi (St Sebastian)
91 Valletta to Qormi (St George)
92 Zebbug to Imghieret (via Qormi)
93 Siggiewi to Imghieret
94 Siggiewi to Ghar Lapsi

GOZO

Bus services on Gozo are less regular than those of Malta. Most of the villages run their own buses and arrange their own timetables. All routes converge on Victoria, and from the terminus in Main Gate Street (Xlendi road)

one can obtain a bus to most parts of the island. Most of these buses are of limited use to tourists, however, as they usually leave the village early in the morning for market and return from Victoria between 09.00 and 10.00, thus making a return journey from Victoria on the same day impossible.

One regular service to Mgarr is timed to meet the ferry from Malta. This service goes to Victoria, and in summer there are services to the resorts of Marsalforn and Xlendi.

Taxis, Horse cabs and Dghajjes

Taxis are white, carry red number plates and are fitted with meters. Charges are fixed by the government, and a board at the airport exit indicates correct fares for various destinations. In Valletta, taxi stands are in Freedom Square (by the bombed Opera House) and by the *Phoenicia Hotel* (Floriana). At Sliema along the Promenade. In Gozo, taxi stands are at Mgarr and It-Tokk Square in Victoria.

Horse cabs (karrozzini) can be found in Valletta outside City Gate, at Great Siege Square in Republic Street and at the Customs House. In Sliema on the Promenade and in Bastion Square, Mdina. Currently the fare is about 50–60 cents for a half-hour's ride. The fare should be agreed at the start.

Dghajjes A *dghajsa* (pronounced 'dicer') or water taxi can be hired from the Customs House, Valletta or the waterfronts of Senglea and Vittoriosa. There are no fixed charges.

Sightseeing tours

More than two dozen travel agents mostly in Valletta and Sliema, offer sightseeing tours to Malta and Gozo. Details may be obtained from your hotel or from the tourist office in City Gate Arcade, Valletta. The price of the tour generally includes lunch.

Examples of tours offered:

1. The Blue Grotto and Prehistoric Temples at Hagar Qim and Mnajdra
2. The Hal-Saflieni Hypogeum and the Tar-xien Temples followed by Marsaxlokk fishing village and the Prehistoric Cave of Ghar Dalam
3. San Anton Gardens, Mdina and Rabat
4. Malta Handicrafts. A tour of workshops
5. Cities of the Knights. A drive around the original 'Three Cities' and a walking tour of the historic buildings of Valletta
6. Harbour Cruises (see below)
7. Gozo. Ferry to Mgarr, then visit to Ggantija Prehistoric Temples, Xlendi Bay and Victoria

Cruises

Harbour Cruises around Marsamxett and Grand Harbours are available from The Strand, Sliema, several times daily (*Captain Morgan, Pleasure Cruises*). There is also a once-weekly trip from St Paul's Bay (summer).

Round Island Daily cruises by *Captain Morgan* (May-Oct, Tue-Sun; Nov-Apr, Tue, Thur & Fri) taking in Blue Grotto and Blue Lagoon, Comino, at 09.15. Also by *Jylland* (May, Wed & Fri; Jun-Sep, Mon-Fri; Oct, Mon, Wed & Fri; Nov, Wed & Fri) at 10.00. Departures from The Strand, Sliema.

Comino Daily trips (summer only) by *Captain Morgan* at 09.00 and *Jylland* at 10.00. Departures from The Strand, Sliema. *Pleasure Cruises* also operate a daily service (summer only) from Bugibba at 10.30.

There are also crossings daily (summer only) from Marfa and from Mgarr, Gozo.

Malta-Gozo Ferries

Details of all ferry schedules are obtainable from the Gozo Channel Co, Hays Wharf, Sa Maison (Tel 603964) or the Tourist Information Office, City Gate Arcade.

From Pietà

Boats daily in summer (May-Oct) from Pietà Creek to Mgarr, Gozo and return. Winter services two or three times weekly. The journey takes approx. 1hr.

From Marfa

Boats also make the crossing daily from Marfa in the north of the island to Mgarr, Gozo. The frequency of services varies greatly, and it is wise to book in advance in the summer. Motor vehicles should be at the quay at least 30min before departure. The ferry service is performed subject to weather and other conditions permitting.

Connecting buses Pietà: Nos 61, 62 (10min). Cirkewwa/Marfa: No 45 (bus timed to leave City Gate 75min before ferry's departure). From Victoria, Gozo, the bus leaves 30min before the ferry's departure from Mgarr.

INCLUSIVE HOLIDAYS

Offering hotel and self-catering accommodation:

Aquasun Holidays 41 Crawford St, London W1

Belle Air Holidays 9 Tudor Parade, London Rd, Hounslow, Middlesex

Burstin Travel Holidays Palace Hotel, Pier Hill, Southend-on-Sea, Essex

C & G Holidays 9 Berwick St, London W1

Exchange Travel 66/70 Parker Rd, Hastings, Sussex

Harlequin Holidays 148 West St, Sheffield

Malta-Gozo Self-Catering Holidays 7 Holland Rd, East Ham, London E6

Malta Tours 21 Sussex St, London SW1

Maltavillas 40/42 Kenway Rd, London SW5

Medallion Holidays 26 Cockspur St, London SW1

Pan World Holidays 8 Great Chapel St, London W1

Sheila Mills Holidays Castle Mews, 29a Castle St, Salisbury, Wilts

Sunspot Tours 2 Hatfields, London SE1

Offering self-catering accommodation only:
Flings Holidays 15 Colbrook Ave, Hayes, Middlesex
Marsascala Holidays 5 Union Rd, Shirley, Solihull, W. Midlands
Solemar Holidays 62 Shirley Rd, Croydon, Surrey
Vella Holidays 1 Nun St, Newcastle-upon-Tyne

Specializing in Gozo:
Il Fawwara 211 High St, Bangor, Gwynedd
Gozo Holidays 17 St Mary's Grove, London W4

ACCOMMODATION

Hotels

Hotels are divided by the Government into seven classes: De Luxe, 1A, 1B, IIA, IIB, III and IV. With the exception of the De Luxe category, all hotels are subject to a maximum fixed charge, which is all-inclusive. The majority of hotels offer reduced winter rates during the low season (1 Nov–31 Mar) but may apply higher rates during the Christmas, New Year and Easter periods.
For details of charges and a list of hotels apply to the Malta National Tourist Organisation, 18 Kensington Square, London W8.

Hotels with classifications (NC: Night Club):

MALTA

Valletta and Floriana

De Luxe
Phoenicia The Mall, Floriana NC
Grand Hotel Excelsior Great Siege Rd, Floriana NC
IIA
Castile Castile Place, Valletta
Osborne 50 South St, Valletta
IIB
Grand Harbour 261 St Ursula St, Valletta
III
British 267 St Ursula St, Valletta
Cumberland 111 St John St, Valletta

Valletta environs
IIA
Kennedy Court The Strand, Gzira
Malta Health Farm Main St, Tarxien
Sa Maison 22 Marina St, Pietà
IIB
Adelphi Victory St, Gzira
Airport Luqa
III
Angela Antonio Sciortino St, Msida
Continental St Louis St, Msida
Isola Bella Clarence St, Msida
Kennedy Fleet St, Gzira
IV
Binamar Bishop Caruana St, Msida
Helena 192 Marina St, Pietà
Taormina 6/7 Ponsonby St, Gzira

Sliema, St Julian's and St Andrew's

De Luxe
Dragonara St Julian's NC
Malta Hilton St Julian's NC
IA
Cavalieri Spinola Rd, St Julian's
Fortina Tigné Sea Front, Sliema
Preluna 124 Tower Rd, Sliema NC
IB
Atlas St Andrew's Rd, St Andrew's
Eden Beach St George's Bay, St Julian's
Le Roy Hughes Hallet St, Qui-Se-Sana, Sliema
Plevna Thornton St, Sliema
Tigné Court Qui-Si-Sana, Sliema
Tower Palace Tower Rd, Sliema
IIA
Capua Court 60 Victoria Ave, Sliema
Eden Rock 117 Tower Rd, Sliema
Europa 138 Tower Rd, Sliema
Green Dolphin St George's Bay, St Julian's
Imperial 1 Rudolph St, Sliema
Marina Tigné Sea Front, Sliema
Metropole Dingli St, Sliema
Plaza 251 Tower Rd, Sliema
St Julian Dragonara Rd, St Julian's
Sliema 59 The Strand, Sliema
IIB
Astra 127 Tower Rd, Sliema
Balluta Main St, St Julian's
Caledonia Dragut St, Sliema
Caprice 2 Victoria Gdns, Sliema
Carina Windsor Terrace, Sliema
Crown 166/7 Tower Rd, Sliema
Day's Inn 76 Cathedral St, Sliema
Debonair 102 Howard St, Sliema
Delphina 72 Dragonara Rd, St Julian's
Eagle Court off St George's Rd, St Julian's
Elba 52 New St, Sliema
Lester Ross St, St Julian's
Meadowbank Tower Rd, Sliema
Midas 45 Tigné St, Sliema
Olympic Paceville Ave, St Julian's
Patricia New Howard St, Sliema
Promenade Tower Rd, Sliema
Regent Milner St, Sliema
Spinola Upper Ross St, St Julian's
III
Adelaide 229/231 Tower Rd, Sliema
Astoria 46 Point St, Sliema
Belmont Mrabat St, St Julian's
Kent 24 St Margaret St, Sliema
Lion Court 9 Nursing Sisters St, Sliema
Neptune Bay Junction, St Julian's
IV
Regina 107 Tower Rd, Sliema
Seacliff 225 Tower Rd, Sliema
Sport St George's Rd, St Julian's

Salina Bay
IB *Salina Bay* NC
III *Lancer* Naxxar Rd

St Paul's Bay/Bugibba

IB
Mediterranea Bugibba Rd, St Paul's Bay
IIA
Concorde Pioneer Rd, Bugibba
Charella Qawra
Flora Pioneer Rd, Bugibba
Hyperion Qawra
Liliana Qawra
IIB
Ambassador Shipwreck Promenade, St
  Paul's Bay
Xemxija Bay Xemxija, St Paul's Bay
III
Blue Mar Xemxija Hill, St Paul's Bay
Carolina Winter St, Bugibba
Cartwheel St Anthony St, Bugibba
Seaview Qawra
IV
Crystal Bugibba
International Islets Promenade, Bugibba

Mellieha

IA
Maritim Selmun Palace Selmun
IB
Mellieha Bay Mellieha Bay NC
IIB
Panorama New St, Valley Rd

Paradise Bay

IA *Paradise Bay* Cirkewwa

Marfa

IA *Ramla Bay*

Golden Bay/Ghajn Tuffieha Bay

IB *Golden Sands*
IIB *Riviera Martinique*

Mdina/Rabat

De Luxe
Grand Hotel Verdala Rabat NC
IIB
Xara Palace St Paul's Square, Mdina
III
Nigret Nigret Rd, Rabat

Balzan and environs

De Luxe
Corinthia Palace De Paul Ave, San Anton
  NC
IIA
Grosvenor Court Balzan
IIB
Albatross Notabile Rd, Mriehel

Birzebugga

III *Sea Breeze* Pretty Bay

Marsascala

IA *Jerma Palace*
III *Cerviola*

COMINO
IA *Comino*

GOZO

Ta'Cenc, Sannat
De Luxe *Ta Cenc*

Victoria
IIB *Duke of Edinburgh* 85/9 Republic St

Marsalforn
IB *Calypso* Marsalforn Bay
III *Ritz* 8/10 Xaghra Rd
IV
Electra 12/13 Valley Rd
Marsalforn Marsalforn Bay

Xaghra
IIB *Cornucopia* 10 Gnien Imrik St

Xlendi
III *St Patrick's* Xlendi Bay

Tourist Complexes/Holiday Villages

I
Mellieha Holiday Centre Mellieha Bay
Mistra Village Xemxija Hill, St Paul's Bay
Riza Qawra, St Paul's Bay
The Galaxy Depiro St, Sliema
The Halland Tal-Ibragg, St Andrew's
Villa Rosa St George's Bay, St Julian's
II
Hal Ferh Ghajn Tuffieha
III
Medisle St Andrew's Road, St Andrew's

Villas and apartments

A wide range of self-catering accommodation is available for all those who prefer the independence that this kind of holiday offers. The cheapest way of booking apartments and villas is through tour operators, many of whom offer them as an alternative to hotel accommodation in their package tours. (See Inclusive Holidays, p.21.)

FOOD AND DRINK

The best place to enjoy traditional Maltese food is the Maltese home. The Maltese are not given to eating out and most restaurants were built for the tourist. Their menus are, accordingly, mainly English and Italian.
With the growing demand from tourists for local food, however, a number of hotels and restaurants are including Maltese dishes in their menus. Maltese food is similar to that of other Mediterranean countries, with a strong Italian bias. The chief ingredients are pasta, rikotta (cottage cheese), vegetables (especially tomatoes, baby marrows, aubergines, peppers and cabbage), fish, pork, rabbit, chicken and eggs. Soup is served with most meals and fruit usually stands in for a sweet. Bread is good, also the *pastizzi* served at bakeries and coffee shops. Fish to look out for are *lampuki*, *dentici*, *tunnagg* (tuna), *kavalli* (mackerel) and *pixxispad* (swordfish).

Some typical Maltese dishes:

Soups

Minestra Akin to the Italian minestrone but more filling. A country favourite

Aljotta Fish soup

Kawlata Vegetable hot-pot with barley and pork

Pasta dishes

Ravjul Ravioli with a rikotta filling

Ross fil-forn Rice baked with minced meat, eggs and cheese

Timpana A very popular and filling dish. Macaroni, eggs, minced meat, rikotta, cheese and tomato purée baked in a casing of puff pastry

Main courses

Bragioli Minced meat, bacon, eggs and breadcrumbs wrapped in thin slices of meat then fried in deep fat

Brungiel mimli fil-forn Stuffed aubergines

Majjal fil-forn Roast pork

Qarnita Octopus stew

Tigiega mimlija Chicken stuffed with minced pork and beef, grated cheese, egg and breadcrumbs then baked

Torta tal-Lampuki Lampuki pie. Fish, vegetables and olives baked in a pastry case

Torta tal-Fenek Rabbit pie

Fenek biz-zalza Casseroled rabbit

Sweetmeats

Almonds are a popular ingredient of cakes and biscuits made for special occasions. These include:

Kwarezimal Biscuit made for Lent with ground almonds, sugar, flour and cocoa powder.

Figolli Easter biscuits cut out into dolls and other shapes and sandwiched together with marzipan

Little almond biscuits Served at weddings and baptisms. Ground almonds, sugar, white of egg and lemon juice

Prinjolata The traditional Carnival sweet. A luscious uncooked conical cake of sponge fingers, butter cream and almonds with white frosting decorated with melted chocolate, glacé cherries and almonds

Almond nougat sold at festivals

Pastizzi

These small oval-shaped pastries make popular snacks. They have a variety of fillings: Rikotta, peas and onions, anchovy or meat.

Cheese

The chief local cheese, made from sheep's milk, is *Gbejna*. The best *Gbejna* comes from Gozo.

Fruit

The finest Maltese fruits are oranges (Dec-Mar) and grapes. Also delicious are strawberries, melons, mulberries, tangerines, pomegranates, figs and peaches.

Wine

The Maltese Islands are not generally associated with wine-making. The visitor who takes the trouble to sample the variety of wines available at the humblest village store will, however, be pleasantly surprised, not only by their quality but their cheapness. Shop prices for a bottle of wine range from 25-50 cents and a glass in a bar usually costs around 25 cents.

There are no *grands vins* or *premiers crus*, and you can occasionally get caught out by a fairly tart concoction in some of the remoter villages. But wine is one of Malta's major products and the larger producers, such as *Emmanuel Delicata* (the *Lachryma Vitis* label), *Marsovin*, *Maltana* and *Farmers* are always consistent. It is a matter of tasting and choosing. The reds are usually very drinkable, while the white wines are sometimes too sweet for many tastes, unless one spends a few cents extra for a 'Special Reserve'.

The Gozitan wines, *Velson's* and *Ggantija*, are worth trying.

Beer and other drinks

Hop Leaf is a light ale made by Simonds, Farsons, Cisk. Their lager *Cisk* (pronounced 'Chisk') is another good drink after a hot day. Malta has its own fizzy soft drink *Kinnie* (again made by Farsons). This contains oranges and aromatic herbs and is an easily acquired taste. It mixes well with white rum or vodka.

Imported spirits It is worth remembering that these are available in the larger grocer's shops at considerably less than UK prices.

Restaurants and night life

Continental dishes predominate in Maltese restaurants: a few specialize in fish. Prices are reasonable. Finding somewhere to eat in the villages is a problem, although coffee, tea and *pastizzi* can usually be bought in village bars.

The following is a list of independent restaurants and night clubs. Most **hotel restaurants** are open to the public, and some of the larger ones have **night clubs**, also open to visitors.

For a list of hotels, see p. 22.

Key

E:Entertainment, i.e. music and dancing

N: Night spot (no food) D: Dinner only

Armier Bay

Belmar

Balzan

Il-Melita

San Anton Gardens

Bahar-ic-Caghaq

Omar Khayyam

Birkirkara

Mayfair ED

Valley Rd

Birzebbuga
Caribbean D
4/5 Hal Far Rd

Gzira
Carriage
The Strand
19 Steps
Ta'Xbiex Seafront
Taj Mahal
122 The Strand

Marsaskala
Coxwain's Cabin
Marina St
L-Awwista
Zonqor St
St Thomas Tower
Zonquor Point

Marsaxlokk
Golden Sun
Tas Silg Road
Hunter's Tower (fish)
Wilga St

Mdina
Medina
Holy Cross St
Palazzo Costanzo
Villegaignon St

Mellieha
The Arches E
113 Main St
Hilltop
13a Main St
Ta' Peter E
76 Main St
Tunny Net (fish) E
Mellieha Bay

Mosta
Whisper (steaks) ED
71 Constitution St

Naxxar
Golden Nugget Tavern
New St

Qawra
Incognito
Qawra Rd
Luzzu
Qawra Rd
Ta' Fra Ben
Qawra Tower

Rabat
Barrel and Basket ED
St Augustine St
Bird Cage ED
Gusman Navarra St
Buskett Roadhouse
Buskett Gardens
Jolly Friar
St Dominic Sq
Nigret Night Club E
29 Nigret Rd
Roman's Den
Main St

St Andrew's
Sunrise Inn
St Andrew's Rd

**St Julian's
and Paceville**
Barracuda
Main St
BJ's ED
Ball St
Chains E
Spinola Bay
China House
8 Spinola Rd
Il Parapett
25 St George's Rd
Ir-Rokna
Church St
La Dolce Vita
St George's Rd
It-Taverna
148 St George's Rd
La Famiglia
Spinola Rd
La Guillotine
49 Paceville Ave
Lighthouse
Ross St
Papillon
108 St George's Rd
Paul's Punch Bowl
St George's Rd
Sardinella
Mensija St
Sharmila
82 Grenfell St
Tigullio
Spinola Bay

**St Paul's Bay
and Bugibba**
Carlo's Hideaway E
Xemxija Hill
Gillieru (fish)
St Paul's Bay
Il-Fekruna
Shipwreck Prom.
Ir-Razzet Grill E
Mistra Village
It-Travi E
Islets Promenade
L'Ambient
Xemxija Hill
Nettuno
Xemxija Hill
Palazzo Pescatore ED
St Paul St (fish)
Papillon
Blacktail St
Portobello
St Luke St
Salad Bowl
St Anthony St
Travellers' Rest
Pioneer Corps Rd
Unique
Upper Conversion St

Woodpecker
St Anthony St
Salina Bay
Ta Saveria
Ghallis Rd

Sliema
Beefeater
Bisazza St
Caravel Night Club ED
Qui-Si-Sana
City Gem (steaks)
St Pius V St
Golden Seven
Tower Rd
Hole in the Wall D
32 High St
Hosteria La Loggia
Mrabat St
Il Bancinu
Tower Rd
Il Barbone
Amery St
Il-Fortizza (Italian)
Tower Rd
Piper Club
Qui-Si-Sana
Ta'Kolina
Tower Rd
Winston
High St
Wyndhams
Tigné St

Valletta
Alexandra's E
35 South St
Britannia
St Lucia St
Bologna
59 Republic St
Cordina's (snacks)
244 Republic St
Lantern
20 Sappers St
Merry Chef
Zachary St
Pappagall
Britannia St

GOZO
Gharb
Sesame
Ta'Pinu

Marsalforn
Il Kartell
Republic
Tritons

Mgarr
Ogygia Palace E

Victoria
Amalfi
Gharb Rd
Eclipse E
Mgarr Rd
Il-Tokk E
Republic St

Xlendi
Il Kenur
Moby Dick

Xaghra
Cornucopia
Gesther
Ulysses Lodge
Ramla Bay

FOLK ART AND CRAFTS

Glassware Although a new industry, the production of glassware is now one of the crafts with which Malta is most identified. *Mdina Glass* produce some fine ornaments and their factory and shop is at Ta'Qali (see below).

Jewellery For generations Maltese craftsmen have fashioned gold and silver into hand-made jewellery. The silver filigree work is particularly beautiful.

Knitting and crochet Very reasonably priced dresses, shawls and jerseys are hand-made in Gozo. They are beautifully made with intricate stitching.

Lace A traditional craft of Gozo. The women work in their own homes, producing intricate and beautiful designs.

Stoneware A highly specialized craft utilizing the calcite onyx found in only a few parts of Malta and Gozo. Most popular items are cigarette and jewel boxes, book-ends, lampstands and ashtrays. The workshops are at Ta'Qali (see below).

String bags These colourful bags, now of nylon, are made in the fishing village of Marsaxlokk.

Weaving demonstrations can be seen at the Ta'Qali Crafts Village (see below) and in Gozo at the Ta'Dbiegi Craft Village, Gharb, Gozo. The cloth is sturdy and is made up into table linen, bedspreads and cushions with attractive multi-coloured patterns.

Wickerwork This small but flourishing craft is centred in the alleys of Main Street in Hamrun.

Wrought iron A craft at which the Maltese are particularly skilful. Small workshops can be found all over the island.

A display of local crafts can be seen at the *Malta Government Crafts Centre*, St John's Square, Valletta (opposite the Cathedral). Opening hours: 1 Oct-15 Jun (Mon-Fri) 08.00-12.30 & 14.00-17.00. 16 Jun-30 Sep (Mon-Fri) 08.00-13.30. In Gozo, the *Gozo Crafts Centre*, St Francis Square, Victoria, has the same opening hours.

Factories open to visitors

Farsons Brewery Malta's only brewery is located at Mriehel, a short distance beyond the Fleur-de-Lys roundabout on the Valletta-Rabat road (Bus 80, 81). Tours of the brewery can be organised by telephoning the Public Relations Officer (Tel: 40331).

Ta'Qali Crafts Village Sign-posted right-hand turning off Valletta-Rabat road beyond Attard. Bus 80, 81 passes the turning, then ¼m walk. Here one can spend a morning watching the manufacture of local crafts. These include glass-blowing, filigree work, ceramics, Malta stone and woodwork. Products are on sale. Visiting hours: Mon-Fri 08.00-14.00

FESTIVALS

Throughout the year, but specially during the summer months, a touch of colour is added to Maltese life by the festivals held in every parish to celebrate the local Saint's day. Street bands, colourful decorations and fireworks are a traditional part of the two or three days of festivities, leading to the climactic procession of the statue of the Saint through the village streets. The parish churches are usually beautifully decorated on these occasions, with damask wall coverings and silverware on display.

There are also national festivals. For exact dates visitors should refer to the useful booklet *What's on in Malta and Gozo*, published fortnightly and obtainable from newsagents. Listed below are some of the more important festivals:

early Feb	**Valletta, Munxar** (Gozo) Commemoration of St Paul's Shipwreck
1st Sun in Lent	**Zabbar** *Had-in-Nies* (People's Sunday) Traditional processions
Fri before Good Friday	**Valletta and elsewhere** *Our Lady of Sorrows* Processions
Good Friday	**Main towns** Solemn evening processions
Easter Sunday	**Main towns** Morning processions. Easter is Malta's most important religious festival, and a time for family gatherings and gifts, such as Easter eggs and *figolli* (a local sweet) to be exchanged
1st Wed after Easter	**Zejtun** *St Gregory* This feast has been celebrated for over seven centuries. The Archbishop, accompanied by the Cathedral Chapter, leads the religious procession from Tarxien to the old parish church of St Gregory, where the Archbishop imparts the blessing. After Mass the pilgrims proceed to Marsaxlokk and picnic
2nd weekend in May	**Valletta, Victoria** (Gozo) and elsewhere *Carnival* These festivities date back to the 16th c. and feature dancing competitions, street bands, decorated trucks and grotesque masks. Special attractions are the *Parata*, a children's sword dance, and *Il-Maltija*, Malta's national dance

Jun (2nd week)	**Zurrieq** *St Catherine* **Qormi** *St George*
(3rd week)	**Siggiewi** *St Nicholas*
(4th week)	**Valletta** (at Co-Cathedral) and **Xewkija** (Gozo) *St John the Baptist*
late Jun	**Buskett Gardens, Rabat** *Mnarja* Folk Festival, held on eve of feast of SS Peter and Paul. Agricultural show, folk music and feasting throughout the night
Jun 29	**Mdina** (Cathedral) and **Nadur** (Gozo) *SS Peter and Paul* Traditional horse and donkey races in the afternoon at Rabat, Malta
Jul 1–15	**Naxxar** Malta International Fair
Jul (1st week)	**Rabat** *St Paul*
(2nd week)	**Qormi** *St Sebastian*
(3rd week)	**Valletta** *Our Lady of Mount Carmel* **Victoria** (Gozo) *St George* Horse races in Racecourse St
Aug (1st week)	**Lija** *Christ the Saviour*
(2nd week)	**Valletta** *St Dominic* **Vittoriosa** and **San Lawrenz** (Gozo) *St Lawrence*
Aug 15	**Valletta, Victoria** (Gozo), **Attard, Ghaxaq, Gudja, Mosta, Mqabba, Qrendi** *Santa Marija* Assumption of the Virgin Mary. Horse races at Victoria (Gozo)
Aug (3rd week)	**Birkirkara** *St Helen*
(4th week)	**Sliema** *Stella Maris* **Valletta** *St Augustine*
Sep (1st weekend)	**Senglea, Mellieha, Naxxar** and **Xaghra** (Gozo) *Il-Vitorja (Our Lady of Victories)* Regatta in Grand Harbour. This day commemorates the victory over the Turks in 1565 and the end of the second siege in 1943
Sep (2nd week)	**Zabbar** *Our Lady of Graces*
Nov (4th week)	**Zejtun** *St Catherine*
early Dec	**Cospicua** and **Qala** (Gozo) *Immaculate Conception*
Dec 13	**Valletta** *Republic Day* This is Malta's National Day, commemorating the foundation of the Republic in 1974. Sports festival, street parade, 'Son et Lumiere' and fireworks.

Public Holidays

Jan 1	New Year's Day
Variable	Good Friday
May 1	May Day
Aug 15	The Assumption (*Santa Marija*)
Dec 13	Republic Day
Dec 25	Christmas Day

LANGUAGE

Maltese is an ancient Semitic language, a legacy from the Arabs who ruled Malta from 870–1090 AD, but with Phoenician origins. Many of the Phoenician words found in the inscriptions on the Marsaxlokk *cippi* survive in the contemporary language. Words from the Romance languages—Norman Sicilian, Italian, Spanish and English—were absorbed during the successive occupations. These modifications are most apparent in the language of the urban community, amongst the more literate trades and professions. Among the country folk, less exposed to external influences, the language is more strongly Semitic.

For centuries *Il-Malti* was only a spoken language. Its written form, using modified Roman characters, was introduced in the 20th century. English is universally spoken, and both *Il-Malti* and English are official languages.

Pronunciation The average visitor need only concern himself with the pronunciation of place names. These are given on p. 58. For this reason, the Maltese accents have been omitted from the text of this book. Most letters are pronounced as in English, but a key to some of the variations, with their accents, is given below:

c	hard c (as k)	j	y
ċ	ch	m	m(im when initial
g	hard g		letter followed
ġ	soft g		by consonant)
gh	silent	x	sh
h	silent	z	tz
ħ	aspirated h (as in ugh!)	ż	z

CLIMATE

Malta has a long hot summer, the heat often tempered by an evening breeze. Spring and autumn are fleeting. The winters are mild, but can be windy with occasional storms: snow is unknown. Rain is frequently of tropical intensity, but the skies soon clear after storms.

Month	Hours sun	Rainfall ins	mm
Jan	5.2	3.26	83.5
Feb	5.1	2.17	55.6
Mar	6.9	1.58	40.5
Apr	8.5	0.87	22.3
May	10.2	0.41	10.5
Jun	11.7	0.08	2.0
Jul	12.6	0.02	0.5
Aug	11.9	0.22	5.6
Sep	9.1	1.19	30.5
Oct	7.1	3.25	83.3
Nov	5.9	3.39	86.9
Dec	5.1	3.81	97.7

Month	Max temp F	C	Min temp F	C	Sea temp C
Jan	63	17.2	46	7.8	14.3
Feb	64	17.8	47	8.3	13.8
Mar	68	20.0	48	8.9	14.1
Apr	72	22.2	51	10.6	15.3
May	78	25.6	56	13.3	17.6
Jun	85	29.4	63	17.2	21.3
Jul	92	33.3	69	20.6	24.4
Aug	91	32.8	70	21.1	26.1
Sep	86	30.0	69	20.6	25.0
Oct	82	27.8	63	17.2	22.5
Nov	74	23.3	54	12.2	19.4
Dec	67	19.4	49	9.4	16.4

BEACHES

MALTA

There are some delightful sandy beaches in the north and north-west of the island suitable for non-swimmers and children, although warning notices at Ghajn Tuffieha and Gnejna should be heeded. Rock bathing is excellent, especially round St Paul's Bay, Sliema and in the south-east (Birzebbuga and Delimara). It is always possible, except in really rough weather, to find a sheltered cove or beach.

Sandy beaches accessible by bus:

Beach	Bus
Armier Bay	50
Ghajn Tuffieha Bay	47, 52
Golden Bay	47, 52
Mellieha Bay	44, 45
Paradise Bay, Cirkewwa	45A
Ramla tal-Bir Bay, Marfa	45, 48
St George's Bay, St Julian's	68

GOZO

Gozo has three accessible sandy beaches: Ramla Bay, Marsalforn Bay and Xlendi Bay.

SPORTS

Water sports

With the warm, clear water and sea breezes round Malta, the most popular summer sports for visitors are scuba diving, water skiing and sailing. Deep-sea fishing can be enjoyed by contacting local fishermen at any of the bays where they keep their boats. Charges are negotiable.

Water sports centres

Malta Hilton St Julian's
Skiing, boat-hire and sub-aqua
Mellieha Bay Hotel
Water Skiing and Sub-Aqua School
Cresta Quay, St George's Bay
Skiing, boat hire and sub-aqua
Dragonara Ski Club
Skiing, boat-hire and sub-aqua
Ramla Bay Hotel
Skiing, boat-hire

Note on scuba diving Malta is a popular centre for the sport of aqualung diving with its stable weather conditions and sheltered bays and creeks. An excellent guide to diving sites in Malta and Gozo is *Diving Around the Maltese Islands* by Fudge and Harris, published by Progress Press, Valletta (1975). The guide also contains information about marine life, diving clubs and suppliers.

Yachts

Berthing facilities are available at the Yacht Marina Harbour (Marsamxett Harbour) to the west of Grand Harbour. Servicing facilities are available from the *Manoel Island Yacht Yard*, London office c/o Malta Drydocks, Marine Engineers Memorial Building, 18 London Street, London EC3.

Yacht and dinghy hire

For those without their own craft, yachts and dinghies can be hired for a half day or longer from *Charles Vella, Hay Wharf, Marsamxett Harbour*.

Competitive and spectator sports

Tennis, squash and golf can be played all the year round. The Malta Sports Club, Marsa, at which one can enjoy all these sports, offers temporary membership to visitors.
Spectator sports include water polo, a popular summer sport, and polo and horse racing in the winter. Polo is played at the Marsa Sports Club. The Malta Racing Club holds race meetings every Sunday between October and May.

MUSEUMS AND MONUMENTS

Museums Except where otherwise stated, the opening hours for museums, etc. is: 1 Oct-15 Jun 08.30-17.00 daily, inc. Sun. From 16 Jun-20 Sep 08.00-14.00 daily, inc. Sun. Closed on public holidays. Entrance is usually about 15 cents.

VALLETTA
National Museum of Archaeology Republic St
National Museum of Fine Arts South St
Grand Master's Palace State Rooms and Armoury Republic St
St John's Co-Cathedral and Museum St John's Sq. Open Mon-Sat 09.30-12.00 & 15.00-17.00
War Relics Museum Fort St Elmo
National Library (Bibliotheca) Republic St. Open Mon-Sat 08.00-12.30 & 13.30-17.00 (closed Sat afternoon & Wed). Summer (16 Jun-30 Sep) closed Wed & afternoons
Mediterranean Conference Centre St Paul St. Open weekdays 10.00-16.30. The *Malta Experience*, a show presenting 5000 years of Maltese history, can be seen Mon-Fri 4 times daily and twice on Sat.

MDINA
National Museum of Natural History Vilhena Palace (Magisterial Palace)
Cathedral Museum Archbishop Sq. Open Mon-Sat 09.00-13.00 & 14.00-16.30

RABAT
St Paul's Catacombs St Agatha St
Roman Villa/Museum Museum Esplanade

BIRZEBBUGA
Ghar Dalam Cave and Museum Zejtun Rd

VITTORIOSA
Inquisitor's Palace Main Gate St

VICTORIA, GOZO
Gozo Museum Citadel
Cathedral Museum and **Folklore Museum** Citadel. Daily 09.00-16.00

Temples are accessible at any time or open at the same time as museums.

PAOLA
Hal-Saflieni Hypogeum Burials St

TARXIEN
Tarxien Temples Old Temple St

QRENDI
Hangar Qim and **Mnajdra Temples**

MGARR
Ta'Hagrat Temple (key from police station)

XAGHRA, GOZO
Ggantija Temples

Churches are usually open in the mornings from 05.30-10.00 and in the afternoons from 16.00-19.00 or later. Country chapels are kept closed, and to see the interior one should contact the parish priest.

CURRENCY AND BANKS

Malta has a decimal currency with one Maltese pound (£M1) being equal to 100 cents, and each cent being divided into 10 mils. There are £M10, £M5 and £M1 notes and 50, 25, 10, 5, 2 and 1 cent coins. Also 5 and 2 mils coins.

Hotels will cash travellers' cheques, but better rates will be obtained from the banks. There are branches in all towns and large villages, and these are normally open Mon-Fri between 08.30-12.30, Sat 08.30-12.00. There is a bank open 24 hrs at Luqa Airport.

SHOPPING

Shops are open daily between 09.00-19.00 (Sat until 20.00) with a two to three-hour lunch break. To alleviate Sunday closing, one food shop in each village is open until 10.00 (also chemists). Prices are fixed on all items. Valletta and Sliema are the two main shopping centres. Hand-knitted and crochet garments should if possible be bought in Gozo where there is a greater variety and cheaper prices.

Shops worth visiting:

Valletta
Artisans Centre, City Gate Arcade
Government Souvenir Shop, Castile Place
Ixtri Malti, Old Market Building, Merchants St

Luqa International Airport
Souvenir Shop

Rabat
Ta'Qali Crafts Village (see p.26)

Mdina
Greenhand Leather Craft, Villegaignon St

Street markets are an attractive feature of Maltese life. Markets are normally open in the mornings between 07.00-12.00, and it is worth going early for the best produce. An interesting market in Valletta, open on Sunday mornings only, is held in the moat below St James' Bastion.

HEALTH

Visitors from the USA, Canada, Australia and Europe do not require certificates of vaccination or inoculation to enter Malta. The island has an excellent health service and there is a reciprocal agreement for medical treatment with the UK providing for immediate medical care to tourists from the UK.

POLICE

The police are very helpful. In villages police stations are in or near the parish church square. All have a map of the village.

TOURIST INFORMATION

Information on all aspects of Maltese travel is available from the Malta National Tourist Organisation, 18 Kensington Square, London W8.

The tourist information office in Valletta is at 1 City Gate Arcade. Hours:

1 Oct-15 Jun
Mon-Sat 08.30-12.30 & 13.15-18.00
16 Jun-30 Sep
Mon-Sat 08.30-13.30 & 15.00-18.00

Archaeology

Malta's prehistoric remains have recently come under fresh scrutiny following new developments in the radiocarbon method of dating (tree-ring calibration of radiocarbon). These findings suggest that the temples may be up to 1000 years older than current estimates: a proposition with challenging implications for historians.*

Long before the dating issue was raised, questions have been asked about the contribution of Malta's prehistoric cultures to the development of European civilization. The wealth of material, fine workmanship and level of artistic achievement are the products of an advanced and highly individual culture, and one that was, apparently, totally indigenous.

The separate evolution of Malta's Temple Culture has intrigued scholars since the giant buildings were first uncovered in the early 19th century. More intriguing, perhaps, is the highly speculative question of their own influence on later European cultures.

Temples The building of the monumental megalithic temples of the Maltese Islands spans a period of 800 years, from c. 2800–2000 BC. These temples are unique, both in their structure and their antiquity, and can be related to no other culture in the Mediterranean or elsewhere.

We know little of the beliefs and rituals of the people who built the temples. Much is guesswork, but the the existence of altars, libation holes and other evidence shows that the buildings were shrines. A fertility cult is evident from the symbolism of carved phalli, reliefs of bull and sow, and the 'fat lady' figures. One statue and numerous figurines have been found of this cult figure or deity to whom, presumably, the temples were dedicated. The statue at Tarxien is immensely fat with tiny feet, and wears a full pleated skirt (proof that the builders of these temples were also skilled at weaving?). There is evidence of animal sacrifice, of votive offerings, of a priesthood.

The temples follow the same plan. With the exception of Tarxien, they all face south-east and have a semi-circular forecourt. They are curvilinear in form with concave façades and central entrances. They are divided into public and sacred areas. In the simplest, or *lobed* form, the passage from the forecourt leads to an internal court expanding into irregular curved chambers. From this simple form, four others evolved, as follows:

Trefoil Three chambers, two lateral and one central, open symmetrically off a court.

5-apse A second pair of parallel lateral apses is added to the first pair with a connecting interior passage.

4-apse The central apse of a 5-apse temple is reduced to a niche.

6-apse A third pair of parallel lateral apses with a second interior passage is added while the central apse remains a niche.

With the exception of Hagar Qim, which is of globigerina throughout, the outer walls of the temples were constructed with coralline to withstand

Hagar Qim temple, entrance

weathering, with internal walls of dressed globigerina. The space between the two walls was packed with rubble or left as a small inner chamber. Doorways are either a *'porthole'* (a rectangular hole in the centre of a slab) or *trilithon* (a stone lintel supported by two stone uprights). Roofs were probably corbelled to a certain level (each stone course stepped inwards to form a 'beehive') then completed with rafters, thatch or brushwood and clay.

The most fascinating prehistoric site in Malta is the underground sanctuary known as the Hal-Saflieni Hypogeum, in Paola. This incorporates many architectural features of the built temples, but has been carved entirely out of the rock. Apart from the Hypogeum, eight temple sites are accessible to visitors: Hagar Qim, Mnajdra, Ggantija (Gozo), Tarxien, Kordin, Ta'Hagrat, Skorba and Bugibba. Of these the first four are the most intact and therefore the most interesting.

Dolmens These Bronze Age burial chambers were surface built and constructed by placing a capstone on two upright boulders. (A shallow depression was first dug in the rock to increase the capacity of the chamber.) The deceased was cremated and his ashes, together with the usual burial offerings, were placed in a large jar inside the dolmen.

Cart ruts Of all the mysteries of Maltese prehistory, there is none more baffling than the 'cart ruts'. These parallel grooves in the rock are found all over Malta and, to a lesser extent, in Gozo. The ruts often run in groups, sometimes crossing one another like railway sidings (one dense concentration near Buskett has been named 'Clapham Junction').

They run for long distances, crossing the ridges between valleys, and often follow the route of modern roads. Where a Bronze Age village has been discovered there are usually cart ruts running up to it. Further evidence

supporting a Bronze Age dating lies in the places where the ruts have been obliterated by the cutting of square Punic tomb shafts.

It is now generally agreed that these tracks were made by 'slide-cars' — two parallel poles, stone shod, with a platform between. The tracks were first chipped out to determine the course and then deepened by the friction of the vehicle. The ruts were roughly a foot wide at the top, narrowing at the base, and of varying depths. The gauge is about $4\frac{1}{2}$ ft. They were obviously a transportation system, and probably used to carry seaweed from the shore and soil from the valleys to turn the barren rocks round the hill-top settlements into fertile land. How they were powered (man, beast or other agency) remains a mystery, as there is no evidence of wear on the surface of the rock either between or at the sides of the ruts.

Rock tombs Much of our knowledge of the inhabitants of the Maltese islands between 3200 BC and the 8th century AD comes from their tombs and tomb furnishings. (Before that date it is presumed that burials were made in the earth, but earlier rock tombs may yet be discovered.) With the exception of the Bronze Age people, who incinerated their dead and placed the ashes in dolmens, the common method of burial was in rock-cut tombs.

The earliest of these tombs were found at Zebbug (c. 3200 BC). They have since been destroyed. Circular in shape and with a sealed entrance, they contained a number of human and animal remains, pottery sherds, flint tools and ornaments of bone or shell.

Tombs were subsequently entered by vertical shafts. These were circular, and the chambers kidney-shaped. (Good examples of this type may be seen at Xemxija near St Paul's Bay, c. 2800 BC).

In later periods, notably the Phoenician and Roman, shafts were square and the chambers rectangular. The shafts varied in depth from 3 ft. to a little more than 10 ft. The rectangular

Main types of grave in Maltese catacombs

Prehistoric sequence (Radiocarbon dating)

Approx. date	Type site	Monument
Neolithic		
3800–3600	Ghar Dalam	Wall (Skorba)
		Ghar Dalam Cave
3600–3400	Grey Skorba	Village hut
		(Skorba)
3400–3200	Red Skorba	Village shrine
		(Skorba)

Temple Culture (Copper Age in neighbouring countries)

3200–2800	Zebbug	Rock-cut tombs
		(now destroyed)
2800	Mgarr	Rock-cut tombs
		(Xemxija)
2800–2400	Ggantija	Kordin III E.
		Kordin III W.
		Skorba W.
		Bugibba
		Ta'Hagrat W.
		Mnajdra E.
		Tarxien far E.
		Ggantija S. & N.
2400	Hal-Saflieni	Hypogeum
		Ta'Hagrat E.
2400–2000	Tarxien	Hagar Qim N.
		Skorba E.
		Tarxien S. & E.
		Tarxien C.
		Mnajdra S. & C.
Bronze Age		
2000–1400	Tarxien	Cremation cemetery
	Cemetery	Dolmens
1400–900	Borg-in-Nadur	Defensive wall
		Village
900–800	Bahrija	Fortified village

See also *Malta in history*, p.12

burial chamber measured about 5ft × 7ft, with a deep trench in the middle, space being left for two bodies, one on either side. When a new interment took place the old remains were placed in the trench. The chamber was shut off from the shaft by a stone slab placed on end and fixed in a mortice cut in the face of the rock. Sometimes the tombs were cut so close to each other that either by accident or design one chamber led into another. Subsequently a single shaft gave access to several groups of burial chambers.

The objects found in the early tombs (pottery, ornaments etc.) were very simple. With successive periods tomb furniture became more elaborate: pottery jugs and vases, metal objects, glassware and lamps.

Catacombs With the coming of Christianity a more elaborate system of underground cemeteries evolved, incorporating halls and chapels. Here followers of the new religion could assemble, and prayers would be offered for the souls of the departed. The first underground cemeteries were introduced to Rome by the Jews

St Paul's Catacombs, Rabat

from Palestine, and the early Christians in Malta adopted many of their religious rites and symbols. Roman law forbade the burial of the dead within a city wall, and in the case of Mdina (the Roman capital Melita) the more extensive catacombs are found outside the old boundary ditch. Smaller catacombs are found in the countryside.

The types of grave in the Maltese catacombs are:

Loculus A horizontal recess cut in the gallery wall. The front was sealed by a stone slab or tiles cemented into place. Many are small, used for children.

Floor grave A rectangular pit cut into the rock floor. Usually for two bodies and with headrests hollowed out at one end.

Canopied table grave A pair of floor graves but at waist height, enclosed by walls with arched openings. The graves would be sealed separately with stone slabs, the final appearance being that of a table.

Saddle-backed canopied tomb In this the surface at waist level is a saddle-backed roof, the chamber beneath being entered through a square cut in one of the sides and sealed with a large block provided with a projecting knob.

Arcosolium tomb or window grave. In this the rectangular chamber is cut at waist level into the gallery wall. The square entrance is set back in an arched niche.

Finally, mention must be made of the *agape table*, a special feature of Maltese catacombs. It consists of a circular table carved from the rock, surrounded by a bench at the same level with an opening for access. The table is sited near the entrance to the catacomb and is thought to have been either the place where religious rites were performed when the body was brought in for burial, or where the mourners reclined for a farewell feast.

For details of prehistoric sites with opening hours, see *Museums and Monuments*, p. 29.

Churches Before the 15th century, many Maltese churches were no more than cave sanctuaries, the troglodyte type of the early Christian era. The great exception to this was the original cathedral built by the Normans at Mdina (later destroyed in the earthquake of 1693).

With the creation of the first parishes in 1436 a few small churches were built. Their design was extremely simple, limited by the absence of timber. Rectangular in shape, they had double walls of stone with a filling of rubble. The interior was spanned by arches which carried horizontal roof slabs. The only source of light was the door at the west end and one or two small windows. These were usually over the west door (a circular light) and sometimes at the east end. Another typical feature was the *zuntier* before the west door, an enclosed space which served as an atrium to the church.

A good example of an early pre-Knights church is St Mary 'Ta'Bir Miftuh' at Gudja. This has two further features also found on many of the country churches: a small bell-cot at the west end and projecting water spouts at roof level. Only churches were allowed to have waterspouts: all other buildings had to conserve their roof water.

Another 15th century parish church, St Gregory at Zejtun, shows how the Knights adapted the Maltese churches to their own conventions with the addition of transepts and a dome at the crossing. This is the oldest example of dome construction in Malta, the low saucer shape quite unlike the high Baroque domes of the 17th century.

Before the advent of Baroque, European styles made little impression on Maltese architecture. The reasons were simple. During the flowering of the Renaissance in Europe the Maltese were struggling to survive the burden of taxation imposed by their feudal lords: at the same time they were suffering the devastating raids of Barbary corsairs. The arrival of the Knights in 1530 brought wealth and protection to the

Art and architecture

Most of Malta's historic buildings were constructed during the period of the Order of St John. The champions of a beleaguered Christendom, the Knights worked with verve and determination to transform a barren undeveloped island into the citadel of their faith: rich, grandiose and cosmopolitan.

Bust of Grand Master Carafa
on Auberge d'Italie, Valletta

island, but another century was to pass before the building of the big new parish churches got under way. In that century the Knights were to concentrate their efforts on building their great new fortress city, Valletta, and the fortifications of the harbour.

The country churches built by the Knights during this period, such as those dedicated to St Roque at Balzan and Zebbug, maintained the vernacular tradition of functional simplicity. Much of this is also seen in the architecture of the Conventual Church of St John in Valletta (1573–77) with its plain exterior, rectangular interior and barrel vault. (The inside, of course, was greatly embellished by successive Grand Masters.)

The architect of this building, *Gerolamo Cassar* (b. 1520), was the the first of a line of distinguished Maltese architects working for the Knights. As the architect of the Order he was responsible for the planning and building of Valletta. He was primarily a military engineer who had worked on the fortifications, and the discipline of his calling shows in the solid lines of his architecture. Two other churches built by Cassar were St Augustine in Rabat and the church of St Catherine in Valletta.

Another architect to express his own style before the tide of Baroque swept the island was *Tommaso Dingli* (b. 1591). His Renaissance façades echo the Rome of the 15th century, and there is no doubt that those he designed for the church of the Assumption, Birkirkara (1617) and St Mary's, Attard (1613) are two of the most beautiful works of architecture in Malta.

By the middle of the 17th century Maltese architecture had fallen in line with the rest of Europe, particularly Italy and Sicily. The style was Baroque, in the Roman tradition, and the ground plan the Latin cross, with a dome raised on a tall drum over the crossing.

A departure from this was the centrally-planned churches of the late 17th century. These churches were usually on very narrow sites, which made transepts impracticable, and were designed in this way to conserve space. The interior plan was based on either a circle, oval, square or octagon. The best examples of this type of church are found in Valletta.

The most important architect of the period was *Lorenzo Gafà* (b. 1630), a Maltese who was trained in Rome and influenced by Bernini. He set the style for Maltese Baroque with his elegant domes set on their tall drums and his majestic façades with their superimposed pilasters. His interiors introduced further concepts that were new to the island. The attic course created an additional vertical stage above the entablature, which served to raise the arches of the vault. The vault was thus loftier than in earlier churches, and though maintaining the barrel shape was intersected by small vaults above the bays, each lit by a side window. The resulting ceiling provided an interesting arrangement of surfaces for the painters to apply their colourful compositions.

Among Gafà's churches are the cathedrals at Mdina and Gozo, St Lawrence at Vittoriosa, St Catherine at Zejtun and St Nicholas at Siggiewi. Of all these the cathedral at Mdina (1697) which replaced the Norman building destroyed by the earthquake, is considered to be his finest work and the one which best expresses the spirit of Maltese Baroque.

Stonemasons cutting limestone blocks

35

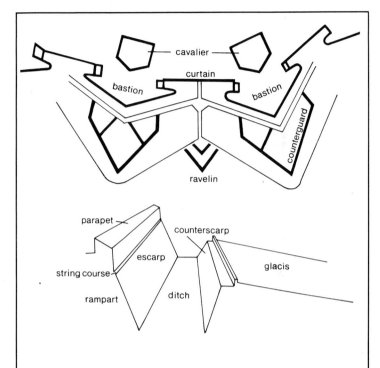

Fortifications: Glossary

Bastion Stone-faced earthwork projecting from fortification

Bulwark Rampart, earthwork

Casement Vaulted chamber in thickness of fortress wall with embrasures for guns

Cavalier Inner defence work higher than other lines of fortification. (In the Knights' fortifications, these are five-sided towers covering the bastions)

Counterguard Protective work in front of bastion

Counterscarp Outer wall or slope of ditch

Curtain Plain wall of fortification usually connecting two bastions

Demi-bastion Half bastion protecting curtain

Demilune Triangular outwork protecting bastion

Enceinte The enclosure of the fortifications

Escarp Outer face of rampart

Fougasse Improvised mortar in hole in rock, charged with stones etc. and fired by gunpowder

Glacis Slope at approach to fort (before ditch) on which attackers are exposed to fire

Hornwork Defence work outside main line of fortifications, usually with two demi-bastions on side open to attack

Outworks Detached defence works outside main line of fortifications

Parapet Low wall at top of rampart to protect defenders

Rampart Broad-topped stone-parapeted defence work

Ravelin Defence work detached from main fortifications with two faces meeting in 'V' at front, and open at the rear to make it exposed in the event of capture. Placed in front of curtain

Sally-port Small opening in fortification from which defenders could sally out and attack besiegers

Tenaille Outwork in main ditch between two bastions, oblong in shape with projecting ends

Gafà's work served as the inspiration for 18th century architects, most notably *Domenico Cachia*, whose St Helen's at Birkirkara (1727–45) is generally considered the finest of the island's larger parish churches. The modelling of the façade is particularly splendid, with an exuberance seen again in the architect's design for the façade of the remodelled Auberge de Castile et Leon (1744).

Fortifications The stronghold of the Knights (Valletta, Grand Harbour and the Three Cities) comprises one of the finest complexes of fortifications in Europe. The construction of these defences continued throughout the Knights' occupation of the islands (1530–1798), but the basic concept lay in the proposals put forward by the Italian military engineer *Francesco Laparelli* to the Grand Master La Vallette in 1566.

This was in the year after the Great Siege of Malta by the Turks, and up to this time the only points to be fortified were Fort St Elmo on the Sceberras peninsula and two peninsulas on the other side of the harbour, L'Isola and Birgu. At the tip of the latter was the citadel fort of St Angelo, the Knights' last line of defence. All these fortifications were badly damaged in the siege, and their inadequacies exposed. Most serious was their vulnerability to the high ground of the Sceberras peninsula (Mt Sceberras) where the Turks had placed their cannon to fire down on St Elmo and the forts across the harbour. The only way to neutralize this high ground was by occupation and fortification: this was the genesis of Valletta.

At the time of the Knights' move to Malta, fortress design was undergoing a major revolution, which in simple terms was the change from the castle with rounded towers placed at the corners and at intervals along the walls to the geometrically designed *enceinte* with angled bastions.

These projecting bastions were located in such a way that the guns mounted on their flanks could not only protect the curtain wall with

enfilading fire but also rake the face of the opposing bastion (see drawing opposite). In Laparelli's plan the western (land) front of Valletta was guarded by four bastions, with three intervening curtain walls. In the central wall was the main entrance to the city (now City Gate). The system of curtain walls with strategically placed bastions continued round the peninsula to the strongpoint of Fort St Elmo at the tip. On the land front, deep ditches were dug in front of the bastions to serve both as an additional defence and as a protected assembly place for any of the defenders' forces carrying out a counter-attack on the besiegers. In front of the ditch a further system of fortifications served to protect the bastions. This included two

counterguards and a central ravelin. To cover the bastions from above, two cavaliers were built. These fortified towers gave a commanding view of the countryside.

Looking at the fortifications of the land front from the Hastings Gardens the visitor will be impressed by the depth of the parapets. A thickness of at least 18 ft of stone wall backed by solid earth was necessary to stand up to the largest Turkish cannon. Such a thickness, of course, had its disadvantages, creating a blind area in front: this was where the viewpoints offered by the flanks of the bastions were so vital.

In less than ten years the fortifications of Valletta were completed, allowing the Knights to concentrate on the building of the city. The subsequent development of artillery, however,

Parapet on land front, Valletta

forced them to look again at their defences, and in 1632 *Pietro Floriani* was commissioned to extend the land front to counteract the increased range of the siege cannon. In this way the fortifications of Floriana were created, involving an even more sophisticated system of defence. A new line of bastions and curtain walls was constructed about 800 yards west of the fortress city and stretching back along the flanks of the peninsula. In front, on the landward side, were two ravelins, open at the back so that they could not be used as forts by the attackers. Finally, a huge hornwork was built on the Grand Harbour side of the defences.

With work completed on Valletta's defences, attention was transferred to the other side of the harbour. Under the direction of another Italian, *Firenzuola*, building commenced on a circle of bastions around Cospicua, the only one of the Three Cities to be unfortified. These defences, the Margherita or Firenzuola Lines, were later interrupted (1670) by a more grandiose scheme, promoted by the Grand Master Nicolas Cotoner, to construct a much wider arc of fortifications (the Cottonera Lines) to totally embrace the landward approach to the Three Cities. The architect was *Valperga*, who also planned the suburb of Floriana.

Another project of Valperga commenced in 1670 was the building of Fort Ricasoli. Sited on the promontory opposite Fort St Elmo, this ensured the protection of both sides of the harbour.

Later works were concentrated on the defence of Marsamxett Harbour, on the other side of the Sceberras peninsula. The principal buildings here were Fort Manoel, commenced in 1722 on the small island in the harbour, and Fort Tigné on the promontory opposite Fort St Elmo (1792). With the last building the fortifications of the Knights had reached a logical conclusion and it is a sad irony that six years later when they might have been put to the test, the city was surrendered without a fight to Napoleon.

Watch towers, small forts and fortified villas The defence of Malta was not confined to Valletta but extended to all the bays and inlets of the island that might be vulnerable to attack. At prominent points the Knights built watch towers which could communicate by signals the approach of an enemy fleet. These were very simple buildings of two or three floors with a communicating ladder or spiral staircase. The most impressive is the Red Tower, built like a miniature fortress, which stands on the Marfa Ridge overlooking the northern approaches to the island.

In addition to the towers, small forts were built guarding the bays which might be used as landing places by an invader. The most important of these were Fort St Thomas,

commanding the entrance to
Marsaskala Bay, Fort St Lucian
protecting Marsaxlokk Bay and Fort
St Mary on Comino, guarding the
channels between Malta and Gozo.
Though small the forts were strongly
built and designed to serve a
permanent garrison who were
required not only to fire on enemy
vessels but to defend their position.

Imitating the forts in their architecture,
the fortified villas provided individual
defence for the nobility. The best
examples of these are the Selmun
Palace near Mellieha and the
Verdala Palace near Rabat, the latter
the country residence of the Grand
Master. Both have crenellation and
corner bastions, but these were
probably more for effect, as it is
doubtful whether either building
would have withstood a major assault.

Villages In the event of a Turkish
invasion or corsair raid, protection of
one kind or another was available to
the Knights and the city dwellers. The
ordinary country folk, however, had to
fend for themselves. Those in the
villages in the south were
particularly vulnerable to armies or
raiding parties marching inland from
the coastal landing places. The main
refuge was the defensive tower in the
centre of the village (a good example
may be seen at Qrendi). Failing that
the only defence lay in the narrow
streets of the village itself. The
intricacy of their layout and the
shortage of exits served a purpose:
to confuse and trap the enemy, who
could then be attacked from roof-tops.
Many of these villages have now been
opened out, but old alleys and cul-de-
sacs remain to baffle the tourist.

Valletta, showing Sceberras peninsula and Fort St Elmo

Domestic architecture The farmhouses and rural dwellings of Malta, so much a feature of the landscape, have their own unique character, prescribed by the available building materials. Without timber for beams, their roofs had to be constructed with stone slabs. These slabs, which could span at the most a width of six feet, were supported on a series of stone arches. To support these arches, walls had to be especially thick and were usually built double with an infilling of rubble. The window openings were very small—a protection against wind, sun and marauder—but their severe appearance is deceptive. Inside, windows open on to a shaded courtyard or garden—one of the most attractive features of Maltese houses.

Decorative features These were applied mainly to the public buildings or to the houses of the nobility. In the auberges of Vittoriosa (Birgu) the only point of interest in an otherwise plain façade is found in the window mouldings. Known as Melitan 'fat' mouldings, these consist of a triple roll and are unique to Malta. In use until 1620, they are also found in Valletta, Mdina and other places.

A distinctive feature introduced by the architect of Valletta, Gerolamo Cassar, can be seen in the Grand Master's Palace, Auberge de Provence and other buildings. This is the binding of the corners of the building with pronounced stonework (rusticated quoins). Such embellishments were borrowed from Roman architecture of the period which Cassar had studied.

Italian influence was predominant and the austerity of the early years gave way to the elaboration of detail occurring in contemporary movements. The apogee of façade decoration was reached in the early to middle 18th century with such buildings as the Castellania in Merchants Street and the remodelled Auberge de Castile et Leon. Here, as

Top: Maltese farmhouse
Above: Melitan 'fat' moulding

on church façades of the period, the soft limestone is carved to maximum effect, making full use of the architectural details (pilasters, cornices, portals, window mouldings etc.). Some of the auberges bear the elaborate escutcheons of Grand Masters who added them during their reign: a fine example is on the Auberge d'Italie in Merchants Street.

Artists No tradition of fine art existed in Malta before the time of the Knights. The island was a province of Sicily from which most of the works of art were imported. When the Knights came they brought their own painters and sculptors to embellish their great buildings. Among these, the most prolific were *Mattia Preti* (b. 1613) from Calabria, who painted the ceiling of the Conventual Church and many fine altarpieces, and the Frenchman *Antoine de Favray* (b. 1706) who in addition to his church paintings produced many fine portraits of the nobility and studies of Maltese habits and costumes. For their services to the Order both artists were made Knights of Grace, a distinction which they shared with a more famous predecessor, Caravaggio.

Caravaggio (1560–1609) came to Malta in 1607 under the patronage of the Knights, to carry out various commissions. His stay was, however, brief, as within a year or so the tempestuous artist had disgraced himself. The most famous of his works in the island is the *Beheading of St John*, in the Oratory of the Conventual Church (Co-Cathedral of St John).

The artistic activity engendered by the Knights created a response in the Maltese. Native talent, already expressed in architecture, asserted itself further in the paintings of *Stefano Erardi* (b. c. 1630) and *Francesco Zahra* (b. c. 1680) who decorated churches in Malta and Gozo. Sculpture, and sculptors, were mainly imported, but there are two distinguished Maltese names.

Melchiorre Gafà (b. 1635), brother of the architect, produced many fine works, most notably the figure of St Paul in the church of St Paul Shipwrecked in Valletta. A more recent sculptor was *Antonio Sciortino* (1883–1947). Many of his works, and of other native-born artists, may be seen in the Fine Arts Museum in Valletta.

The Beheading of St John *by Caravaggio*

The Knights of St John

The Sovereign Military and Hospitaller
Order of St John of Jerusalem
of Rhodes and Malta

In the full title of the oldest order of chivalry lies a summary of its history and purpose.

The title 'Hospitaller' relates to the primary function of the Order, which was to maintain a hospice in Jerusalem for the care of the Christian pilgrims visiting the shrines of the Holy Land. The hospice, founded c. 1080 by merchants from Amalfi, was dedicated to St John and administered by Benedictine monks who called themselves the 'Frères Hospitallers de St Jean de Jerusalem.' Their leader was Brother Gerard, Prefect of the Hospital, who was effectively the first Grand Master of the Order.

At this time Jerusalem was in the hands of the Turks, who though lenient to Christian worship in the Holy Places were persistent in their harassment of the pilgrims *en route*. This brought the eventual retribution of the First Crusade, and in 1099 the city fell to the Christian armies after a six-week siege. The Hospitallers, on hand to welcome the conquerors, were able to tend their needs, and in so doing establish themselves as saviours in the eyes of the grateful Christians.

The rewards for their services were numerous: money and gifts of land from the estates of the European nobility who had fought in the Crusade and—no less important— the physical support of the many Knights who now joined the Order.

In 1113 the Order acquired, through a Papal Bull, the status of a religious foundation, with all members taking vows of poverty, chastity and obedience. (This historic document can now be seen in the National Library in Valletta.) Subsequently, as the struggle with the Moslems intensified, the Order assumed its military role. To their monastic vows the soldier-monks added a pledge to protect the Holy Places and to wage a continuing war against the infidel.

For two centuries the Knights maintained this role in the defence of the Kingdom of Jerusalem, assisting in successive crusades and adding to their prestige both by their knightly deeds and their increasing wealth. After the recapture of Jerusalem by Saladin (1187) the Christians were in retreat, but their final expulsion from the Holy Land (1291) though marking the end of the Kingdom, was no more than a temporary setback for the Knights.

By this time the consolidation of their wealth and land holdings in Europe had provided them with the material support necessary to tide them over until they were able to find a new base for their endeavours. Temporarily this home was Cyprus, but in 1309 the Knights moved to the island of Rhodes, off the west coast of Turkey, which they had wrested from the Byzantines. Here, in what was to be their first sovereign territory, they created a fortified city and built a powerful navy which they used both to defend their shores and to harry the Turkish fleet.

In 1480 the Turks laid siege to the island, but after several months were repelled with great losses. In 1520 they tried again, this time under the leadership of Suleiman the Magnificent. The Knights put up a heroic defence, but the odds were against them. Not only were they vastly outnumbered by the Turks but a long way from their allies in Europe, who were unable to send them either the supplies or reinforcements necessary to maintain the siege. In the end, after six months, they were forced to capitulate to Suleiman. Impressed by their valour, the Sultan granted the Knights the honours of war, allowing them to leave the island unharmed and in their own ships.

For the next seven years the homeless knights wandered the Mediterranean. Initially they sought funds to mount an expedition to Rhodes to recapture the island, but when this was not forthcoming they petitioned their allies for a new base in the Mediterranean. Their efforts were finally rewarded with the offer of Malta by the Holy Roman Emperor, Charles V. For the next 270 years this was to be their home. (For the history of the Knights in Malta, see p. 14.)

Members of the Order of St John at the 400th anniversary of the Great Siege, Valletta

Constitution of the Order in Malta

Convent This was the seat of the Order where the Grand Master, the Council and the Langues had their official residence.

Council The Order's governing authority, presided over by the Grand Master.

Chapter-General This was the supreme legislative authority, responsible for drawing up the statutes of the Order. It could be summoned only by the Pope or Grand Master. It consisted of the following members, who represented the hierarchy of the Order:

Grand Master

Bishop

Prior of the Conventual Church

Grand Treasurer

Piliers (Heads of the Eight Langues)

Grand Priors, Bailiffs and
   Commanders

(These officers were in charge of the Order's properties. The more important were known as Priories, the lesser as Bailiwicks and Commanderies.)

Provincial Chapters dealing with local matters were held in every Priory, presided over by the Grand Prior. Appeal could be made to the Council of the Order.

Grand Master The head of the Order, who was also Prince of his own sovereign state, was elected by his fellow knights and served for life.

Langues The Order was divided into eight Langues, or 'tongues'. These were Aragon, Auvergne, Castile and Leon, England, France, Germany, Provence and Italy. Each was given a section of the fortifications to defend, and specific duties. The heads of the Langues (the Piliers) were designated special responsibilities:

Aragon Grand Conservator:
   transport and supplies

Auvergne Marshal: military
   administration

Castile and Leon Chancellor: the
   Chancery

England Turcopilier: mounted forces
   and coastguard

France Hospitaller: the Infirmary

Germany Grand Bailiff: fortified
   outposts

Provence Grand Preceptor: the
   Treasury

Italy Admiral: head of the Navy

Each Langue had its own church, and a chapel in the Conventual Church of St John.

Members The order was divided into three classes: Knights of Justice, Chaplains and Serving Brothers.

Knights of Justice The military knights, who were required to produce proof of nobility on both the father's and mother's side, going back (in the case of the German Langue) as many as five generations. On admission to the Order the knight took vows of poverty, chastity and obedience. He also paid an admission fee (*passaggio*) and willed four-fifths of his possessions to the Order. In this way the Order acquired the allegiance—and wealth—of some of the most distinguished families in Europe.

Chaplains The priests of the Order were associated with the work of the church and hospital. They were not expected to be nobly born; merely 'respectable'.

Serving Brothers The duties of this third class (not nobly born) were both military and domestic.

In addition to the above were the honorary *Knights of Grace*, appointed for some meritorious service to the Order.

Residence The Magisterial Palace was the official residence of the Grand Master. Here also was the Council Chamber (the present Tapestry Room) and the hall used for state functions (now the Hall of St Michael and St George).

Until a knight was given a Commandery he lived in the Auberge (Inn) of his Langue. Formerly, in Rhodes, the knights lived in a segregated area known as the *Collachio*. The same segregation had been attempted, less successfully, in Birgu, but in Valletta the idea was thought impracticable for the defence of the city and the auberges were more strategically located.

Escutcheons of the Grand Masters of the Order of St John in Malta 1530-1798

DE L'ISLE ADAM
1530-34

DEL PONTE
1534-35

DE ST JAILLE
1535-36

DE HOMEDES
1536-53

DE LA SENGLE
1553-57

DE LA VALLETTE
1557-68

DEL MONTE
1568-72

DE LA CASSIERE
1572-82

DE VERDALLE
1582-95

GARZES
1595-1601

ALOF DE WIGNACOURT
1601-22

DE VASCONCELLOS
1622-23

DE PAULE
1623-36

DE LASCARIS
1636-57

DE REDIN
1657-60

DE CHATTES GESSAN
1660

RAFAEL COTONER
1660-63

NICOLAS COTONER
1663-80

CARAFA
1680-90

ADRIEN DE WIGNACOURT
1690-97

PERELLOS
1697-1720

ZONDADARI
1720-22

DE VILHENA
1722-36

DESPUIG
1736-41

PINTO
1741-73

XIMENES
1773-75

DE ROHAN
1775-97

VON HOMPESCH
1797-98

45

Plants and flowers From autumn to spring Malta's rocky landscape is relieved by an astonishing variety of wild flowers. The earliest bloom after the autumn rains, and many remain in flower for three or four months. A few of the familiar species are listed below, with the month of flowering:

October Buttercups and wood daisies spring up in woodlands and valleys. The narcissus (*N. tazetta*) is also found in the valleys under the carob trees. This lovely fragrant flower is widely marketed, especially at Christmas.

November The field marigold (*Calendula arvensis*) can be seen in most rural areas.

December The Mediterranean heather (*Erica multiflora*) is conspicuous in exposed coastal areas. The cape sorrel (*Oxalis cernua*), also known as the 'English weed' is said to have been introduced to the island by an Englishwoman in 1806. Although it brightens the countryside, this attractive lemon yellow flower has now become a nuisance for farmers and gardeners alike.

A particularly delicate flower is the asphodel (*Asphodelus ramosus*). A member of the lily family, it grows in profusion on rocky and exposed places, a lovely sight with its tiny pale pink flowers carried on tall rigid stems. Wild thyme (*Thymus capititus*) is also common in exposed places, where it covers the rocks with a sheet of mauve.

January From now until early May the countryside is at its loveliest. The first month of the year brings some of the most colourful species:
Borage (*Borrago officinalis*). This bright blue flower with its hairy stems and leaves, so like the anchusa of English gardens, is found along roadsides and on wastelands.

Crown daisy (*Chrysanthemum coronarium*). This is the most spectacular of Malta's wild flowers, growing in great clumps of dazzling yellow often 3ft tall. The flowers resemble the Korean chrysanthemum and do well as a cut flower.

Red snapdragon (*Antirrhinum majus*). A tall branching plant which complements the blue of the borage and the yellow of the crown daisy.

Anemone (*A. coronaria*). The beautiful windflower blooms in the valleys.

February This is the month of crocuses and the exquisitely scented freesia (*F. refracta*) now naturalized in Malta (particularly in the Buskett valley). At this time the first wild grasses appear, and until June's hot sun shrivels them up the island is clothed in green in all but the rocky areas. There are around 20 common species, some growing to a height of 3ft or more.

March The crimson corn flag (*Gladiolus segetum*) will be familiar to all those who have seen the Mediterranean countryside in the spring. This lovely wild gladiolus is common among the crops and along the country roads. Wild irises and orchids may also be seen at this time. The scarlet corn poppy (*Papaver rhoeas*) and the tall opium poppy (*Papaver somniferum*) with its beautiful pink and purple flowers, bloom in both the valleys and the uplands. A naturalized plant is the silla (*Hedysarium coronarium*), the tall purple clover grown as fodder. A field of silla rippling in the breeze is an unforgettable sight.

May A familiar climbing plant is the caper (*Capparis spinosa*), seen trailing from the crevices in fortifications and cliffs. The white flower with its long violet stamens is attractive. The buds are cut young and pickled.

Garden plants Semi-tropical shrubs and climbers thrive in gardens and courtyards. Hibiscus in all its varieties, pittosporum with its sweet-scented white flowers and orange berries, French lavender (*Lavendula dentata*), the pale blue *plumbago capensis*, tecoma with its yellow and orange trumpet-shaped flowers, honeysuckles, stephanotis and bougainvillaea are seen everywhere. Roses flourish in partial shade, while almost all the lime-tolerant plants seen in an English garden will grow in Malta.

Trees The olive, carob, evergreen oak (*Quercus ilex*), wild almond and wild fig are natives of Malta. The conifers —*Cupresses sempervirens*, *Pinus pinea* and *Pinus halepensis*—do well, as do the ficus and casuarina, but only in localities where there is a sufficient depth of soil. The beautiful blue-flowering jacaranda will flourish in a sheltered situation, while the spring-flowering Judas tree (*Cercis siliquastrum*), with its lovely pinkish-violet flowers, grows all over the island. The eucalyptus and mimosa, seen everywhere, are recent Government plantings.

Rural landscape, Malta

Cultivation Much of Malta's farm land is terraced, the high rubble walls built to retain the precious soil. These walls usually have a thickness of several stones, to allow the rain to trickle through without causing erosion. Many of the fields have been painstakingly built up over the years, the customary method being to lay crushed stone on the rock and then to cover it with soil brought from nearby earth pockets, household refuse and manure. Nowhere, except in the valleys, is the soil more than a few feet deep.

The farms are very small, the largest around five acres. There is little irrigation, and most of the land is devoted to potatoes, tomatoes, cereals and silla—all winter and early spring crops. Citrus fruits, peaches, plums, pears, melons and high quality vegetables are grown in the valleys. Most crops are consumed locally, and only potatoes and onions are exported in any quantity. Vines are mainly cultivated in the north of the island.

In recent years there has been a rapid increase in greenhouse cultivation. Cut flowers, particularly carnations and gladioli, are exported to Continental markets.

Wild life There are few wild animals in Malta. The rabbits which replaced the medieval conies have been decimated by farmers. Contrary to popular belief, there are no poisonous reptiles. The snakes are not only harmless but virtuous, as they eat mice. A familiar species is the golden leopard snake, about 18 ins. long. A wide variety of lizards includes the skink and the ghekko, also a rare species found only on the islet of Filfla (see entry).

An insect to beware of is the scorpion. It has the same putty colouring as the tropical variety (occasionally it is black) but is neither as large nor as deadly. It can, however, inject enough poison from its tail to produce a painful swelling. Another tropical insect is the praying mantis, a fascinating and quite harmless creature.

Although the summer months bring the mosquitoes they are not malarial, and picnickers are rarely bothered by wasps. The wild thyme brings out the honey bees, and the lantana bushes are often surrounded by clouds of butterflies. Of the two dozen species found in Malta, more than half are natives: these include the Red Admiral, Painted Lady and Swallowtail. Of the many moths, the Humming-bird hawk moth is the most fascinating to study, darting and hovering amidst the flowers.

With its scarcity of water and vegetation Malta has few resident bird species. The most common is the Spanish sparrow, seen everywhere in the island. Another common resident is the Sardinian warbler, and the spectacled warbler, Cetti's warbler, short-toed lark and tree sparrow also breed here. The barn owl, kestrel, Mediterranean peregrine and European quail have been known to rear their young in Malta and Gozo, but they are rare. Of the gulls only the Mediterranean herring gull is native to the islands. Filfla is the most important breeding ground in the Mediterranean for the stormy petrel, while the Levantine and Mediterranean shearwater also breed on Filfla and the cliffs of the archipelago. The national bird of Malta is the blue rock thrush which nests in cliffs and inaccessible places.

As in Italy and other Mediterranean countries, bird netting and shooting is practised on a large scale. A popular method of attracting the wild birds is by the use of decoys, mostly caged finches.

The migrant birds are particularly vulnerable. Flying in exhausted over the coast they are easy targets for the waiting guns. A total of 346 species have been logged, some wintering in the islands and some passing through. It is hoped that bird protection regulations which already protect a number of birds and certain areas will soon be updated to give better protection to bird life.

Maltese curiosities The observant visitor will notice many individual features of the Maltese scene, most of them unique to the island, which will arouse his curiosity. Things to look out for:

Balconies The enclosed wooden balcony (*galleria*) is an attractive feature of the older Maltese houses. Beautiful carved stone balconies of the Knights' period are found in Gozo.

Bollards round the harbours made from old cannons.

Bull horns on farmhouse to ward off the evil eye and protect cattle from disease.

Cross in the countryside marking the limit of a parish.

Dghajsa Gaily-painted Grand Harbour water-taxi with a high prow. Propelled with long oars, the rower standing facing forward. Many now have an outboard motor.

Eye of Horus painted on Maltese fishing boats goes back as far as the ancient Egyptians, who painted the eye of the falcon god on the bows of Nile vessels as a talisman. Later the Phoenicians adopted the symbol and brought it to Malta.

Bull horns, balconies, eye of Horus

Faldetta or *ghonella* (half skirt) Traditional black cloak with a wide stiffened hood. Still occasionally seen worn by old countrywomen.

Girna Beehive-shaped stone field huts. An ancient construction.

Karrozzin Horse-drawn cab, introduced in the 19th century.

Ledges beside the upper windows of a village house held pots of sweet basil if there were marriageable daughters in the family (one pot for each daughter).

Luzzu Fishing boat.

Olive branches on farmhouses to avert the evil eye.

Plaques on old rural churches and chapels reading 'Non Gode L'Immunita Ecclesiastica' denote that the buildings did not enjoy the right of ecclesiastical sanctuary. This right of asylum was abolished in 1828 by Governor Ponsonby to assist the civil authority in maintaining law and order.

Round towers in town and country are the shells of corn grinding mills without their sails.

Shrines on houses Probably dating back to the building of Valletta, when it was decreed that all corner houses must have a shrine or statue.

Shrines in buses

Tal-Fenek Rabbit dog. Honey-coloured greyhound-type dog bred by farmers.

Water spouts projecting from the sides of old churches. Unlike dwelling houses, churches and chapels were not required to have a well to store water from the roof.

Zuntier Enclosed forecourt to an old country chapel.

Exploring Malta

A great misconception of travellers to Malta is that in such a small island there can be little to see, and what there is to see can be quickly appraised in a couple of short excursions. On both counts they would be wrong. Malta possesses, per square mile, more monuments than any other country in Europe, and although distance is hardly a problem the traveller can never lose his sense of exploration. The treasure has still to be found, whether an early Christian catacomb dug into a hillside or a Dingli church lost in the labyrinth of a rural village.

For such pursuits a car is, of course, invaluable, but those who are not hiring their own transport have a congenial alternative in the buses whose routes cover the island in a spider's web, spreading out from the capital of Valletta. Services are frequent to most parts of the island, and the drivers usually speak English. For a general impression of the countryside, a seat in a bus offers a better viewpoint than a car. Many of the roads are narrow and winding, with low stone walls obstructing the car driver's view. This, and the lack of signposts, makes orientation difficult, particularly in the west of the island. The villages, with their maze of streets, are similarly confusing, and here the bus traveller is at a distinct advantage. He has no need of directions, and at his destination (the bus usually stops in the main square) he knows he has reached his objective: the historic centre of the old village.

The car driver's advantage is, of course, his flexibility. Not only can he reach the remoter spots beyond the range of the buses but he can plan an itinerary to take in the natural attractions of the island: primarily the northern valleys and the varied coastline.

View from west coast looking towards Gozo

A morning spent exploring the fantasies of the Blue Grotto can be followed by an afternoon puzzling over the ruins of the prehistoric Hagar Qim, with a swim in the sea pools at Ghar Lapsi as a sundowner. A trip to Mdina and Rabat can include an excursion to the dramatic Dingli Cliffs on the western coast—a replica of the White Cliffs of Dover. And trips to St Paul's Bay or Marfa can be stretched to the luxuriant Pwales Valley or the windswept Marfa Ridge.

Malta's first settlement has been traced to *c.* 4000 BC. Most knowledge of these early settlers has been gleaned from two **Neolithic** sites: *Skorba* and *Ghar Dalam*. Excavations at Skorba, in the north-west of the island, revealed the site of the island's oldest village. In the cave at Ghar Dalam, in the south, the remains of Neolithic men were of secondary interest to the huge cache of bones belonging to the Pleistocene fauna who roamed the prairies and swamplands of Europe, and which came here when Malta was still connected to the continental land mass.

A preoccupation with Classical antiquity, both by archaeologists and travellers, is inevitable in the Mediterranean. But as more work is being done in the prehistoric field the significance of Malta's megalithic temples is growing and their role in the evolution of Western European civilization raising many perplexing questions. New dating techniques, as yet unconfirmed, put the temples amongst the earliest buildings of stone. By conventional techniques they are dated between 2800–2000 BC, which places them before Stonehenge and the palaces of Crete. This is known as the **Temple Culture** period. Although contemporary with the Copper Age elsewhere in Europe, it is interesting that the temples were built with Stone Age tools; an indication of the isolation of Malta from her neighbours at this time.

Despite this, the construction of the temples is highly sophisticated. The massive building blocks are skilfully shaped and laid, the decoration delicate. Twenty-three temples are known in the islands of Malta and Gozo, the ruins of some standing to a considerable height. The most important groups in Malta are *Hagar Qim* and *Mnajdra* on the south coast and the *Tarxien* complex on the outskirts of Paola.

A short walk from the Tarxien temples, in the centre of Paola, is the famous *Hal-Saflieni Hypogeum*. This remarkable cemetery-temple of the third millenium BC was discovered by accident in 1902 when workmen cutting cisterns for a new housing estate broke through the roof. In it were found the bones of some 6000 to 7000 people, together with their funerary ornaments and offerings. A maze of chambers was cut out of the rock on different levels with architectural details similar to those of the built temples above ground. Among the artifacts recovered from the Hypogeum and megalithic temples were altars, carved blocks, stone cult statues, terracotta figurines, temple models, personal ornaments and pottery. Most of these objects are now in the National Museum of Archaeology in Valletta.

The **Bronze Age** people (*c.* 2000–800 BC) produced nothing comparable with the buildings of the Temple Culture, but the mysterious 'cart ruts' found all over Malta are evidence of their industry. These parallel grooves in the bare rock run in pairs, often in groups, and sometimes in combinations like railway sidings (one dense concentration near Buskett has been named *Clapham Junction*). They run for long distances or disappear under houses and roads, reappearing again on the other side. Invariably they run up to the hill-top sites of Bronze Age villages. At Borg-in-Nadur overlooking Marsaxlokk Bay they approach the remains of a massive Bronze Age defensive wall, standing on the neck of a promontory. In places the ruts have been cut by square Punic tomb shafts: further proof of their antiquity. The mystery of their function remains unsolved, and will no doubt provide an eternal guessing game for archaeologists and laymen alike.

Apart from some dolmens and bell-shaped cisterns, few other vestiges of the Bronze Age can be found in Malta. There is a similar dearth of material from the succeeding period, the colonization of the island by the **Phoenicians and Carthaginians**. Of these people, whose influence on the island continued well beyond the Roman conquest, little now remains but their tombs and tomb furnishings and a few inscriptions such as those on the Marsaxlokk *cippi*.

These layers of successive occupation are a typical feature of Maltese archaeology. The scarcity of good sites compelled the new inhabitants to destroy or bury much left by their predecessors. A great deal of Malta's antiquities have been discovered by chance, and we are left with the temptation of what still lies beneath the surface. This is particularly true of the **Roman** period, of which little has so far come to light.

At *Ghajn Tuffieha* (Spring of the Apple Tree), near the bay of the same name, an extensive set of Roman baths and the remains of a villa were discovered accidentally. Restored in 1961, the site includes a fine example of a Roman mosaic floor.

On a hill-top about a mile from St Paul's Bay is the little church of *San Pawl Milqghi* (St Paul Welcomed). According to tradition this church was built on the site of the villa of the Roman governor Publius. 'In the same quarters were possessions of the chief man of the island, whose name was Publius, who received us, and lodged us three days courteously.' Recent excavations by the Italian *Missione Archaeologica* have brought to light the remains of a Roman villa of the 1st century AD. There is some question as to whether San Pawl Milqghi was, in fact, the actual meeting place, but no other villa has as yet been discovered so close to the scene of the shipwreck.

Like their later successors the Knights of St John, the Roman over-lords of Malta were prosperous. Traces of their villas are found all over the island, but at Rabat, outside the walls of the ancient city of Mdina, a whole Roman town lies buried. The most important discovery here was the *Roman Villa* which lies immediately to the west of the moated citadel.

The most venerated **early Christian** shrine in Malta is the ancient *Grotto* under the parish church of St Paul in Rabat, where it is believed the Apostle stayed during his three months on the island. Rabat is a town of monasteries and churches. It is noted, too, for the many Christian catacombs which honeycomb the rocks in and around the town. The most extensive group is the *St Paul's Catacombs*.

Several rock-hewn chapels of unknown antiquity are found in different parts of the island. All are highly venerated, but none more than the *Sanctuary of the Virgin, Mellieha*. This is built around an ancient rock church, and according to legend the mural of the Virgin and Child was painted by St Luke. The little church has been the object of many pilgrimages since the Middle Ages.

The **Arabs** were in Malta for 200 years, but their influence is found more in Malta's language than her architecture. Their work as builders is best seen in the walls of *Fort St Angelo* in Grand Harbour and in the moated city of *Mdina*, which was their major stronghold in the island. It is at Mdina that we linger for the traces of the **Normans** and their successors, the rulers of Sicily, who included, for 250 years, the **Spanish**. Little remains: the parts of the Norman cathedral to survive the earthquake of 1693 and the palaces of the Maltese nobility, built in the Siculo-Norman or Renaissance style. Similar vestiges may be found in the back streets of *Vittoriosa*, the old settlement of Birgu.

Malta before the Knights was a beleaguered and neglected island. The people, harassed and robbed by corsairs and absentee landlords, led a meagre existence. Their places of worship were mainly caves until, with the formation of the ten parishes in 1436, a few simple churches were built. *St Mary Ta'Bir Miftuh* near Gudja is the best preserved of these 15th century parish churches. Of great interest is the old parish church of *St Gregory, Zejtun*. Built in 1436 it has a fine vaulted east end added to the medieval nave by the Knights. At the abandoned hamlet of *Hal Millieri* near Zurrieq the ancient little church of the Annunciation contains a remarkable series of murals, the best surviving example of pre-Knights painting in Malta.

These small rectangular churches with their unobtrusive charm are often hard to find: either tucked away in the back streets of a village that has long ago outgrown them or isolated like a rustic ornament in the remote countryside. Their simplicity, though, provides a pleasant contrast to the more elaborate churches in the Baroque tradition that continues to this day.

In 1530 the Great Carrack of the **Knights of St John** sailed into the deep waters of Grand Harbour, bringing with it the most celebrated refugees of medieval Christendom, the knight adventurers who in the next two and a half centuries would bring Malta securely into the orbit of the Christian continent not just as a defensive outpost but eventually as a sovereign state fully involved in European commerce and culture.

With the defeat of the Turks in the Great Siege of 1565 and the building of the new capital of Valletta, the Knights were able to establish the wealth and reputation necessary to attract the best of Europe's artists and craftsmen. The military engineers from the continent designed and built the greatest complex of fortifications known to the western world, while the Knights, scions of the most exalted families in Europe, enriched their new homeland with their own possessions and the commissioned work of imported painters and sculptors. In addition to this the increased prosperity and safety of the island brought a remarkable flowering of native artistic talent. This is seen largely in the island's churches, almost exclusively the work of Maltese architects.

The fortifications of *Grand Harbour* and *Valletta* are without doubt the Knights' greatest achievement. There is nothing to compare with the view of Grand Harbour from the Upper Barracca Gardens, especially at dawn or sunset when the sheltered waters of the harbour reflect the changing colours of the sky and the fortresses rise like the prows of giant ghostly ships.

Most impressive of the harbour's individual strongholds is *Fort St Angelo* at the end of the Vittoriosa peninsula. It is also historically the most important. Built by the Arabs on earlier foundations and subsequently rebuilt by the Knights, it played an important part in the Great Siege. At the moment it serves the Royal Navy (as HMS St Angelo) but is open to the public once a week.

In Vittoriosa (Birgu), the first home of the Knights in Malta, two important monuments escaped serious damage in the last war. These are the *Inquisitor's Palace* and the church of *St Lawrence*, the first Conventual Church of the Order of St John in Malta. A walk round the fortifications of Vittoriosa is recommended, both for the splendid views and the sense of history it conveys.

If the Knights' fortifications were a triumph of strength, their church was a triumph of devotion. The Co-Cathedral of Valletta, formerly the *Conventual Church of St John*, is the masterpiece of Gerolamo Cassar, the Maltese who became architect to the Order. In contrast to the austere exterior, the interior is a feast to the eye. Successive Grand Masters devoted their wealth to its embellishment, with beautiful paintings, sculptures and other treasures. Its survival of the bombs, as near-miraculous as that of St Paul's in London, can be seen as a testimony of the faith of its builders and benefactors.

The Order built many other churches in Valletta, but the visitor's impression is more of a city of palaces and grand houses. Many now have shops at ground level, others are Government buildings, but this detracts little from the elegant, 17th century character of the city. Though not the most impressive architecturally, the *Grand Master's Palace* in Republic Street is a primary attraction for visitors with its state apartments and armoury. There are also the *Auberges of the Knights*, five of which survived the war. One of them, the Auberge de Provence, contains the interesting *National Museum of Archaeology*.

Outside Valletta and Mdina, the most important palaces are the romantic *Verdala Palace* (near Buskett, Rabat) built for the Grand Master Verdalle, the *Inquisitor's Summer Palace* at Girgenti (also near Buskett), the *Selmun Palace* (overlooking St Paul's Bay) and the President's Palace at *San Anton* (Attard). At present none of these palaces is open to the public, although the exteriors of all are on view. Located either on a dominant site or in an attractive setting, their surroundings alone must justify a visit. The wooded Buskett Valley, with its orange groves and conifers, makes an ideal setting for Verdala, a refreshing area of greenery and shade on a hot summer's day. No garden lover should miss the lovely early 17th century gardens of the San Anton Palace, the greater part of them open to the public.

The architects of the Mdina of the Knights (*Città Notabile*) added many fine palaces to those of earlier periods. Its most important building is however the late 17th century *Cathedral* built by another of Malta's great native architects, Lorenzo Gafà. Gafà also contributed to the nearby parish church of St Paul in Rabat.

To choose outstanding examples among the parish churches of Malta's other towns and villages is almost impossible. Many of them are spectacular, lavishly endowed by their parishioners. The cathedral-like *St Catherine, Zejtun* (1692) dominates the town, as does its neighbour at *Zabbar, Our Lady of Grace* (1641). Equally powerful, but more exuberant, is the superb *St Helen's, Birkirkara* (1735). This was the work of the Maltese Domenico Cachia, and replaced the earlier parish church of the *Assumption* (1617) by Tommaso Dingli. The latter church has one of the few Renaissance-style façades in Malta: a composition of extreme elegance and beauty. A similar church by Dingli—one of Malta's original architects—is that of *St Mary, Attard*. Mention should be made of three other churches which for different reasons make a lasting impression: *St Nicholas, Siggiewi, St George, Qormi* and *St Saviour, Lija*.

The tradition of the small country church, established in the 15th century, was maintained by the Knights in their own small churches and chapels, employing the characteristics of the indigenous architecture. Among the most delightful are the little *St Roque, Balzan, St Peter, Qormi* and *St Roque, Zebbug.* With the exception of the *Anglican Cathedral* in Valletta and the huge domed church at *Mosta*, there was little church building of note after the departure of the Knights. The arrival of the **British** (1800) renewed a concentration on the island's defences. The forts of the *Victoria Lines* and those south of Grand Harbour are fine examples of 19th century military architecture.

The use of local stone and the traditional 'cubic' form has brought a happy blending of 19th and early 20th century domestic architecture with the old. One can only hope that the newly independent Malta will escape the concrete development seen elsewhere in the Mediterranean, and preserve its many unique qualities.

Itineraries for motorists from Valletta

Bold type: Major sites
Names in brackets: Points on route for signpost direction only

HALF DAY TOURS

1 *Hypogeum & Tarxien Temples*
(Marsa)—**Paola**—**Tarxien** and return

2 *Three Cities*
(Marsa)—(Paola)—Senglea—Cospicua—**Vittoriosa**—Kalkara

3 *Three Villages*
(Hamrun)—Birkirkara—Attard—San Anton Gardens—Lija—Balzan—(Birkirkara) and return

WHOLE DAY TOURS

4 *Rabat & Mdina*
(Hamrun)—**Rabat & Mdina** and return
Restaurants at Rabat and Mdina

5 *East*
(Marsa)—(Tarxien)—Birzebbuga for **Ghar Dalam** & Borg-in-Nadur—Marsaxlokk—Delimara—(Marsaxlokk)—Zejtun—Marsaskala—Zabbar—(Paola) and return
Restaurants at Birzebbuga, Marsaxlokk and Marsaskala

6 *South*
a) Major sites only
(Marsa)—(Luqa)—(Zurrieq)—**Blue Grotto** (Wied-iz-Zurrieq)—**Hagar Qim** & **Mnajdra** and return
Restaurant at Blue Grotto

More detailed tours
b) (Marsa)—(Luqa)—Zurrieq—**Blue Grotto** (Weid-iz-Zurrieq)—Il Maqluba—Qrendi—St Catherine Tat-Torba—Hal Millieri—(Luqa) and return

c) (Marsa)—Qormi—Zebbug—Tal Hlas—Siggiewi—Tal Providenza—Ghar Lapsi—**Hagar Qim** & **Mnajdra**—(Qrendi)—(Mqabba)—(Luqa) and return
Restaurant at Ghar Lapsi

7 *West*
(Hamrun)—(Rabat)—Verdala Palace & Buskett Gardens—Clapham Junction—Inquisitor's Summer Palace—Dingli Cliffs—(Rabat)—Bingemma Gap—Mgarr—Ghajn Tuffieha (Roman Baths)—Zebbieh (Skorba)—(Rabat) and return
Restaurants at Buskett and Rabat

8 *North*
(Sliema)—(Birkirkara)—Mosta—St Paul's Bay—Mellieha—Marfa—(St Paul's Bay)—(Sliema)—Tal Lunzjata Catacombs—(Msida) and return
Restaurants at St Paul's Bay and Mellieha

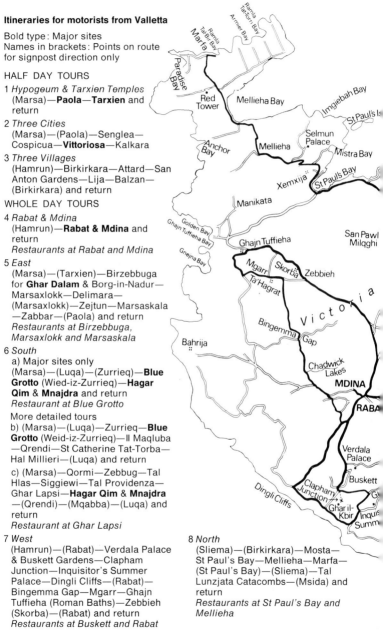

56

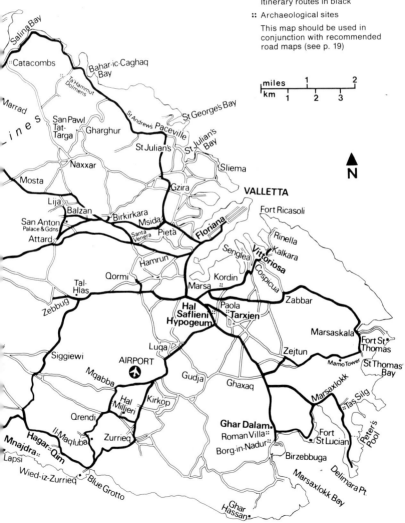

Malta road map

Itinerary routes in black

:: Archaeological sites

This map should be used in conjunction with recommended road maps (see p. 19)

miles 1 2
km 1 2 3

N

Salina Bay
:: Catacombs
Bahar-ic-Caghaq Bay
:: Ta'Hammut Dolmens
Marrad
San Pawl Tat-Targa
Gharghur
St Andrew's
Paceville
St George's Bay
L i n e s
Naxxar
St Julian's
St Julian's Bay
Sliema
Mosta
Gzira
VALLETTA
Lija
Balzan
Birkirkara
Msida
Floriana
Fort Ricasoli
San Anton Palace & Gdns
Santa Venera
Pietà
Rinella
Attard
Hamrun
Senglea
Vittoriosa
Kalkara
Qormi
Kordin
Cospicua
Tal-Hlas
Marsa
::
Zabbar
Zebbug
Hal Saflieni Hypogeum
Paola
Tarxien
Marsaskala
Siggiewi
Luqa
Zejtun
Fort St Thomas
AIRPORT
Mamo Tower
St Thomas' Bay
Mqabba
Gudja
Ghaxaq
Marsaxlokk
Hal Millieri
Kirkop
Tas Silg
Qrendi
Mnajdra ::
Hagar Qim
Zurrieq
Ghar Dalam ::
Roman Villa ::
Fort St Lucian
Peter's Pool
Lapsi
Borg-in-Nadur ::
Birzebbuga
Wied-iz-Zurrieq
Blue Grotto
Delimara Pt.
Marsaxlokk Bay
Ghar Hassan

Gazetteer

This Gazetteer contains information on the location, history and main features of the places of interest in Malta. Information about hotels, restaurants, etc. will be found in the Practical Information Section.

Museum opening times are shown where they vary from official hours. For details of the latter, see Museums and Monuments, p. 28.

Populations (approximate) are for towns and villages of 4500 or more inhabitants.

Accents have been omitted from Maltese place names. For details of pronunciation see below and note on *Language*, p. 27.

Pronunciation of place names With the following exceptions, place names are spoken as written:

Maltese	Pronunciation	Maltese	Pronunciation
Bahrija	*Bahreeya*	Marsaxlokk	*Marsashlock*
Balzan	*Baltsan*	Mdina	*Imdeena*
Bighi	*Beeghee*	Mnajdra	*Imnighdra*
Bingemma	*Binjemma*	Mqabba	*Imabba*
Birzebbuga	*Beerzeebooja*	Msida	*Imseeda*
Borg-in-Nadur	*Borje-in-Nadur*	Naxxar	*Nashar*
Dwejra	*Dwayrah*	Qala	*Arla*
Ggantija	*Jganteeya*	Qawra	*Aura*
Ghajnsielem	*Ine-seeaylem*	Qormi	*Ormee*
Ghajn Tuffieha	*Ine Tuffeeha*	Qrendi	*Krendee*
Gharb	*Arb*	San Pawl Milqghi	*San Pawl Milee*
Ghar Dalam	*Ar Dalam*	San Pawl Tat-	*San Pawl Tat-*
Ghar Hassan	*Ar Hassan*	Targa	*Tarja*
Ghar il-Kbir	*Ar il-Kbeer*	Saqqajja	*Sahayeear*
Ghar Lapsi	*Ar Lapsee*	Siggiewi	*Sijjeewee*
Gharghur	*Ghargoor*	Ta Cenc	*Ta Chench*
Ghaxaq	*Arshark*	Ta Hagrat	*Ta Hajrat*
Ghasri	*Arsree*	Tal Lunzjata	*Tal Lunzeeata*
Gnejna	*Jnayna*	Tas Silg	*Tas Silj*
Gudja	*Gudya*	Tarxien	*Tarsheen*
Hagar Qim	*Hajar Eem*	Ta'Xbiex	*Tashbeeish*
Kercem	*Kerchem*	Xaghra	*Shahra*
Lija	*Leeya*	Xewkija	*Shookeeya*
Luqa	*Lu-ar*	Xlendi	*Shlendee*
Mgarr-ix-Xini	*Imjar-ish-Sheenee*	Zebbug	*Zebooj*
Maqluba	*Ma-luba*	Zejtun	*Zaytoon*
Marsamxett	*Marsamshett*	Zurrieq	*Zurrea*

Geographical features occurring in place names

Maltese	English	Maltese	English
bahar	sea	marsa	harbour, inlet
borg, torri	tower	qala	creek
buskett	small wood	ramla	sandy
ghajn	spring or well	ras	headland
ghar	cave	wied	wadi, valley
hal	village	xaghra	rocky plateau

Anchor Bay West coast, at narrow neck in north of island, 1 m west of junction 1 m north of Mellieha.

This little inlet used by fishermen is recommended for good swimmers only. Steep steps lead down from the cliff-top to the rocks below. (No amenities.)

Armier Bay North coast, 1½ m east of junction with Marfa road, 1½ m north of Mellieha. The sandy beach here is ideal for small children. Like all the beaches served by bus it can be very crowded, especially at weekends, but this is more than compensated by its amenities and the fine view across the channel to Comino and Gozo. There is no shade, but umbrellas can be hired. (Parking alongside beach.)

Little Armier Bay to the east is also ideal for children. It can be reached either by road or on foot from Armier Bay, and has similar amenities.

Attard Village 4 m west of Valletta reached by turning off Rabat road.

One of the ancient 'Three Villages' (Attard, Balzan and Lija) situated in the centre of the island in what was once the heart of the orange-growing district. Although the old village is much the same, modern villas and bungalows now stand on the site of the groves.

The parish of Attard, founded in 1575, has two important monuments:

Parish Church of St Mary This graceful church in the main square was designed by Tommaso Dingli and built in 1613. Attard was Dingli's native village and the church is probably his most notable achievement. The façade is exquisitely carved; the giant orders and pediment suggesting a Roman temple. The foliage decoration of the portals is particularly fine, and here one should note, in addition to the main entrance, the exterior doors of the transepts on either side of the building. The campanile adjoining the north transept was added to the church in 1718.

The church is cruciform in plan with a coffered barrel vault. The side altars are in arched recesses in the nave. Dingli was only 22 when he designed this church, one of the very few Renaissance-style buildings in Malta.

San Anton Palace Residence of the President of the Republic of Malta, situated on the Attard–Balzan road. (The gardens can also be reached from the Rabat–Valletta road, turning off at the San Anton sign.)

At the end of the 16th c. Antoine de Paule, Knight of the Order of St John, acquired a house near the village of Attard. By 1693, when he was elected Grand Master, the pleasure-loving de Paule had developed this modest house into a comfortable villa. 600 guests dined here on the day of his installation, an indulgence for which he was censured by the Inquisitor Fabio Chigi, later to become Pope Alexander VII. A lover of luxury, de Paule set about enlarging his villa into a palace suitable for a Grand Master. In addition he planted orange groves around the palace and laid out elaborate formal gardens.

It is these 17th c. **gardens**, with their terraces, fountains, great trees and flowering shrubs that the visitor sees today. (Opening times vary according to season, but are usually 8 am to one hour before sunset. The exact closing time is posted at the palace entrance. The palace and private gardens are closed to the public.)

One wing of the palace arches over a narrow public roadway (no cars) leading from the palace entrance to the public gardens. Abutting this old wing of the palace is the tiny chapel of the *Virgin of Pilar*. Rectangular in plan, and roofed with a ribbed barrel vault, it is a characteristic early 17th c. Maltese chapel.

De Paule's original house now forms the stables of the palace.

Bahar-ic-Caghaq Bay 3 m north of Sliema, at the point where the coast road reaches the sea.

A popular rocky bathing area with a small patch of sand. (No amenities.)

Bahrija Bronze Age village site on west coast, 4 m west of Rabat.

Follow the St Martin signposts from the Roman Villa at Rabat. Just after the hamlet and church of St Martin (3½ m) a new road bears right to the Bronze Age site. (The road ahead ends at the hamlet of Bahrija.)

The settlement site is a rocky crescent-shaped plateau high on the Ras-ir-Raheb promontory. The climb up is rugged, but rewarding for those in search of views and atmosphere (the promontory commands a panorama from Dingli Cliffs in the south to Gozo in the north).

Apart from the water cisterns cut in the rock, little can be seen in the way of archaeology. The keen-eyed might catch sight of a Bronze Age sherd, but most of the retrievable material of this site, which represents the last prehistoric phase (900–800 BC) is in the National Museum in Valletta.

Balzan Village 3½ m west of Valletta, approached via Birkirkara.

One of the attractive old 'Three Villages' (the others are the nearby Attard and Lija). The main square is dominated by the parish church of the *Annunciation* (1669–95). The façade, a Baroque treatment but with a single giant order, is unlike any other in Malta. It shows a strongly Spanish influence.

In Three Churches Street off the main square (the left hand fork viewed from the east end of the church) stands an architectural gem,

the little church of **St Roque**. It was built in 1593, probably to commemorate the great plague of that year (St Roque is the patron saint of the plague-stricken).

The elegant façade of this rectangular church has a decorated doorway. The circular window with an infilling of overlapping semi-circles is a novel detail. It is enclosed in a square moulded panel, surmounted by a small triangular pediment enclosing a flower. The sides and east end of the church are plain, with three waterspouts on each side.

This church does not have the usual enclosed space or *zuntier* in front of its door, common to most early Maltese churches and chapels, but the road widens to form a little square with a stone cross on a tall pillar in the centre. It is possible that the cross marks the site of an early cemetery.

Beside St Roque is the little church of the *Annunciation* built in the 15th c. It is a typical example of pre-Knights ecclesiastical architecture in Malta, consisting of a plain rectangular nave divided into bays by slightly pointed arches rising from wall piers. The original arched doorway in the west front was subsequently heightened and made rectangular. This was the first parish church of Balzan until the present church was completed (see above).

Adjacent is the third small church of the group, which now forms part of a private house. This church, contemporary with St Roque, was known as *St Leonard* and dedicated to the victims of slavery.

Bingemma Gap Viewpoint 2½ m north of Rabat where Rabat-Mgarr road crosses Great Fault.

Perched high on the rim of the valley below the jagged escarpment of the fault is the little church of the *Madonna tal-Lettera*. This is a typical wayside church of the 18th c., rectangular with a shallow pitched roof and a ribbed barrel vault. Beneath the church is a cave with a small two-chambered *Punic tomb* scooped out of the rock at the back. Note also the cart ruts near the church.

In the hillside across the valley are many small catacombs, known as *Gherien il-Ihud* (the Jewish caves). Above the catacombs can be seen a section of the Victoria Lines.

Birkirkara (pop. 16,800) Town 2½ m west of Valletta on Valletta-Mosta road (via Msida).

Founded in the 16th c., Birkirkara retains many old houses of the period tucked away in the side streets. Two of the finest church façades in Malta—of her old and new parish churches—may be seen in the town. They are well worth visiting, but in view of the congestion of narrow streets it is recommended that motorists should leave their car at the Church of the Assumption and go to the other church (St Helen) on foot.

Church of the Assumption To reach this church motorists approaching from Valletta should go through the traffic lights on the main road through Birkirkara (there is only one set) and then immediately left up Old Church Street (slope facing) and turn left. Those travelling by bus (No. 71) should walk to the church through the public gardens adjoining the bus terminus.

Birkirkara's first parish church was designed in 1600 by Vittorio Cassar but completed under the direction of Tommaso Dingli in 1617. It was replaced by the parish church of St Helen in 1727. The old church was allowed to fall into disrepair, but is now being restored. Its most remarkable feature is the façade topped by a broken pediment. The lavish and intricate carvings, particularly the fine details of the entablature, are typical of the Dingli's work. Much of the interior was the work of Cassar, who also built the tower.

Parish Church of St Helen To find this church after visiting the Church of the Assumption walk down Old Church Street and cross the main road to the market opposite. At the top of the alleyway beside the market turn left and then right into Main Street. At the end is the police station and beyond, St Helen.

This has been described as the finest parish church in the island. Built between 1727-45, it was designed by Domenico Cachia, chief architect of the Order, at the age of 27. St Helen was the first of his major works: he was later responsible for the Auberge of Castile and Leon in Valletta.

The spectacle of the façade, only partially visible at the end of the narrow street, is almost overpowering as one steps into the wide square. Happily the impact is lightened

Above: Detail of entablature, Church of the Assumption, Birkirkara
Right: Church of St Helen, Birkirkara

by some fanciful details: the statues at roof level and the scrolls and curves of the centre-piece and spires. A Sicilian influence is apparent.

The church has a Latin cross plan with aisle chapels, but the apse is more deeply set than usual. The coupled pilasters on high bases are characteristic of Malta. The twin ribs of the vault have engraved and gilded panels. The vault and apse and the domes of the aisles are sumptuously painted.

Birzebbuga (pop. 4700) Village on coast 5½ m south of Valletta.

Once a fishing settlement, Birzebbuga has expanded into a pleasant small resort. It lies on the west shore of Marsaxlokk Bay and stretches from St George's Bay round Pretty Bay to Kalafrana.

In the vicinity of the village are three important sites of different periods. These are Ghar Dalam and the Roman Villa (see **Ghar Dalam**) and the Bronze Age village of Borg-in-Nadur (see below).

Entering the bay from the main road, the route curves to the right. On the right by the bus stop is the small church of *St George* (1683) at the head of St George's Bay, to which an earlier medieval chapel on the same site gave its name. The fortified church stands in the centre of a redoubt built in the form of a crescent facing out to sea. Access to the church and redoubt was through a portcullis at the back of the church. A number of interesting graffiti of ships dating from the period of the Knights are incised on the outside walls of the church. The galleys of the Order of St John used to winter in St George's Bay and it was customary for the crews to attend Mass in this church before setting sail. A salute to the Saint would be fired before the galleys left the bay.

Borg-in-Nadur At the top of the lane running behind St George's Church and then across a field are the remains of this Bronze Age village. (Take care to keep to the edge of cultivated fields.)

The first ruins, in the first field, are pre-Bronze Age. These are of a 4-apse *temple* (c. 2000 BC), which was probably used for domestic purposes by the Bronze Age people. Further on, on the far side of the next field, are the remains of a huge *defensive wall* lying across the neck of the promontory between the two valleys running down to St George's Bay and Pretty Bay. In the centre of the wall is a massive redoubt facing landwards. Behind the wall the stone foundations of huts were discovered.

Blue Grotto see **Wied-iz-Zurrieq**

Bugibba see **St Paul's Bay**

Buskett (Boschetto) Gardens 1½ m south of Rabat. Open daily.

The Buskett valley planted out by Grand Master Verdalle is the greenest part of Malta. Here a woodland of pines and conifers and groves of citrus trees provide a refuge from the rocky landscape of the island. It is the setting for the Mnarja folk festival held in late June (see p.27). The *Buskett Forest Restaurant* and the *Buskett Roadhouse* are open all day.

Chadwick Lakes Small 19th c. artificial reservoirs 1 m north of Roman Villa at Rabat. Dry for most of the year, these 'lakes' are only worth visting in the winter.

Clapham Junction Bronze Age cart ruts 2 m south of Rabat. Buskett Gardens ¼ m.

The ruts fan out over the rocky plateau south

of Buskett Gardens, to the east of the Buskett-Dingli Cliffs road, and are reached by a track running south-east from the junction with the Girgenti road (see map).

This is Malta's most complex and baffling concentration of cart ruts. The number of pairs has never been accurately calculated, and their extent gives the mystery of their origin a greater complexity (see p. 31). Near the stone boundary wall of an adjacent field can be seen the square shafts of *Punic tombs*. To the south of the ruts, on the same plateau, are the remains of what was once Malta's largest troglodytic dwelling (see **Ghar il-Kbir**).

Comino (area 1 sq m) Island in narrow channel between Malta and Gozo. For details of boat services, see p. 21.

Coralline limestone, jagged cliffs and a pretty lagoon are the features of this largely infertile island. The small farming community consists of only four families.

History Archaeological finds show that Comino was inhabited during the Roman period, but when the Knights arrived it was abandoned scrubland, abounding with hare and wild boar. For some years it was used by the Order as a hunting ground. After the erection of Fort St Mary in 1618, and again during the 19th c., farmers were brought into the island, and cummin (from which the island takes its name), cotton and honey were produced. However, reclamation of the land proved too burdensome and the population declined.

The island In the south-east corner of Comino stands the powerful *Fort St Mary*, a landmark for many miles. The fort was built by Grand Master Alof de Wignacourt as part of the coastal defences against a possible Turkish invasion.

Throughout the Middle Ages Comino was used as a base by pirates preying on the Maltese islands and capturing voyagers between Malta and Gozo. In 1418 the Maltese petitioned King Alfonso V of Spain for the erection of a fortified tower to prevent pirates occupying Comino. Consent was given and a tax on wine imposed to raise funds for the building of a tower. However, work was never carried out and the money raised went into Alfonso's pocket. The manuscript petition with the King's consent, dated 1418, is extant in the Archives of the Cathedral at Mdina.

The present fort was designed by Vittorio Cassar and commands the channel between Malta and Gozo. Like Cassar's other forts (St Lucien and St Thomas) in the south of Malta, Fort St Mary stands foursquare with corner turrets. The fort, armed with ten heavy and eight light guns, could house a garrison of 120 men.

There is one chapel on Comino, that of *Santa Marija* dedicated to 'The Flight from Egypt'. Of little aesthetic quality, the importance of

this chapel lies in its antiquity. Predating the fort, its exact origins are unknown. It was desecrated in 1667 and reconsecrated in 1716.

Comino's attraction for the summer visitor is its excellent bathing and turquoise sea. It has two small sandy bays and a lagoon of brilliant blue separating it from the tiny islet of *Cominotto*. During the summer the rocky interior is bleached and arid, but in the spring the pink and mauve flowering thyme is springy underfoot and scents the air; no sound is heard but the murmur of bees and from the thickets, the song of the nightingale. It is a magical transformation, and this is the time to visit Comino.

A ferry connects Comino with Malta and Gozo. There is one modern hotel (see p. 23), closed in winter.

Cospicua (Bormla) (pop. 8900) Town 3 m south of Valletta on opposite side of Grand Harbour.

This was the last of the Three Cities of the Knights to be founded, the other two (Birgu and L'Isola, now Vittoriosa and Senglea) being already established on their fortified promontories.

The development of the Knights' first settlement at Birgu was so rapid that by 1562 a new settlement, Bormla, had grown up outside its fortifications. During the Great Siege of 1565 Bormla, lying in no-man's land, was heavily damaged. Enough survived, however, to form the nucleus of a flourishing harbour town, re-named Cospicua.

The vulnerability of Cospicua (lying outside the fortifications of Vittoriosa and Senglea) and the consequent gap in the landward defences of Grand Harbour, worried the Knights. In 1638 Grand Master Lascaris invited the Italian military engineer Vincenzo da Firenzuola to advise on the island's fortifications.

Firenzuola recommended a line of bastions to encircle Cospicua. These, the Margherita Lines, were begun in 1645. However, when Grand Master Nicolas Cotoner decided to build the Cottonera Lines (see entry), work on the Cospicua fortifications was suspended and not resumed until 1733.

The greater part of the **Margherita Lines** still stand, together with the three gates. The *Margherita Gate* and the *Rock Gate* are on the road leading out to Zabbar, *St Helen's Gate* at the top of New Street leading out of Gavino Guilia Square. These fortifications are the only part of the old city to survive the war.

Cospicua is hilly, with steep narrow streets and stepped alleys. The main street (St Theresa) skirts the dockyard from Gavino Guilia Square ascending steeply to St Theresa's Gardens and the Vittoriosa bus terminus, with a road leading down into Vittoriosa. A few yards further up the hill is a roundabout

Clapham Junction

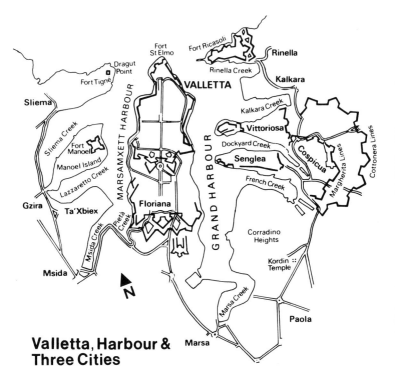

Valletta, Harbour & Three Cities

with a second road into Vittoriosa, a road to Kalkara and Bighi and the road out to Zabbar. Off this last road, just inside Rock Gate, are the imposing *Verdala Barracks* (1853), recently restored and converted into housing. **Church of the Immaculate Conception** (1637). Cospicua's parish church, which miraculously escaped the bombing, dominates the dockyard and lower part of the town. It is approached by steps leading up from St Theresa Street (see map). The church is especially rich in silver artifacts which are displayed on 8 December, the Feast of the Immaculate Conception. It also contains a large number of paintings by Maltese and Italian artists. The charming painting behind the high altar of the *Madonna and Child with St John* is by Polidoro Veneziano of Abruzzi (17th c.).

Cottonera Lines Fortifications enclosing landward side of the Three Cities on south side of Grand Harbour.

The magnificent line of fortifications with eight bastions and connecting curtains which defends the Three Cities from French Creek

to Kalkara Creek was designed by the Italian military engineer Valperga and named after the Grand Master who inspired the work.

Although the Margherita Lines (see **Cospicua**) were considered by many to be sufficient safeguard for Cospicua and the Grand Harbour, Grand Master Nicolas Cotoner on his accession decided to build, with his own funds, a massive outer defence work. This would not only afford additional protection to the Three Cities from landward attack, but would also provide asylum to 40,000 people and their cattle in the event of siege. Work on the Margherita Lines was stopped and the foundation stone of the new fortifications was laid with great pomp and ceremony on 28 August 1670.

The grandiose scheme was never completed. On the Grand Master's death in 1680 funds ran out, and the construction of ravelins had to be abandoned.

In the centre of each curtain is an ornate gateway. All these gateways are now filled in, with the exception of the **Zabbar Gate** on the Zabbar road. This gate, built in 1675, is a splendid Baroque monument to a Grand

Dingli Cliffs Beauty spot on south-west coast, best approached via Rabat and Dingli village (signposted from Rabat).
These 800ft cliffs are a 10min. walk from Dingli village and afford breath-taking views. A motor road skirts the cliffs for 2½m. This is being extended to the west.
Perched on the edge of the cliff 1m to the south-east of the village is the lonely little chapel of *St Mary Magdalene* (1646). Mass is celebrated once a year on the Saint's Day, 22 July.

Filfla Rocky islet 3m off south coast.
Once a fisherman's sanctuary with a troglodytic church, Filfla has until recently been used as a gunnery target by the Royal Navy. Temple Period material can be found and—a living link with ancient times—a dark green lizard with red spots (*Lacerta muralis var. filfolensis*) peculiar to the island. Filfla is also known as an important breeding ground for the stormy petrel.
Legend links the origin of Filfla with the phenomenon of Il-Maqluba (see **Maqluba, Il-**).

Floriana (pop. 4600) Suburb of Valletta.
This town of open spaces and gardens lies behind the massive fortifications of the Floriana Lines, an extension to the landward defences of Valletta.
In 1634 Grand Master de Paule, fearing an imminent Turkish attack, appealed to Pope Urban VIII who sent the Italian Pietro Floriani to Malta to advise on its defences. This brilliant military engineer designed the line of fortifications with lunettes, ravelins, tenailles and bastions lying across the neck of the Sceberras peninsula with a great hornwork thrust out beside Grand Harbour. Although his plans were opposed by many of the Knights and leading European engineers, they were reluctantly accepted by the Council of the Order. Work began in 1636 but Floriani, offended by the adverse criticism, returned to Italy. He was replaced by Vincenzo da Firenzuola, who introduced new proposals. These were for the construction of the Margherita Lines (see **Cospicua**). Work on the Floriana Lines was then suspended until 1640 when the work was re-appraised and the work completed.
Soon after Manoel de Vilhena became Grand Master in 1722 the Council decided to build a suburb to Valletta, with the stipulation that the new town should not interfere with the defence of the city or Floriani's fortifications. An open space (glacis) was to be left between the Valletta fortifications and the first houses. The town was to be laid out in a grid pattern with wide access roads running between the two lines of defence.
Floriana was largely destroyed in the bombing of 1941–42, but the layout of the town is much as it was in the 18th c.

Master. It is richly carved, inscribed with a tribute to Nicolas Cotoner's generosity, and surmounted by his bust in bronze.

Delimara Tip of promontory enclosing Marsaxlokk Bay 7½m south-east of Valletta. Best reached by car via Marsaxlokk (6m, signpost to Delimara). Bus to Marsaxlokk only).
Perhaps the most attractive swimming area in Malta. The views are spectacular and the beach seldom over-crowded. Steep steps lead down from the parking area to flat rocks. The sea is not suitable for toddlers, but there is a patch of shallow water over rocks for older children and non-swimmers. Swimmers can picnic along the cliff-top where ladders lead down to the water. Shade is available throughout the day. (No amenities). An alternative bathing place ½m north of the point is *Peter's Pool* (see entry).
Fort Delimara On the west side of the peninsula, this fortress was constructed by the British in 1881 to guard the entrance to Marsaxlokk Bay. It houses four 38-ton muzzle-loading guns. (Not open to the public.)

Dingli Cliffs

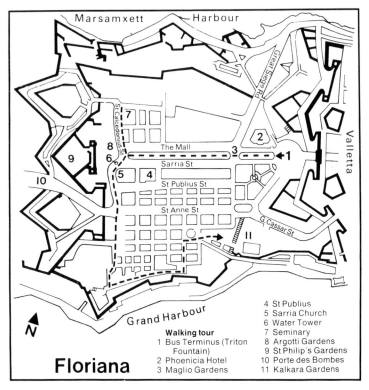

Marsamxett Harbour

The Mall

Sarria St

St Publius St

St Anne St

St Caledonius St

Valletta

Great Siege Rd

G. Cassar St

Grand Harbour

N

Floriana

Walking tour
1 Bus Terminus (Triton Fountain)
2 Phoenicia Hotel
3 Maglio Gardens

4 St Publius
5 Sarria Church
6 Water Tower
7 Seminary
8 Argotti Gardens
9 St Philip's Gardens
10 Porte des Bombes
11 Kalkara Gardens

Walking tour (see map) Starting point: **City Gate**. From the bus terminus, pass the *Triton Fountain* and continue straight ahead down a tree-lined walk with the *Phoenicia Hotel* on the right. Opposite the hotel is the *Monument to Christ the King* by Antonio Sciortino, commemorating the Eucharistic Congress held in Malta in 1913. To the west, across the road, are the *Maglio Gardens*. At the entrance stands a fine statue of Grand Master *Manoel de Vilhena*, who did much to improve the fortifications of Floriana.

Maglio (Mall) Erected by Grand Master Lascaris in 1656, this was originally a walled enclosure, used by the young Knights for the game of pall-mall (*palla a maglio*). An inscription on the left-hand gate adjures the young men to keep physically fit for battle and away from gambling, wine and women. The Maglio was turned into a garden by Sir Alexander Ball, first British Civil Commissioner. Down the length of the gardens are monuments to prominent Maltese citizens. To the right of the gardens is *Independence Arena*, once a parade ground. Beyond are

the *Lintorn Barracks*, now Government offices. This area was used for recreation by the crews of the galleys moored in Marsamxett Harbour. To the left of the gardens are the *Granaries*. These circular pits (also at Fort St Elmo) were used by the Knights to store grain. Lined with wood and then sealed by a circular slab, they kept grain fresh for two or three years. A two years' supply was always in reserve. The Order held a monopoly on grain (imported from Sicily) and made a good profit on the sale.

Overlooking the Granaries is the parish church of **St Publius**, built to the memory of the Roman governor of the island who was converted by St Paul and made the island's first bishop. This church, dive-bombed and nearly demolished in the war, has been reconstructed. The foundation stone was laid in 1733 and the church completed in 1768. The architect was Giuseppe Bonici. The side chapels were added in 1856 and the portico flanked by two towers in 1882.

At the end of the Maglio on the opposite side of the road behind St Publius' Church is the little church of **Sarria** (1678). This escaped the bombing and was used as the parish church until St Publius was rebuilt.

It is a delightful circular chapel on the site of a church built by the Knight Martino de Sarria Navarro for the sailors of the Order. It was dedicated to Our Lady of the Galleys. By 1670 the church had fallen into disuse, and when the Black Plague of 1675–76 struck the island the Knights vowed that if they were delivered from it a new chapel would be built and a yearly pilgrimage made here from the Co-Cathedral of St John. This procession is still held every year on 8 December by the Canons of the Co-Cathedral.

The new chapel was designed by Lorenzo Gafà. The exterior is simple and shows the grouped dome ribbing and coupled pilasters typical of Gafà's work. The dome, flowing down into the circular exterior wall with only a very shallow cornice, is much more pronounced than the usual Maltese dome, which is often partly obscured by the cornice.

The chapel was endowed by Grand Master Nicolas Cotoner, who entrusted its decoration to Mattia Preti. It is embellished with seven of Preti's most vigorous paintings, including the altar-piece of the *Immaculate Conception* and the large canvases of *St Sebastian* and *St Roque*, patron saints of the plague-stricken. The Grand Master's emblem of a cotton plant is carved on the pilasters. The chapel is now administered by the Jesuits.

Near Sarria Church is Grand Master de Wignacourt's *water tower*, a staging post of the aqueduct leading into Valletta. The tower bears the elaborate arms of the Grand Master.

Beside the tower is the entrance to the Argotti Gardens, and a few yards away steps lead down to St Philip's Gardens. A diversion can be made here (a few minutes' walk along St Calcedonius Street) to St Calcedonius Square and the *Seminary*. This building is an enlargement of a 16th c. residence of the Knights. A Baroque chapel replaces the original and the façade, with its richly carved Baroque doorway and flanking windows, is 18th c.

Argotti Botanical Gardens The Argotti owes its existence to the Bailliff Ignatius de Argote who built a house here (now used as offices) and planted out the surrounding area in 1774. It contains specimens of local flora, exotic trees, rare plants and a collection of 2000 varieties of cacti. (These can be seen on application to the head gardener.) The large building visible from the gardens is St Luke's Government Hospital.

St Philip's Gardens lie below the Argotti on St Philip's Bastion. They were opened in 1974. Here one has reached the limit of Valletta's landward fortifications, and there are fine views to be enjoyed from the ramparts.

Porte des Bombes, Floriana

On leaving the gardens continue south past the pseudo-Gothic church and downhill to the main road (St Anne Street). Turn right for the **Porte des Bombes**, a few hundred yards down the road. Built between 1697 and 1720 this was one of the two gates piercing the curtain walls between the three bastions of the Floriana Lines. The other has been destroyed. The gate originally had a single archway, with drawbridge and ditch. The archway was doubled in 1868 and the adjoining curtain walls cut away to enable traffic to flow round it. The carved emblems are those of Perellos, who was Grand Master when the gateway was constructed.

After leaving Porte des Bombes walk back up the right-hand side of St Anne Street and turn to the right. Go to the end of the street, follow the route to the left along the bastions overlooking Grand Harbour, then up through *Kalkara Gardens* to Duke of York's Avenue and Castile Place. These pleasant gardens with their view over Grand Harbour are worth a visit on their own.

Fort Delimara see **Delimara**

Fort Manoel see **Manoel Island**

Fort Rinella Coastal battery $\frac{1}{4}$ m east of Fort Ricasoli (Grand Harbour).

This small late-19th c. fort houses a 100-ton muzzle-loading gun that is almost unique. One other is at the Napier of Magdala Battery in Gibraltar.

Some years ago the Youth Section of *Din L'Art Helwa* (Malta National Trust) cleaned the abandoned gun and site. Every summer the group holds its annual camp on the site and spends a week or two looking after the gun. Drawings of both the gun and fort are extant and little money would be needed to restore the fort, which could become a monument of considerable interest.

Fort Ricasoli Overlooking Rinella Creek at the entrance to Grand Harbour. Approached by the Bighi road (signposted at the Kalkara turning) or on foot ($\frac{1}{2}$ m) from Kalkara. Although the promontory on which Fort Ricasoli stands was used to great effect by the Turks in their bombardment of Fort St Elmo during the Great Siege of 1565, it was not until Nicolas Cotoner was elected Grand Master that the Knights decided to construct a fortress on this strategic point.

The powerful Fort Ricasoli was erected in 1670 to the designs of the Italian military engineer Valperga at the expense of Fra Francesco Ricasoli, who also endowed it with an annuity. Grand Master Cotoner contributed to the maintenance of the garrison with funds derived from his property in Valletta.

The fort faces Fort St Elmo and together they defended the entrance to Grand Harbour. The seaward bastions of this longitudinal fort covering the whole of the promontory rise sheer from the water, while on the landward side it is protected by ravelins and three bastions. It could maintain a garrison of 2000. The fort suffered several direct hits in the bombing of Grand Harbour in 1941–42. Its fine Baroque *gateway* was damaged and unfortunately rather indifferently restored. The fort is not open to the public.

Fort St Angelo see Vittoriosa

Fort St Elmo see Valletta

Fort St Lucian
On central promontory of Marsaxlokk Bay between Marsaxlokk ($\frac{1}{2}$ m) and Birzebbuga (1 m).

In the early 17th c., under the rule of Grand Master Alof de Wignacourt, several powerful forts and defensive towers were built. Fort St Lucian guarded the vulnerable bay of Marsaxlokk. It was designed in 1610 by the Maltese military engineer and architect Vittorio Cassar, son of Gerolamo Cassar the 'architect of Valletta'. The massive curtain walls rising above a wide ditch add to the impressive bulk of the fort.

The fort proved its worth in 1641 when the Turks landed a force of 5000 men in Malta. The Turkish advance was halted by Maltese cavalry, and 60 galleys were driven from the beaches of Marsaxlokk by the guns of the fort. In 1798 it attained fame as the last of the coastal forts to surrender to the invading French troops.

The fort originally had a drawbridge and portcullis. Sympathetically restored, it has been used by various educational establishments. (Not open to public.)

Fort St Mary see Comino

Fort St Thomas
On tip of peninsula between Marsaskala Bay and St Thomas Bay, 1 m from Marsaskala.

The second of the two powerful forts built south of Grand Harbour by Grand Master Alof de Wignacourt. As with the earlier Fort St Lucien the architect was Vittorio Cassar. The fort was erected in 1614 to guard the two bays. It is square, with corner bastions and a moat. The two floors have barrel-vaulted rectangular chambers. The central doorway is approached by a drawbridge and a flight of steps. (Not open to public.)

Fort Tigné see Sliema

Gardens
Open 8 am to sunset. **Argotti** and **St Philip** (see *Floriana*); **Buskett** (see entry); **Hastings** (see *Valletta*); **Kalkara** (see *Floriana*); **Maglio** (see *Floriana*); **Sa Maison** (see *Pietà*); **San Anton** (see *Attard*); **Upper and Lower Barracca** (see *Valletta*)

Ghajn Tuffieha
Ancient site 5 m northwest of Rabat, reached by road to Ghajn Tuffieha Bay (see below).

Roman Baths Ghajn Tuffieha (The Spring of the Apple Tree) is famous for its Roman baths, the best example of their kind in Malta.

They are situated to the left of the road about 1 m before Ghajn Tuffieha Bay. When the site is not open, the key is available at the farmhouse down the lane.

The spring is one of the most copious in Malta and today is piped into the island's water system. Stone Age man, too, made use of this spring, for when the Roman Baths were excavated by Sir T. Zammit in 1929 Temple Period sherds were found. The Baths were extensively restored with UNESCO funds in 1961 and enough survives to give the visitor a fair idea of the layout and function of a Roman *thermae*.

These were not only baths but social centres for meeting friends and for idling away the day. The main rooms were the *caldarium*, a room where the water was very hot and the first entered, the *tepidarium* with warm water and benches where patrons could relax and gossip, and a *frigidarium* where a cold plunge would be taken before leaving the baths.

To the right of the entrance gate (**A**) lies a rectangular hollow (unexcavated) which was the *piscina* or open-air bathing pool. Beside it are some low concrete structures (**B**) built to preserve what is left of the tiled and mosaic floors (alternating) of the *changing rooms*. Seven of these were found. The one to the west with a pelta and swastika mosaic has been completely enclosed and roofed.

Behind the line of changing rooms is the remains of a tiled passage (now a path) with the water conduit running alongside. On the north-west corner of this path is the exposed *frigidarium* (**C**) with the remnants of a tiled floor and stone steps. This adjoins the second restored room, the *tepidarium* (**D**). which has a fine mosaic floor with a marble drain in the centre. Facing the entrance to the *tepidarium* across what was once a tiled passage are the remains of the *caldarium* (**E**), one end of which is apsidal. The *caldarium* was built on

pillars with a furnace underneath, while the cooler water of the *tepidarium* was heated by a fire outside the room (the pit for this can be seen by the north wall with the water conduit running into it).

To the north of the site is the *latrine* (**F**), in the main restored. Flanking it are the foundations of an unidentified building.

Ghajn Tuffieha Bay

On the north-west coast, 5½ m west of Mosta. Signposted roads from Mosta (by the church) and St Paul's Bay. This long sandy bay is approached by a steep flight of steps. It is seldom overcrowded. Visitors should take note of the warning that swimming here is dangerous in rough seas when there are undercurrents, and non-swimmers and children should only venture into the sea when it is calm. There are no amenities but these can be found at *Golden Bay* to the north (see entry). The *Riviera Martinique Hotel* overlooks the bay.

Ghar Dalam

Prehistoric cave and museum 5 m south of Valletta on Birzebbuga road (entrance on hill just outside village). For opening hours, see p. 28.

To visit Ghar Dalam is to go back 250,000 years. In the underground cavern are innumerable fossilized bones, some embedded in the walls, of Pleistocene fauna which once roamed the swamps and rich pastures of northern Europe. As the succeeding Ice Ages gripped the land these animals retreated southwards until they reached the Mediterranean basin, once part of the European land mass. At the end of the last glaciation the climate changed, water from melting ice raised the level of the seas, the uplands emerged as islands, and here the animals were trapped.

There is no agreement as to how these bones came to be deposited in Ghar Dalam. However, geological evidence shows that the cave was once a subterranean rock fissure lying at an angle under the ravine of *Wied Dalam*. It is likely that waters from heavy rainfall and melting snows broke through the floor of the ravine, gradually eroding the rock and enlarging the fissure. The bones and detritus carried by the waters would then have been sucked down into the cavern. Stalactite and stalagmite formations, and the fact that large quantities of bones were found to be rolled out into pebbles, support this theory.

The cave of Ghar Dalam, opening on to the north bank of the *wied*, was discovered by Professor Arthur Issel in 1865. At this time it was half-filled with field soil and used as a cattle pen by farmers. Excavations were carried out at intervals and the cave opened to the public in 1933. In 1934 a further section of the cave was found on the opposite side of the *wied*, but excavations were deterred by rockfalls.

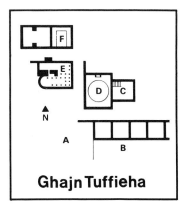

Ghajn Tuffieha

The main passage of the excavated site varies from 20–60 ft in breadth and 10–18 ft in height. It has a penetrable depth of over 270 ft and then divides into narrow passages and crevices. Excavations revealed a narrow coralline rock floor covered with clay. Then came a layer of bone breccia (mainly of dwarf elephant and dwarf hippopotami) under loose earth in which were embedded fragments of hippopotami bone, the bones of giant swans and the tusks and molars of elephants. Above this was a deep layer of field earth yielding the bones of bears, wolves and foxes, and the antlers of stags. Finally there was a much disturbed deposit of earth and pebbles in which were found early Neolithic flints, slingstones, personal ornaments and pottery dating from c. 4000 BC.

Tour The visitor to the cave passes through a small *museum* housing a collection of the semi-fossilized bones, tusks, molars and antlers of the fauna, with a few restored skeletons. (The Neolithic finds are in the National Museum in Valletta.) A railed walk runs down the centre of the cave. A pillar shows the level and nature of the original deposits. To the right of the walk is the bone breccia layer. Flanking the walk are trenches containing fossilized bones of Pleistocene mammals still embedded in loose soil, or solidified in the breccia.

Opposite the cave on the other side of the valley (ascend slope by rough path) are the scattered remains of a *Roman villa* (*Ta Kaccatura*). The site has been disturbed by earth movements and the floor plan is not clear. Of greater interest is the **Roman cistern** further up the slope. This is marked by a walled entrance, with steps leading down into the chamber, cut to a depth of 18 ft. The roof, at ground level, is of stone slabs, supported on square pillars. It is interesting to note the maximum span (6 ft) which the local limestone could tolerate when used as a cross-beam.

Ghar Hassan

Cave and beauty spot $1\frac{1}{2}$ m south of Birzebbuga. Reached by taking Kalafrana-Hal Far road and turning left after 1 m (signpost).

This waterworn cavern was once a subterranean tunnel with two outlets to the sea. A cliff path (with railings) leads down to the main outlet, now the entrance. It is for the dramatic view from the lesser outlet that Ghar Hassan is worth a visit. The secondary 'arm' bears off to the right in the cave, ending in a window in the sheer cliff face with the sea, a brilliant blue, 400 ft below.

Beside the window is a tiny room with a stone couch carved out of the rock. Here, it is said, the legendary Hassan, the last Saracen left on the island after its conquest by the Normans, held a Maltese maiden hostage. At the last, to avoid capture, he jumped with her into the sea. The truth is more likely to be that it was a guardroom for the local Maltese militia, who undoubtedly watched the horizon for enemy sails from this spectacular natural lookout. A weekday morning visit is advisable as this cave is a great local attraction. A torch is necessary.

Ghar il-Kbir

(The Big Cave) $2\frac{1}{2}$ m south of Rabat near *Clapham Junction* (see entry). These caves, once Malta's largest troglodytic hamlet, were occupied over many centuries. In 1835, when the caves were considered by the authorities to be too insanitary, the inhabitants were moved to Siggiewi.

Ghar Lapsi

Beach on south coast 3 m south of Siggiewi, $4\frac{1}{2}$ m west of Zurrieq.

This cliff-girt inlet, with its small beach, is a popular picnic and bathing place. Unfortunately the modern approach road has destroyed a great deal of its charm, and the improved access has brought the crowds, particularly in high summer. There is a car park and restaurant.

Gharghur

Village 5 m north-west of Valletta, 2 m north-east of Mosta.

This medieval hill-top village is on the Naxxar ridge overlooking the Victoria Lines. A steep winding road leads down to the 19th c. *Fort Madliena*, built to protect the eastern flank of the Victoria Lines, and continues on to join the coast road.

The village has a number of 17th c. churches: the church of the *Assumption* (1655), *St Nicholas* (1656), *St John the Baptist* (1678) and the parish church of *St Bartholomew* (1636) designed by Tommaso Dingli.

Roman cistern, near Ghar Dalam
Right: Golden Bay

Ghaxaq Village 4m south of Valletta.
The village, though old, has little of interest.
The church of *St Mary* (1655) is one of the
many parish churches designed by Tommaso
Dingli.

Gnejna Bay On north-west coast 5m west
of Mosta, approached via Mgarr.
A remote bay with a sloping sandy beach,
ideal for children. There is also good rock
bathing. The bay is cut off from Ghajn Tuffieha Bay by a headland, and is rarely
crowded, being only accessible by car. The
steep valley leading down to the bay is one
of the most attractive drives in the island.
There is parking by the beach, but no
amenities.
A Knights' *tower* stands on the cliff-top overlooking the bay.

Golden Bay On the north-west coast adjoining Ghajn Tuffieha Bay. Follow signs
from Mosta (5½m) and St Paul's Bay (3m)
to Ghajn Tuffieha.
One of the most popular sandy beaches in
Malta, which offers all amenities. The *Golden
Sands Hotel* (see p. 23) overlooks the beach,
and an old barracks complex close by has
been converted into a tourist village, *Hal
Ferh.*

Gudja Village 4m south of Valletta, reached
via Luqa.
This village has three 17th c. churches, one
of them the work of the prolific Tommaso
Dingli. This is the parish church of *St Mary*
in the main square, built to serve the village
in succession to the remote 'Ta Bir Miftuh'
(see below). The nearby *St Catherine* was
built in 1661 and to the south of the village, off
the Safi road, is the church of the *Virgin of
Loretto.* This fine domed church with a pleas-
ing façade was originally 16th c. but rebuilt
after the plague of 1676. An arcaded loggia
beside the church carries an inscription
dated 1550.

St Mary 'Ta Bir Miftuh' (St Mary of the Open
Well) This ancient church once served as the
parish church for several hamlets including
Gudja. To reach it take the Luqa road from
Gudja and branch left after 500yds.
Although of primitive structure this church is
one of Malta's most valuable monuments, a
fine example of a pre-Knights parish church.
Established as a parish church in 1436 its
origins were probably in the Norman period.
Interesting architectural details, such as the
low Siculo-Norman door on the south side,
point to its antiquity.
Traces of foundations around the church indicate that it was once a much larger building, and there is further evidence in the
width of the low-walled atrium in front of the
church, which is greater than that of the
church. (Note also the vestiges of an adjoining building to the north.)
The church has a shallow pitched roof (hid-
den externally by the parapet wall) and projecting water-spouts. These spouts were a
privilege denied to non-ecclesiastical buildings, which had to incorporate some system
of conserving roof water. The graceful bell-
cot was added in 1578.

Gzira (pop. 9500) Town 2m north-west of
Valletta.
A modern industrialized town, part of the
ribbon development on the west side of
Marsamxett Harbour. From the Strand, a
bridge runs out to *Manoel Island* (see entry).

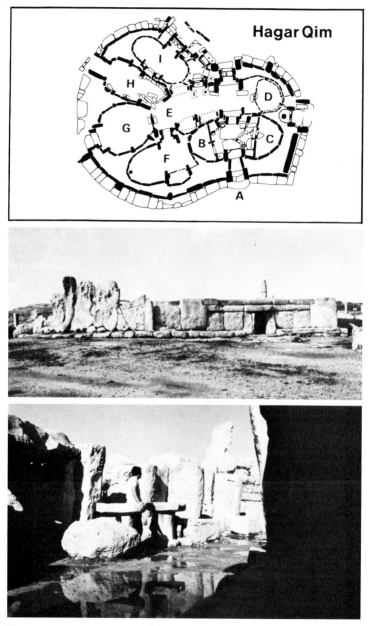

Hagar Qim, façade and entrance and pedestalled altars

Hagar Qim Megalithic temple (2400–2000 BC) on south coast, 6½ m south-west of Valletta.

The temple complex known as Hagar Qim stands on high ground overlooking the sea. This is unique among the Maltese temples in that the local globigerina limestone was used throughout in its construction, and the great orthostats have consequently been eroded by wind and rain. The slabs used in the outer wall are often extremely large and include an enormous megalith 23 ft high. The site was cleared in 1830.

The original temple was a 5-apse structure but with a rear door instead of a niche. The temple has the usual trilithon entrance (**A**) with a bench on either side. The orthostats flanking the doorway are huge, as are the horizontal blocks: some of these have been replaced since the site was first cleared. Inside the entrance passage the side apses (**B**, **C**) were almost completely walled off from the central court. Access to the apses was through porthole slabs which could be closed by screens (hung from the V-perforations in the jambs).

It was in the left-hand apse that the fine decorated altar in the National Museum was found. The inner right apse (**D**) is lined with small upright stones. Here there is an 'oracle hole' connecting with an external shrine. Where the central niche would be is a doorway leading to the outside.

The inner left apse (**E**) has special features: three slab-roofed niches and two pedestalled altars. Between the latter there is access to two chambers within the wall, one of them with a further altar.

From **E** there is access to three oval chambers. The first (**F**), up three steps, contains a court, central niche and right apse. Against the rear wall of the apse is a *betyl*—a cylindrical column—its purpose unknown. It was under the great slab at the entrance to this chamber that the 'fat lady' statues of Hagar Qim were found. The entrances to the other two oval chambers (**G**, **H**) are through breaks in the wall. There is a fourth chamber (**I**) north of these three which is walled off and can only be entered from the outside. It is recognisably a temple fragment with two apses.

The huge blocks of stone, the imposing façade and the temple's commanding position make Hagar Qim an impressive site, both for the casual visitor and the student of temple architecture.

Hal-Millieri see Zurrieq

Hal-Saflieni Hypogeum (c. 2400 BC)

Paola. 400 yds south of main square (follow signs). For opening hours, see p. 29.

The Hypogeum is Malta's most important monument, for it is unique. This subterranean sanctuary, one of the most remarkable works of prehistoric man, was discovered by accident in 1902 when workmen digging a cistern for new houses above broke through into the upper chambers. The discovery was deliberately concealed until the houses were finished, and in the meantime considerable damage had been done to the upper level. The investigation of the site was entrusted to Father Magri, S.J., who excavated the central chambers. It was later completed (1905–9) by Sir T. Zammit.

As the foundation walls of the houses had sealed off the original entrance, a new one was constructed enabling the site to be opened to the public. The modern doorways are modelled on temple trilithons. Before descending the staircase leading to the heart of the Hypogeum visitors should note the casts of the more important pieces found, and study the scale model of this complex site.

Antechamber to Holy of Holies
Hal Saflieni Hypogeum

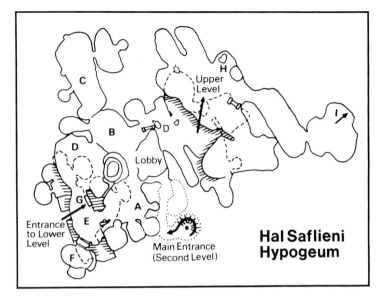

**Hal Saflieni
Hypogeum**

Tour The hypogeum is on three levels. The spiral staircase leads down to a passage; thence, via the bottom of the bell-shaped cistern cut by the modern builders, to a 'lobby'. This is the *Second Level* of the site some 16 ft below the street. The most interesting part of the Hypogeum is on this level. The top damaged level, the oldest part of the site, can be returned to later.

On the left of the lobby is the *Main Chamber* of the sanctuary (**A**). The circular wall has been carved to imitate the masonry of a built temple, and most of the wall surface is washed with red ochre. The advanced architecture of the chamber astonishes the modern visitor, especially with the knowledge that the sanctuary was carved out of the rock with no tools but flint, obsidian and horn, and no mechanical aids. It was in this chamber that the two 'sleeping lady' figurines—now in the National Museum—were found.

From the lobby one enters an *Unfinished Chamber* (**B**). On the right is a complete trilithon. The walls of this chamber are marked by deeply cut holes illustrating the method of excavation. This was by the use of flint borers, fixed to wooden hafts, to drill a V-pattern of holes in the rock surface. The rock was then prized out and the surface smoothed with mauls (flint hammers). Although the smoothing has not been carried out in this chamber, there are traces on the ceiling of the red ochre which was used as a finishing touch elsewhere.

From the Unfinished Chamber three steps lead down to the rectangular *Oracle Chamber* (**C**). This has three oval side chambers of different sizes. The first on the left has the appearance of a burial chamber. Opposite, at a lower level, is the second and largest chamber which itself has a small inner chamber. The third, at head level in the left-hand wall, is little more than a niche. This, when spoken into, causes a man's deep voice to reverberate around the chamber. (There is no echo when a woman speaks into the aperture.) The end wall of the main chamber has a moulding cut at ceiling level. This may have been constructed to enhance the acoustic effects. The ceiling of the chamber is decorated with spirals of red ochre. Returning through the Unfinished Chamber and bearing right one reaches the *Decorated Chamber* (**D**). This has an ochre-painted vault and walls with spirals and a honeycomb pattern. On the right of the entrance is the impression of a hand on the wall. Within a niche in the left-hand wall is a concave pit, 6 ft deep, with a sloping shelf around the circumference. The purpose of the pit has given rise to much speculation, but it is generally thought that it was used for offerings. This theory is supported by the small window above the edge of the pit which opens into the Main Chamber. The latter may well have served as the congregation chamber of the sanctuary, from which alms were passed. Amulets and ornaments found in the pit would seem to confirm this. The opening at the far end of the chamber leads down steps to the wondrous climax of the tour—the semi-circular *Antechamber to the Holy of Holies* (**E**). On the left are the stairs to the third and lowest level of the Hypogeum, and the central niche of the Main Chamber. But it is the magnificent façade to the Holy of Holies which commands our attention.

This consists of a 'porthole' slab with a rectangular opening beneath a lintel supported by four uprights. This is framed within a larger trilithon and topped by a course of corbelling beneath the flat ceiling. The tooling is fine and executed with great care. In the face of such skilled and imaginative work, achieved in such difficult circumstances, it is impossible not to revise one's conception of the 'primitive' stone-age man.

In the floor of the Antechamber are two libation holes. The walls are ochre-washed. The so-called *Holy of Holies* (**F**) beyond the porthole slab is a semi-circular chamber with an unfinished look, containing two roughly-carved pillars flanking a niche.

The lintel over the steps (**G**) leading down from the Antechamber to the *Lower Level* is one of the few cut blocks in the sanctuary. It is fitted into a specially cut groove in the rock and slopes inwards, following the curvature of the walls. The lower steps are separate blocks too, and irregular. They lead to a variety of chambers, culminating in a tall final chamber with openings to four niches. This is the deepest part of the site, nearly 36 ft below the surface. The whole of this level has been hammer-dressed and washed with red ochre.

The much-damaged *Upper Level* with the now blocked original entrance (**H**) is to the right of the central 'lobby'. On the left of this level is a chamber with the remains of human debris, the original deposit having been returned to the site after the extraction of numerous amulets, ornaments and sherds. All the chambers here are rough-hewn and the ceilings collapsed at many points. The original entrance is blocked by house foundation walls at the highest point of the site. Here, too, is a bell-shaped *cistern* (**I**) cut to a depth of 26 ft.

The purpose that the Hal Saflieni Hypogeum served in the lives of prehistoric man in Malta continues to baffle archaeologists. The decoration of the chambers, and the beautifully-carved architectural features which echo those of the standing temples, indicate an important place of worship. Evidence of burial, however, is equally significant, and the remains of no less than 6000–7000 people were found here. Whatever its true purpose, one function of the Hypogeum had a strange reversal in the last war, when the resting place of the dead became a refuge for the living. During Malta's second great siege the Hypogeum was used as an air raid shelter: fortunately it suffered little damage.

Hamrun (pop. 13,500) Town 1 m west of Valletta.

The old part of Hamrun has been swamped by the dull modern development which stretches for 1 m to the Fleur de Lys roundabout. The narrow little church of *St Mary of Porto Salvo* (1736) in the main street (between Nos. 636 and 637) near the central square is noteworthy for its rich façade and elaborately carved doorway.

Imgiebah Bay On the north-east coast, approached by a narrow road from Selmun village (off the main coast road to Marfa, 1 m north of St Paul's Bay).

This attractive little bay is part rock and part sand. The path down the cliff is strictly for the energetic. (No amenities.)

Inquisitor's Summer Palace Girgenti, 1½ m west of Siggiewi and ½ m from Dingli Cliffs.

At the head of the fertile Girgenti Valley, on a long flat ridge of rock, stands the most attractive of Malta's minor palaces. This beautifully proportioned building, harmonising so perfectly with its site, must have provided a cool and pleasant summer retreat for the Inquisitors, in contrast to their forbidding palace in Vittoriosa.

The palace was built by the Inquisitor Onorati Visconti between 1625–27. It has been recently restored and will eventually be opened to the public, but for the moment the site and exterior alone justify a vist.

Kalkara Village on east side of Grand Harbour, 3½ m from Valletta.

Situated at the head of the creek of the same name, this small fishing village was severely damaged during the bombing of the convoys in the last war. Its parish church was destroyed, to be rebuilt after the war entirely with voluntary labour. The creek is bounded on one side by the bastions of Vittoriosa and Fort St Angelo and on the other by the Bighi peninsula. Beneath the hornwork of Castile, part of the Vittoriosa fortifications, is the little Kalkara boatyard, where many of the Grand Harbour's traditional craft, the *dghajjes*, are made.

Behind the boatyard, through a tunnel in the fortifications, one can enter the *Great Ditch* below the walls of Vittoriosa. The ditch is planted with olives and one can walk along it as far as the St John's Cavalier. The exit is up some steps and through the Advanced Gate to the Vittoriosa bus terminus. Air raid shelters can be seen cut into the walls of the ditch. (An alternative and quicker way into Vittoriosa is by the steps at the tunnel entrance leading up to the Gate of Auvergne.) Kalkara Creek is also known as 'English Creek', for when Henry VIII offered Grand Master de L'Isle Adam the gift of two shiploads of armour to replace that lost by the

Knights in Rhodes, he stipulated that English ships should be allowed to anchor in Kalkara Creek. The British link with Kalkara was renewed with the establishment here of the residence of the C-in-C Mediterranean.

Bighi Peninsula This separates Kalkara Creek from Rinella Creek to the north. At the tip, on the Salvator Heights, is the old *Royal Naval Hospital*, which is now a Government school. The nucleus of this building is a villa built in 1650 by Prior Giovanni Bichi, Knight of the Order. The villa was converted to use as a hospital in 1805, and enlarged 40 years later.

At the top of Rinella Street (the street running up to the peninsula from Kalkara) a turning to the left by the Coronation Bar leads to the chapel of *Salvatore*, now derelict. It is of ancient foundation and was Kalkara's first parish church. It was severely damaged during the siege of 1565 and afterwards restored by Grand Master La Vallette. Prior Bichi, who rebuilt the chapel in 1650, is buried here. When the parish church in Kalkara was destroyed in the last war, little Salvatore this time escaped and resumed its original role of parish church. On the front of the church is a statue of the *Madonna of the Snows*.

Kirkop
Village 4½ m south-west of Valletta, 1 m north-east of Żurrieq.

This 16th c. village suffered severe bomb damage and has been largely rebuilt since the war. Its 16th c. parish church of *St Leonard* escaped.

Kirkop's most interesting monument is the *menhir* beside the road just to the north of the village. Several of these *menhirs* or standing stones are found in Malta and Gozo. Their age and function are unknown, but they are certainly prehistoric. This one is popularly known as 'Is-Salib' ('The Cross') as it has a small cross on the top, probably to mark the limits of the parish. It is approx. 10 ft high, the top having been chipped away to fit the cross.

Kordin
Ancient site on Marsa–Cospicua road 2½ m south of Valletta.

In the grounds of the Government Technical School in a walled enclosure are the remains of the **Kordin Temple** (Kordin III). Key at the National Museum.

The Corradino Heights rise from the sea at the south-west corner of Grand Harbour and reach as far as the Hypogeum in Paola. Traces of megalithic buildings have been found all along this plateau, but little now remains except this site—the remnant of a three-temple complex largely destroyed by the building of RN hutments.

This is one of Malta's earliest Neolithic temples. Although its walls stand only to the height of a few feet the trefoil plan can clearly be seen. A cobbled forecourt fronts a concave façade, the entrance leading into an inner court (also cobbled) with three apses. Behind the temple are the remnants of a number of small rooms of contemporary date, probably used as storerooms. Excavations have shown that there was an earlier occupation of the site. Every type of Neolithic artifact—mallets, slingstones, scrapers, borers, personal ornaments—was found.

The interest of this site is confined to the enthusiast. There is, however, one unusual feature to be found in the left-hand corner of the inner court. This is a unique communal grindstone or quern 9 ft long with seven grooves. The use of a sanctuary for the grinding of corn shows how the security of the holy place was utilised for an everyday activity.

Lija
Village 4 m west of Valletta, reached via Birkirkara (take Balzan exit).

One of the historic 'Three Villages' of Malta, Lija has a sedate 18th c. atmosphere, with many houses and churches of the period.

The parish church of *St Saviour* in the main square was designed by Giovanni Barbara in 1694. The façade is graceful and unusual,

with a single Corinthian order mounted on high pedestals and supporting a strong entablature. The decorative moulding of the central window is echoed by the Spanish-style spires on the twin bell-towers. The dome is typical of Maltese Baroque, apparently diminutive behind the high cornice of its supporting drum. The most impressive feature of the interior is the rich painting of the vault, dome and semi-dome of the apse. From the steps of the church a white-painted statue of *St Peter* can be seen on the left. It stands beside the delightful little Baroque chapel of the same name (1728). Continue past the statue down Main Street. The first turning on the left (St Saviour Street) leads to the old parish church of *Our Saviour* (early 16th c.) surrounded by olive trees. It originally consisted of only a long rectangular nave roofed with a barrel vault supported on arched ribs. The transepts and dome were added in the early 17th c. The 16th and 17th c. tombstones inside the church are of special interest.

Tal-Mirakli (Church of Our Lady of Miracles) Lija's most venerated church stands ½ m outside the village on the road to Ta'Qali, at the exact geographical centre of the island.
The church is of ancient foundation but rebuilt by Grand Master Nicolas Cotoner in 1664. There is a fine altarpiece by Mattia Preti representing the *Virgin and Child with St Peter and St Nicolas of Bari*. In a niche on the right of the altar is the central panel of an old *triptych* (probably 16th c.) showing the Virgin and Child, which is credited with a miracle. It is said that during an earthquake in 1743 tears were seen to flow from the eyes of the Madonna.

Luqa (pop. 5000) Village 2¾ m south-west of Valletta.
The airfield which puts this village on the map served almost to destroy it in the last war. Happily the 15th c. twin churches of the *Assumption* survived, and the wrecked

parish church of *St Andrew* (1650) by Tommaso Dingli has been rebuilt. It contains the original *altarpiece* by Mattia Preti.

Mamo Tower see **Marsaskala**

Manikata Village in north-west, ½ m north of junction on Ghajn Tuffieha–St Paul's Bay road, 2⅓ m west of St Paul's Bay.
A nondescript village, but possessing Malta's most exciting piece of modern architecture, the parish church of *St Joseph*. Designed in the '60s by the young Maltese architect Richard England, the church was consecrated in 1974.
England's architecture combines functionalism with beauty and a feeling for the indigenous architecture of the Maltese Islands. This church, with its curvilinear form, is reminiscent of the megalithic temples. Its earth-brown colour unites it with the landscape.
Richard England's architecture may be seen elsewhere in the north of the island (Ramla Bay Hotel, villa at Gharghur).

Manoel Island   Marsamxett Harbour, north of Valletta.
The Yacht Marina offices, yacht slipways and the Royal Malta Yacht Club are all on Manoel Island, which is connected to the Strand at Gzira by a bridge.
Fort Manoel In 1726 Grand Master Manoel de Vilhena commissioned the building of a fortress on the island to protect Valletta and Floriana from attack across the waters of Marsamxett. The fort, designed by the French military engineer de Tigné, is square with four corner bastions, a wide ditch and ravelins protecting the curtain walls. It has a fine Baroque *gateway*.
The fort could accommodate 500 men. Much of it, including the chapel, was destroyed in the last war. It is not open to the public.
Below the fort is the long line of buildings erected in 1643 as the *Lazaretto* of the Order. It was used as an isolation hospital during the British occupation and as a submarine base during the war, when it was badly damaged.

Maqluba, Il- Geological fault on southern outskirts of Qrendi off the Qrendi-Wied-iz-Zurrieq road, 6½ m south-west of Valletta.
Il-Maqluba, a pit 330 ft long by 200 ft wide and 130 ft deep, is an enormous dissolution pocket in the rock, a deep waterworn cavern whose roof has collapsed, probably as the result of an earthquake. Its inaccessible floor is an evergreen garden of trees, bamboos and shrubs.
The legend of Il-Maqluba, 'the turned upside-down', tells of how a small village once existed on this spot whose inhabitants were so sinful that the wrath of God caused an earth tremor to engulf them. However (the

Kalkara Creek

story goes on), they were too sinful even for Lucifer's realm, so he launched the village skywards and it landed upside down in the sea. Thus was created the uninhabited islet of Filfla!

At the edge of the pit stands the tiny chapel of *St Matthew*, which is reputed to have survived the tremor (dated as St Catherine's Day, 1343). Whatever the truth of this, the chapel is of unknown antiquity. It has room for only 16 worshippers, but attached to it is a larger 16thc. *church*. The present altarpiece representing the *Martyrdom of St Matthew* was painted in 1680 by Mattia Preti. The old altarpiece hangs in the Sacristy.

Marfa Landing stage for the Gozo ferry, 15 m north-west of Valletta. Reached by the coast road via Sliema or via Mosta and St Paul's Bay. Nearby is the *Ramla Bay Hotel* (see p. 23).

For boat services to Gozo, see p. 21.

Margherita Lines see **Cospicua**

Marsa (pop. 9000) Town 1½ m south-west of Valletta.

Embracing the wharves of Marsa Creek, this town with its power station and factories is the most concentrated industrial zone in Malta. There are no monuments of interest, but the Marsa Sports Club with its encircling race track provides a pleasant green area.

Marsamxett Harbour The second harbour of Malta, lying to the north of Valletta and Floriana, but without the depth of water of Grand Harbour. Lazzaretto and Msida Creeks have been developed as a Yacht Marina. Pleasure boats cruising to Grand Harbour, and up to Comino, berth in Sliema Creek. Sailing races, and in particular the Middle Sea Race, start opposite the Royal Malta Yacht Club at Fort Manoel.

Marsaskala Village on south coast 6 m south-east of Valletta.

Although there has been some resort development, this modest fishing village is still comparatively unspoilt. It was in the sheltered Marsaskala Bay that the Turks landed a force of 5000 men in 1614. They marched inland to attack Zejtun, but were driven off by Maltese cavalry. As a result of this, *Fort St Thomas* was built to guard the bay (see entry).

½ m south on the road to Zejtun is the *Mamo Tower*. The plan of this 17th c. tower is unique in the Maltese Islands. Built in the form of a cross of St Andrew, it has a circular room covered with a shallow vault occupying the crossing of the arms. The arm on the left of the gate has two storeys, the others one story. The tower is surrounded by a ditch excavated from the rock (not open to the public).

Marsaxlokk (Marsascirocco) Village on eastern inlet of Marsaxlokk Bay, 5½ m south of Valletta.

The name of this village is derived from *Marsa* (Arabic for 'harbour') and *scirocco* (south wind from the Sahara). It is the biggest fishing village in Malta, where one can see every kind of Maltese fishing craft. The gaily-painted boats, set against the vivid blue of sea and sky, are unforgettable. In the summer months the fishermen's families can be seen making the brightly-coloured string bags which are on sale all over the island.

Marsaxlokk Bay On south-east coast. 1 m wide at its entrance, and 1½ m in length and breadth, this bay is a safe anchorage for ships of all sizes. The coast round the great bay with its inlets and beaches has always been vulnerable to attack from the sea. In medieval times it was sparsely populated, and although the Knights in the 17th and 18th c. built their forts and batteries to defend the bay, it was not until the 19thc. that settlers felt safe on its shores. In the Great Siege of

Harbour, Marsaxlokk

1565 the Turkish admiral Piali Pacha disembarked his infantry and guns on the beaches of Marsaxlokk; more than two hundred years later, in June 1798, Napoleon's troops were landed from ships anchored in the bay.

The most important strongpoints guarding the bay are *Fort Delimara* and *Fort St Lucien* (see entries).

Mdina Ancient capital of Malta, 6¼ m west of Valletta.

History There can be little doubt that the commanding heights graced by the walled city of Mdina have been occupied since early times. A Bronze Age village site has been indicated by sherds of the period, and Phoenician tombs have also been found. It was the Romans, however, who left the strongest imprint.

The ancient Roman city of *Melita*, seat of the Roman governor Publius, was three times the size of Mdina today, covering much of the area of the present suburb of Rabat. When the Arabs conquered the island in 870 AD

they reduced the city to its present dimensions, encircling it with defensive walls with a moat on the southern front. They renamed it *Medina*.

In 1090 Count Roger of Normandy overran the country. One of his first acts was to build a cathedral in Medina, on the site of the ruined sanctuary where once stood the house of Publius, the Roman governor converted by St Paul to Christianity.

Throughout the Norman, Swabian, Angevin and Aragonese dominations Medina remained the capital city. Here the rich built their palaces. By the 14th c., although part of the Sicilian kingdom with the Viceroy as overlord, Malta had a form of local government, the Università, with its seat at Medina. The head of the governing body of the Università was the Captain of the Rod, or Chief Justice. In 1427 Medina became *Notabile*, a title bestowed by King Alfonso V of Aragon. But with the coming of the Knights of the Order of St John in 1530 the status of the city was reduced. The Order, now a maritime power, established itself in the settlement of Birgu

by the waters of Grand Harbour. The powers and privileges of the Università were gradually whittled away. Then, with the building of Valletta, Notabile lost its status of capital city and became *Città Vecchia*, the Old City. The old nobility and leading Maltese families retired into their stone palaces, aloof from their new masters.

Not until the 18th c. did Città Vecchia assume any degree of importance. Grand Master Manoel de Vilhena, who succeeded in 1722, was a man sensitive to the feelings of the Maltese. He decided to restore the old city, much of which (including Count Roger's cathedral) had been destroyed by the earthquake of 1693.

In 1798 the ancient capital once more took its place in the island's history, for it was here that the Maltese first rose in rebellion against the French, who under Napoleon had ousted the Knights. Finally, with British interests centred round Valletta and the Grand Harbour, *Mdina* (as it was now called) sank into peaceful obscurity. And so it has remained, a city in miniature dreaming within its protecting walls.

Walking tour Starting point: **Mdina Gate** (see map). The main entrance to the city is across the moat dug by the Arabs and through the fine triumphal gateway erected by Grand Master Manoel de Vilhena and adorned with his arms. Vilhena blocked up the original entrance to make room for his palace inside the gate—its outline can be seen on the wall to the right.

Inside the gate is the little square of St Publius. The splendid Baroque *gateway* on the right is the entrance to the **Magisterial Palace** (c. 1732) designed by Giovanni Barbara. The palace, showing the influence of French Baroque, is built round three sides of a square and has a fine doorway and carved windows. Grand Master de Vilhena's escutcheon adorns the gateway and his portrait in bronze is over the doorway. The palace is now a Natural History Museum.

Facing the palace is the *Torre dello Standardo* (16th c.), originally the city gatehouse and now the police station. At the head of the square are the massive walls of the *Nunnery of St Benedict* (1418, altered in the 17th c.). The Order lives in strict seclusion, entry being forbidden to all men except the doctor and whitewasher.

To the left of the nunnery, round the corner, is Villegaignon Street, which divides the city in two. The most ancient buildings lie to the left (or west), the part least damaged in the

Mdina Gate

Walking tour
1 Mdina Gate
2 Magisterial Palace
3 Torre dello Standardo
4 Nunnery of St Benedict
5 St Agatha
6 St Benedict
7 Casa Inguanez
8 Palazzo Gatto-Murina
9 Casa Viani
10 House of Notary Bezzina
11 Casa Testaferrata
12 Banca Giuratale
13 Cathedral
14 Cathedral Museum
   (former Seminary)
15 Palazzo Santa Sofia
16 Palazzo Falzon
17 Carmelite Church
18 Corte Capitanale
19 Arengo

20 Greeks' Gate
21 St Nicholas
22 St Peter

Mdina

earthquake of 1693. The first building on the right in the walls of the nunnery is the little church of *St Agatha*, founded in 1417 but re-modelled in 1694 when the architect was Lorenzo Gafà. Then comes the entrance to the chapel of *St Benedict* with a fine altarpiece of the *Madonna with Sts Peter, Benedict and Scholastica* by Mattia Preti.

Opposite is the *Casa Inguanez*, seat of the most ancient of the Maltese nobility. Created barons in 1350, they were the hereditary governors of the city and Captains of the Rod. Their coat-of-arms can be seen on the inside of the main gateway. King Alfonso V of Aragon stayed in this palace in 1432, and Alfonso XIII of Spain occupied the same room in 1927. The palace has a modern façade, but the beautiful Renaissance door-knockers should be noted.

A few yards down Mesquita Street, bounding the north wall of the Casa Inguanez, turn right into Gatto Murina Street. Here is the *Palazzo Gatto-Murina*, with a 14th c. façade. It has fine double windows and an arcaded string course.

Returning to Villegaignon Street, two buildings to be noted on the left are the *Casa Viani* (17th c.) at Nos. 6/7 and the *House of Notary Bezzina* (No. 11) remembered for the part it

played in the uprising of the Maltese against the French in 1798. It was from the balcony of this building (originally the offices of the Captain of the Rod) that the commander of the French garrison, Captain Masson, was thrown to his death by a mob infuriated by the looting and auctioning of tapestries from the Carmelite church. The death of the French commander was the signal for a general assault by the Maltese on the citadel, which fell to them after a brief resistance.

Opposite the Casa Viani at No. 34 is the 18th c. *Casa Testaferrata*, and beyond that, overlooking the south side of St Paul's Square, is the *Banca Giuratale* (1730), erected by Grand Master de Vilhena.

Cathedral On the east side of the square is the building which replaced the devastated Norman cathedral. Designed by Lorenzo Gafà, who created many of Malta's finest Baroque churches, the cathedral was built between 1697-1702.

The façade of the cathedral is one of Gafà's most harmonious compositions, a beautiful example of restrained Baroque. The short ornate towers are in perfect proportion to the rest of the building and the whole is crowned by the magnificent dome which dominates the skyline of Mdina.

On either side of the west front are two 17th c. bronze *cannon*. These were retrieved in 1888 from the Artillery Museum in Woolwich, where they had been taken by the British earlier in the century.

The interior is a Latin cross with three bays on either side of the nave, wide transepts and aisle chapels. The chancel is flanked by two chapels. On the left, in the *Chapel of the Blessed Sacrament*, is an ancient painting of the *Madonna and Child*, probably 13th c. but traditionally ascribed to St Luke. The *Chapel of the Crucifix*, on the right, contains a painting on wood of *St Paul*, the central panel of the polyptych now in the Cathedral Museum (formerly the altarpiece of the old cathedral). The *crucifix* is early 17th c., by Fra Innocenzo de Petralia.

The only part of the old cathedral to survive the earthquake was the apse, which retains a fine fresco by Mattia Preti of the *Shipwreck of St Paul* (1681) in the semi-dome of the apse. A modern cross by the high altar replaces the precious *Crusader Cross*, removed for safekeeping. Brought by the Knights from Rhodes, the cross is thought to have been carried by the Crusaders into Jerusalem.

The paintings in the aisle chapels are of no great importance. The ceiling *frescoes* (1794) are by the Sicilian artists Vincenzo and Antonio Manno, and those of the dome by Francesco Zahra. A further painting by Preti of *St Paul Appearing During the Saracen Raid, 1442* is in the north transept. Looking at the mosaic medallions of St Peter and St Paul on the chancel arch one has the impression of paintings.

Of special interest are the multi-coloured marble *tablets* paving the nave and aisles, marking the graves of dignitaries of the cathedral and those members of the nobility entitled to be buried within its walls. The fine carved oak *door* leading into the sacristy

from the north aisle was originally the main door of the Norman cathedral. The marble *baptismal font* just inside the west door also survived the earthquake. It was presented by Bishop Giacomo Valguarnera in 1495.

On leaving the cathedral turn left. Across Bishop's Square is the *Seminary* (1733). Designed by Giovanni Barbara it is very different to his Magisterial Palace, the influence here being of Italian rather than French Baroque.

The Seminary now houses the **Cathedral Museum**, an accumulation of the treasures of 800 years (for opening hours, see p. 29). The collection owes its origin to the Marchesi Bequest. The Marchesi family from Provence, who settled in Malta in the 17th c., were great patrons of the arts and acquired a wealth of works, including many engravings and drawings by Old Masters. A third of the collection was left to the cathedral by Count Saverio Marchesi in 1833. In addition, throughout the rule of the Order of St John, donations were made to the cathedral by the Knights, and bequests by the clergy.

The treasures owned by the cathedral include etchings, lithographs, engravings and paintings by artists as diverse as Guido Reni, Van Dyck, Goya, Salvator Rosa, Lucas van Leyden, Tiepolo and Antoine de Favray. Part of the extensive collection of woodcuts by Albrecht Durer is always on display.

In the centre of a room containing paintings and triptychs rescued from abandoned country chapels are the remaining panels of the beautiful 14th c. *polyptych* from the old cathedral. Also in this room is a painting of *St Agatha*. Legend relates that in 1551, when Mdina was under siege from North African corsairs, a nun from St Benedict claimed that she had had a revelation from St Agatha. The saint had foretold that if her picture were shown on the bastions Mdina would be saved. The painting was subsequently hung on the battlements, and the siege raised.

As well as vestments bequeathed by the Bishops of Malta, the museum contains old damask and traditional Maltese lace. Among the manuscripts are codices from the 11th c., an ancient Antiphon Book and illuminated 16th c. Psalters.

Unfortunately many of the gold and silver articles belonging to the Conventual Church of St John in Valletta were looted and melted down by Napoleon, but the church's magnificent set of *silver statues* of the Virgin and the Apostles was ransomed from the French by the Cathedral Chapter. The statues were sent to the cathedral but the ransom—their weight in silver—was never handed over, as by that time the French were blockaded in Valletta. The statues are early 17th c., all donated by Knights (the names are on the back) and are of chiselled – not cast – silver. They are kept in the museum and displayed on the high altar during religious festivals.

Returning to Villegaignon Street from St Paul's Square, the first building on the left is the *Palazzo Santa Sofia*. This is thought to be 13th c., and the oldest building in Mdina. The first floor was added in 1938. The string course decoration of pendant triangles with small balls at the apex is typical of buildings of the 13th and 14th c. The same decoration can be seen on the *Palazzo Falzon*, or Norman House, further up the street on the right. The house was originally of one storey (14th c.) the second storey with its attractive double windows being added in the 15th c. On the opposite side of the street is the octagonal *Church of the Carmelites*, built in 1570 but modified in the next century.

Villegaignon Street leads out into Bastion Square with a wonderful view of the countryside. Below is the Hemsija Valley with Imtarfa and its tall clock tower on the far side. To the right is the dome of Mosta Church and, in the distance, St Paul's Bay. Beyond the disused airfield of Ta'Qali can be seen the fortifications round Grand Harbour.

To return to St Paul's Square walk along the bastions and then through Bastions Street. Cross the square to the Seminary and then turn right into St Paul's Street. The 17th c. *Archbishop's Palace* is on this corner, forming a wing of the cathedral. At the end of St Paul's Street is a delightful little square in front of the *Xara Palace*, now an hotel. Facing the Xara Palace is the *Corte Capitanale*, once the Courts of Justice presided over by the Captain of the Rod. The third side of the square is a graceful loggia, the *Arengo*, from which the town herald made his proclamations. The road to the right leads back to St Publius Square.

The visitor with time to spare should wander round the narrow streets to the west of Villegaignon Street. Inguanez Street runs down

Villegaignon Street, Mdina

from St Publius Square to **Greeks' Gate**, the other entrance to Mdina. This was reconstructed by Grand Master Vilhena, whose arms are above the archway. Here can be seen the old vertical Arab walls (the base of the Knights' walls was angled). A few yards to the north, off Magazine Street, is a third gate, in effect a sally port.

Close by in St Nicholas Street (running up from Greeks' Gate) is the church of *St Nicholas* (1692). At the end of St Nicholas Street is St Peter Street and on the left is the church of *St Peter* (1617). In these little streets there are houses dating back in part to the 14th c., often with double windows. Magazine Street on the perimeter leads up to Bastion Square.

Mellieha   Village 13½ m north-west of Valletta.

This attractive village lies on a high ridge overlooking Mellieha Bay. It was one of the original ten parishes created in 1436, but was abandoned early in the 16th c. as a result of corsair raids. The parish was then joined to that of Naxxar, and not re-established until 1841.

The parish church of *Our Lady of Victory*, situated at the highest point of the village, was erected in 1897 to take care of the needs of the expanding agricultural community. It was designed by Vincenzo Sammut, and finished after his death by Gio Maria Camilleri. The interior is not yet complete, but one can see the painting which celebrates the great event in Maltese history commemorated in the name of the church. This is *The Victory of the Great Siege* by the Maltese artist Giuseppe Cali (1846–1930).

At the northern end of the village, on the left-hand side going down to Mellieha Bay, is the graceful domed structure of the *Sanctuary of Our Lady*. This was the original parish church, and is built round a rock-hewn church of unknown antiquity. The *murals* in this little troglodyte church are of great interest. According to legend the one of the *Virgin and Child* was painted by St Luke when he was shipwrecked with St Paul in 60 AD; recent research, however, has shown that this could not have been painted earlier than the 3rd c. AD. Also portrayed are the *Seven Bishops* who consecrated the rock sanctuary in the early Christian era. Adjoining the sanctuary is a small vestry with a number of ex-voto paintings. This little church has always been held in great veneration and since the Middle Ages, at least, has been the venue of pilgrimages from all over the island.

Cave Facing the church are steps leading down to a cave with a spring and a statue of the *Virgin and Child*. The water of this spring was held to be miraculous, its healing powers related particularly to children's diseases. Votive offerings of infants' garments hang on the walls.

Mellieha Bay North-east coast.
This long narrow sandy beach with shallow water is ideal for small children. Although easily accessible (the coastal road follows the bay) it is large enough not to become overcrowded, except at weekends. A disadvantage is the closeness of the road, which makes it less attractive (and less clean) than other beaches. Amenities include restaurants and the *Mellieha Bay Hotel* (see p. 23).

Mgarr Village 8½ m north-west of Valletta. Signposted from Mosta Church.
This small agricultural village is dominated by its modern, big-domed church of the *Assumption*—popularly known as the 'egg church'. It was built by voluntary labour, funds for the fabric being mostly raised through the sale of eggs and other local produce.
At the entrance to the village on the left-hand side (signposted) is the ancient temple of Ta'Hagrat (Key at the police station).
Ta'Hagrat ('The Big Stones') is a double temple comprising a small trefoil and a very small lobed, side by side. Although the site is very much a ruin the setting is delightful, with views south to the escarpment of the Victoria Lines.
Entrance is to the *western* temple of the pair (c. 2600 BC). This started as an open trefoil, but subsequently its central apse was walled off. The court with a surrounding bench has

a well-made stone floor. The ruins of the little *eastern temple* (c. 2400 BC) show that it was irregularly lobed. Ta'Hagrat is perhaps the most primitive of the surviving temples.

Mistra Bay Inlet on north shore of St Paul's Bay reached by narrow signposted road left of main coast road ½ m beyond St Paul's Bay. Rock bathing, but no amenities. To the north of the bay is the *Pinto Redoubt*, built in 1658 by Grand Master de Redin to guard the entrance to St Paul's Bay. Grand Master Pinto enlarged the redoubt in the 18th c. to provide shelter for cavalry based on Mdina.
Armorial Gate Near Mistra Bay, ½ m beyond St Paul's Bay, at the junction of the main coast road with the minor road on the left to Mistra Bay.
This handsome ornamental gateway, now sadly in need of restoration, was erected during the Grandmastership of Manoel Pinto. It marked the entrance to property owned by the *Monte di Redenzione* (see **Selmun Palace**).

Mnajdra Megalithic temples (c. 2600–2200 BC) on south coast 6½ m south-west of Valletta. The temples lie about 600 yds west of the temple complex of Hagar Qim, on a beautiful gently-shelving site overlooking the sea.
There are three temples, two adjacent 4-apse and niche temples with a little trefoil temple

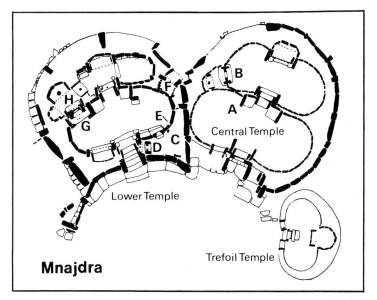

Mnajdra

Mnajdra

to the east. The three temples are grouped round a semi-circular forecourt. The little *trefoil temple* was the first to be built (c. 2600 BC); it has an unusual triple entrance. The **Central Temple** (c. 2000 BC) was the last to be built. Its entrance echoes that of the little trefoil, with a huge 'porthole' slab over 9 ft high offering a fine view through to the central niche. The first course of slabs round the apses are regular and well-fitted.

The temple has two special features. The largest upright to the left of the inner passage (**A**) has an engraving of a temple façade on the side facing the passage. Through the passage, the left-hand inner apse has a porthole slab within a trilithon (**B**), opening into a small chamber with a pillar altar.

The third **Lower Temple** (c. 2200 BC) is of all the temples the one that creates the feeling of the original structure. The walls retain much of their original height, while the upper courses (particularly in the first right-hand apse) slope inwards, giving the impression of roofing.

The concave façade of rough coralline has a trilithon entrance with benches on either side. On the right of the main doorway, inside, is another little doorway with steps and a 'porthole' slab leading to a small chamber within the wall (**C**). Here is a complex altar niche—a porthole slab within a trilithon leading to an inner altar (**D**). In the stone next to the stepped doorway is a small square hole opening into the apse (**E**). Three blocks

further on in the wall of the right apse there is another square aperture with a small intra-mural chamber behind (**F**), reached only from the outside. The exact function of these apertures is unknown, but a reasonable guess is that they were oracle holes, enabling a priest inside the chamber to communicate with the congregation in the apse. In the far corner of the left-hand apse, facing the main doorway, is a large 'porthole' slab framed in a trilithon, the whole decorated by close-spaced pitting (**G**). The great threshold slab was carefully cut to fit round the orthostats of the trilithon. V-perforations cut in the orthostats suggest a door or screen. On either side of the doorway are free-standing pitted slabs, widening upwards. The chamber through the doorway (**H**) is, in effect, the left-hand inner apse. Here are three altars: a double pillar altar to the right, another double one facing the doorway, and a third altar, pitted but without a pillar, to the left.

Mosta (pop. 7900) Town 5m west of Valletta.

Much of this town, situated near the military airfield of Ta'Qali, was destroyed by wartime bombing. The church, however—a landmark for miles around—had a miraculous escape. **Parish Church of St Mary** This church, with its huge dome (the largest in Malta and the fourth largest in Europe) was completed in 1860. It was built largely with voluntary labour and without the use of scaffolding.

This was achieved in part by building the new church around the old—a device used elsewhere in the islands.

While imitating the design of the Pantheon, the church lacks the harmonious proportions of the Roman building. The portico seems strangely at odds with the squat towers and immense dome. The scale of the dome is best appreciated inside the church. The impression of space, enhanced by the light from the windows of the drum, is overwhelming. The effect is further dramatised by the frescoes, the work of the Maltese artist Giuseppe Cali, which have a three-dimensional quality.

In 1942 the church was hit by three bombs. The first two bounced off the dome and dropped into the square without exploding: the third penetrated the dome but by a similar miracle—after hitting the interior wall twice and rolling across the floor—did not explode. Nor was anyone killed—although a service was being conducted in the church at the time. (The bomb can be seen in the vestry.)

Tal-Isperanza Here is a very different church, the little country chapel of 'Our Lady of Good Hope'. It can be found about ¼ m from Mosta Church to the right of the Zebbieh road, off Hope Street.

This charming little octagonal chapel, built in 1760, owes its name to a touching legend. Some girls from Mosta were working in the fields one day when suddenly a band of cor-

sairs appeared in the distance. The girls ran towards the safety of the village but one, not so fast as the others, was left behind. She hid in a cave and prayed to the Madonna for help. She remained undiscovered, and her salvation was seen as a miraculous intercession.

The chapel is built over the original cave, as a tribute to the Madonna. It has a Renaissance façade and the niche over the main entrance contains a statue of *Our Lady of Good Hope*. In front of the church is the *zuntier*, or walled sanctuary, found in many of the country churches.

Steps outside lead down to the *Cave of the Visitation* beneath the chapel. Records show that this much-venerated cave was dedicated before the year 1575. In the cave are statues of *St John* and *St Luke* and the legendary girl kneeling in prayer.

Mqabba Village 4½ m south-west of Valletta.

Traces of Spanish or Moorish decoration can be seen in the surviving 16th c. houses of this village. Typically Moorish are the intricate roundels carved on the façades. These motifs have supernatural associations. Like the head of Minerva carved on the lintel of some Maltese doors, or the lion knockers, they were supposed to have the power of averting the evil eye.

At the southern edge of the village are the *Tal-Mintna Catacombs* (key at the National

Museum). These catacombs provide some of the most interesting examples of early Christian tomb architecture in Malta. They have carved arcosolium and canopied tombs, some beautifully decorated with a scallop shell in low relief. Their estimated date is 5th c. AD.

Msida (pop. 11,500) Town between Floriana and Sliema $1\frac{1}{4}$ m west of Valletta.

Once an old fishing village (the name Msida comes from the Arabic *msayda* 'a fisherman's dwelling'), the town is now part of the ribbon development which starts with Pietà and ends with Sliema. The parish church of *St Joseph* (1893) overlooks Msida Creek.

A short distance along the road to Birkirkara (on the right) is an 18th c. *washing place*, vaulted and arcaded. It was built over a spring at the expense of the German knight Fra Wolfgang von Guttenberg, a great benefactor of the Maltese. The troughs have been covered in.

Naxxar (pop. 4500) Village 6 m north-west of Valletta, 1 m north-east of Mosta (signposted from Mosta Church).

The old village of Naxxar, a parish since 1436, has lost much of its character in its development as a wealthy residential area. It retains, however, some attractive old streets.

The parish church of *Our Lady of Victory* (founded 1616) is one of the many parish churches designed by Tommaso Dingli. The façade and side aisles are later additions (1912).

San Pawl Tat-Targa (Steps of St Paul) $\frac{1}{4}$ m to the north of Naxxar, this little village contains the church of *St Paul* (17th c.). Standing high on the Naxxar Ridge with a fine view of the Burmarrad Plain, this church is on the site of an earlier one built at the spot where traditionally St Paul preached to the local inhabitants after his shipwreck.

Behind the church is *Gauci's Tower*, one of the earliest towers erected during the period of the Knights of St John. The tower, which is privately owned, was built in 1548 by Cikko Gauci of Naxxar.

During one of the sporadic attacks by corsairs on this part of the island, members of Gauci's family had been carried off into slavery. Gauci petitioned Grand Master Juan de Homedes to allow him to build and maintain a tower at his own expense, and to retain it for his private use. His petition was granted. The tower is square with three single drop boxes (through which missiles could be showered) on each side. Within the garden is a chapel dedicated to St Simon.

Across the road from the church stands the *Captain's Tower* (*Torri tal-Kaptan*), built in 1558. This square fortified tower, used as a lookout, commands views of St Paul's Bay and Salina Bay, together with the Burmarrad

Plain. From its roof the islands of Comino and Gozo are visible. It is called the Captain's Tower from the period of the Knights when it was under the supervision of the Captain of the Maltese cavalry based on Naxxar. Within the three-storied tower are carved the coats-of-arms of both Grand Master La Vallette and Grand Master Hompesch. (No access.)

A pleasant winding road runs down from San Pawl Tat-Targa to Salina. On the way, $\frac{1}{2}$ m north of the village at the Naxxar Gap (where the road crosses the Victoria Lines), are some of the island's most clearly marked *cart ruts*.

The *Annunciation Chapel* and the *Tal Lunzjata Catacombs* (see **Salina Bay**) can be found on the right just before this road meets the main coast road.

Paola (Pawla) (pop. 11,300) Town 2 m south of Valletta.

In 1626 Grand Master Antoine de Paule founded the new town of Paola in the hope that its elevated position would attract those seeking cool breezes in summer. Like Valletta it was laid out on a grid plan. However, it never became popular during the Knights' period, perhaps because it was unfortified. The old parish church of *Santa Ubaldesca* (1626) was designed by Vittorio Cassar and enlarged at the beginning of this century when Paola had become a prosperous centre. It is reached by Ninu Gremona Street, opposite the new parish church (see below). In the main square stands the great new parish church of **Christ the King** (1924), designed by Giuseppe Damato, a prominent landmark (Damato was also responsible for the vast new domed church at Xewkija, in Gozo). The *interior* is one of the most unusual in the island. Although a Latin cross, the transepts are wide, the bays almost nonexistent. Ionic columns separate the nave from the aisles, soaring up to shallow arches beneath the vault. The amber Maltese stone is left unadorned by paint or gilding to create a feeling of warmth and space.

On the square opposite the church is the open air *market*, particularly good for fruit and vegetables (closing time 11 am).

400 yds to the south of the square is the **Hal Saflieni Hypogeum** (see entry). Within a short distance of this are the **Tarxien Temples** (see entry).

Paradise Bay (Cirkewwa) In the northwest corner of the island. Signposted road from Marfa.

This pretty cliff-girt bay, with its sandy beach, is suitable for all ages. The view of Gozo adds to its charm. There is a car park on top of the cliff, and steep steps down to the beach. There is only one small café-bar, but the *Paradise Bay Hotel* and *New Paradise Bay Hotel* (see p. 23) are nearby.

Peter's Pool Beauty spot on east coast of Delimara peninsula, 7½ m south-east of Valletta. A sign on the side of a small building on the Marsaxlokk–Delimara road marks the turning, 1½ m from Marsaxlokk.

The most attractive of Malta's rocky bathing coves has much to commend it. It is seldom crowded, but on such occasions one can also bathe from the long flat rocky beach to the south of the pool. The water is deep and clear blue.

The cove is reached by a steep path, and is suitable for swimmers only. There is shade from the rocks, but no amenities. There are occasional cliff falls after winter gales, so care should be taken early in the year in the choice of a picnic spot.

Pieta Town comprising part of the ribbon development between Floriana and Sliema, 1 m south-west of Valletta.

Pietà takes its name from the church of *Our Lady of Sorrows* in Our Lady of Sorrows Street, the second turning on the left past the Ta Braxia Cemetery on the road from Valletta. It is typical of the small village churches of the late 16th c., with one variation. Instead of the central bell-cot there is a pedestal and a tall statue of the *Pietà* topping the pediment. The bell-cot is on the parapet at the side. The Baroque doorway is a later addition.

Overlooking Marsamxett Harbour are the *Sa Maison Gardens*, reached from Valletta by taking the turning to the right by the children's playground (nearly opposite the *Sa Maison Hotel*). The entrance to the gardens is a short way up on the left-hand side. It is a cool and shady place in summer, with a fine view of the Valletta fortifications from the upper walk. The gardens were laid out in the early years of British rule. A number of badges of British regiments once stationed in Malta are carved on the bastion above the lower garden. Below a restored Knights' octagonal sentry post are the gun emplacements of anti-aircraft guns used during the war. At the end of the gardens is Giovanni Barbara's 'skew arch', an amazing architectural feat. It served as a sally port in the Floriana Lines.

Qormi (pop. 14,500) Town 2 m south-west of Valletta.

Created a parish in 1436, Qormi was raised to the status of a town (*Città Pinto*) by the Grand Master of that name in 1743. It was once known as *Casal Fornaro* ('village of the bakers'), for traditionally the best bread on the island was baked here. Bread for the auberges of the Knights was supplied from Qormi in the days before the Order's bakery was established. Although today much of Malta's bread is machine-baked, towns and villages still use their old bakeries, where the doorway opens straight into a large room with ovens built into the walls.

Although Qormi has expanded in recent years, some of the old 16th c. buildings remain. Main Street and St Catherine Street have many houses with fine balconies and carved masonry, a few displaying the coats-of-arms of Grand Masters. The best starting point for a tour is the main square and parish church of St George (see below) where the buses stop. This is on the east side of the town, but motorists are advised to ask directions, as Qormi is a 'rabbit warren'.

Parish Church of St George The architect of this elegant Renaissance-style church, built on the site of an earlier parish church of 1456, is unknown. Built in the 1580's, shortly after the Conventual Church of St John in Valletta, its façade has many similarities to that of Cassar's church, with its pediment, superimposed orders and twin bell towers (here the spires are intact). In detail, however, it is more graceful. The cornice is crowned by balustrades and the three round-arched doors set within Corinthian portals. The upper order is deeper than the lower, lending an impression of height to the façade, and the panelling of the pilasters gives them an effect of slenderness. The interior of the church is cruciform, with Doric pilasters and a coffered vaulted roof.

Behind the church the narrow St George's Street (keep bearing left) leads to Dun Marju Street. From here one reaches Stagno Alley in which stands the elegant *Palazzo Stagno* (1589).

From the church, enter Main Street. The second turning on the right leads up to St Catharine Street, in which one can see three delightful small churches. First on the right is the cubic *St Mary*, (16th c.) with its beautifully carved doorway. Next on the left is *St Peter*, also 16th c. This church, with its elegant Renaissance doorway surmounted by an oval window, has a special charm. At the top of the street is *St Catherine* (17th c.).

Returning to Main Street, turn right and continue to another square (St Francis Church). The road forks here, but following Main Street to the right one sees an interesting old house immediately on the left (No. 31 St Paul Street) with two fine carved balconies. Three others, lost in the war, have been replaced by iron balconies.

Qrendi (pop. 2200) Village 5 m south-west of Valletta.

This is a very ancient village. Up to the middle of the 17th c. the coastline of Malta, with the exception of Grand Harbour, was largely undefended. Consequently many domestic buildings within raiding distance of the sea were heavily fortified against marauders.

Octagonal tower An outstanding example is the group of 16th c. buildings with an octagonal tower (the only such tower in the Maltese Islands) at Qrendi. It can be found in a side street to the right, going out from the church square to Siggiewi (follow Siggiewi signs and look out for beginning of stone country wall on left at exit to town. Opposite this is the side street leading to the tower.)

The tower has three storeys with octagonal rooms on the first two and a square room on the third. The roof terrace is octagonal and has four double and four single drop boxes jutting out from the sides of the tower. These

were used to shower missiles on attackers. Qrendi has two 17th c. churches which could almost be models for the ecclesiastical architecture of rural Malta. The larger parish church of *St Mary* is cruciform with two bell towers and a central cupola, the smaller *St Saviour* is rectangular with a bell-cot and simple front with a Baroque doorway and circular window.

More interesting is the little church of *St Catharine Tat-Torba* (rebuilt 1625) on the northern outskirts of the village on the Mqabba (Valletta) road. This has an unusual façade for the period. Rectangular blocks of projecting masonry give an impression of solidity, strengthened by the crenellated parapet.

South of the village, on the road to Wied-iz-Zurrieq, is the unusual feature known as Il-Maqluba (see entry under **Maqluba-Il**).

Off the road to Mqabba, just outside the village, is a right turning to the churches at *Hal-Millieri* (see **Zurrieq**).

Rabat (pop. 11,300) Town 6 m west of Valletta.

The name 'Rabat' is Arabic for 'suburb'. Mdina's present suburb was, in fact, originally part of the Roman city of Melita before the Arabs created the citadel (see **Mdina**). It is best known for its catacombs and Roman remains, and has some interesting old streets. It is also a centre for lace-making and weaving.

If time is limited to one day Rabat can be explored after visiting Mdina. For a tour of either, one can start from the bus terminus or nearby car park, close to the old city.

Octagonal tower, Qrendi

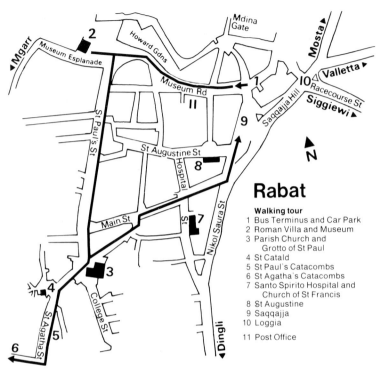

Rabat

Walking tour

1 Bus Terminus and Car Park
2 Roman Villa and Museum
3 Parish Church and
    Grotto of St Paul
4 St Catald
5 St Paul's Catacombs
6 St Agatha's Catacombs
7 Santo Spirito Hospital and
    Church of St Francis
8 St Augustine
9 Saqqajja
10 Loggia

11 Post Office

Walking tour starting point: *Bus Terminus* or *Car Park*. From Howard Gardens, which lie south of the walls of Mdina, follow Museum Road to Museum Esplanade.

Roman Villa and Museum The ruins of the villa (probably the town house of a Roman magnate) were discovered and excavated in 1881, and a small museum was added in 1923.

Museum The finds were recovered from tombs or local building sites. The entrance hall contains mainly Hellenistic and Roman objects, including terracottas and glassware, funerary monuments, architectural fragments and inscriptions. The finest Roman monument is that dedicated to the *Lyre-player* from Pergamum (150AD). Also in the entrance hall is a ground plan of the villa and some of the buildings of ancient Melita, whose excavations can be seen to the rear of the museum.

The large oil *pipper* at the end of the hall was found at Marsaxlokk. The olives were crushed between the stone wheels and the side of the basin, the wheels being so balanced that the pips were left undamaged. Alongside are conical axles of Roman flour mills made from lava imported from southern Italy.

A staircase descends from the museum to the ground floor of the *Villa*. On the landing is a large stone block found in Mdina in 1747. It appears from the inscription to be the pedestal for a statue erected to a Roman public benefactor.

The room entered at the foot of the stairs is the *atrium* or central court of the Roman house. This was roofed over except for the usual opening in the centre through which rainwater fell into a basin (*impluvium*) to be channelled off into a cistern. The *impluvium* here shows a charming mosaic of two birds perched on a bowl. The *peristyle* (the columns surrounding the court) has been partially reconstructed. A few of the blocks are original. Opening off the *atrium* are two smaller rooms. One, the *triclinium* (dining room) has a mosaic floor of white, green and black cubes. Hung on the walls round the atrium are panels of floor mosaic lifted during excavation, and on shelves and in showcases are marble statues, amphorae, pottery, glassware and other Roman objects found at the time. In one showcase can be seen finds from the remains of a Roman tower (2nd c. AD) near Safi, including a little gold ring and a carbonised bread roll. On shelves are Arab tombstones with Kufic script found near the site of the villa.

St Paul's Street runs south from the junction of Museum Esplanade and Museum Road; at the end is Rabat's historic parish church. **Parish Church of St Paul** Founded in 1575, this is the first of the large parish churches to be built using the plan of a Latin cross with the crossing spanned by a dome. All earlier churches in Malta were based on a simple rectangle. The architect of the church, which has been altered several times, is unknown. It is possible that Lorenzo Gafà worked on it at some stage, for in 1692 he was employed in rebuilding the *Sanctuary of St Publius*, which forms part of the church. The sanctuary owes its existence to a Spaniard, Giovanni Beneguas, who in 1600 came to Malta to join the Order but instead turned hermit, living in the Grotto of St Paul beneath the sanctuary. It was enlarged by Grand Master Lascaris before being rebuilt by Lorenzo Gafà. The main altarpiece is by Mattia Preti.

Grotto of St Paul Steps descend to one of Malta's most famous ancient shrines, where according to tradition St Paul lived as a prisoner (though with freedom to preach) during his three-month stay on the island. The fine 17th c. *statue* of the Apostle was presented by Grand Master Manoel Pinto. From the same period is a *model galley* of gold which bears the arms of the eight Langues of the Order.

The church of *St Catald* opposite is built over a small but interesting early Christian *catacomb*, remarkable for its elaborate canopied tombs and *agape* tables. These catacombs are the nearest to the old Roman walls of Melita, and were hewn just outside the perimeter of the moat. The church of St Catald was built on earlier foundations in 1745. The *altarpiece*, which shows St Catald in episcopal robes, is attributed to Antoine de Favray. **St Paul's Catacombs** (For opening hours, see p. 28.) A short distance from the church along St Agatha Street, these form the largest complex of early Christian catacombs in Malta. Entrance is down a steep flight of steps cut into the rock, with small *loculus* graves for children on either side. At the foot of the stairs is a rock pillar. To the left of this, lower down, is a chamber identified as a *chapel*. To the right of the pillar, adjoining the chapel, is the *main hall* with an *agape table* (see p. 33) at each end. Passages lead from the main hall into a labyrinth of narrow galleries cut at different levels, forming several storeys which communicate by narrow flights of stairs. The lowest are the most recent.

On the first storey the main gallery extends about 220 ft. In two places in this gallery traces of inscriptions in red on white plaster can be seen. One is the Greek letters EYTYXION, probably the name of the interred.

With the exception of the *arcosolium* tomb all the types of grave described on p. 33 may be seen in the main part of these catacombs. More than 25 separate catacombs are grouped around the main one, honeycombing the rock. Some of these belonged to families, some to Guilds, and others were Jewish. **St Agatha's Catacombs** Further along the street on the right is an extensive group noted for its *arcosolium* tombs. The walls of some retain traces of murals. The burial chambers were excavated between the 4th–6th c. The connecting rock-hewn *chapel* is of unknown antiquity. It is decorated with murals said to have been executed in the mid-15th c. Tradition links St Agatha (a patron saint of Malta) with these catacombs, for she is believed to have lived here after fleeing from the Roman persecutions of the Christians in Catania, Sicily.

After leaving the catacombs return to St Paul's Church, then through a tree-lined walk to Main Street. Bear right in Main Street and continue to Hospital Street (first right). On the left is Malta's oldest hospital, the *Santo Spirito*, founded in 1347. Used by the Knights of St John, the hospital has now been closed and will be converted into a medical museum. The building is part of a Franciscan friary, and adjacent to it is the 18th c. church of *St Francis*.

Returning to Main Street, turn left at the end (Nicol Saura Street) then left again into St Augustine Street.

Church of St Augustine (1571) This was Gerolamo Cassar's first important church, and his training as a military engineer is revealed in the architecture of the interior. The Renaissance-style façade, with its charming doorway and rose window, is a screen hiding the irregularities of the building behind.

The *interior* is impressive, the design similar to that of Cassar's later masterpiece, the Conventual Church (Co-Cathedral) of St John in Valletta. The main features—strength and simplicity—are shown in the massive masonry and arched barrel vault, which springs straight from the Doric pilasters. (Note also the thickening of the vault rib marking the division of nave and chancel.)

To return to the bus terminus or car park, walk back to the beginning of St Augustine Street and turn left. On the way is the square known as the **Saqqajja**. At the foot of Saqqajja Hill, to the right, is the road to Siggiewi. This is known as Racecourse Street, from an event which has occurred here every year since the time of the Knights. On 29 June, at the height of the festival of *Mnarja*, there are races between horses, mules and donkeys, reminiscent of the *Palio* of Siena, in which many villages compete. The winning post (located at the entrance to Racecourse Street) is marked by the old arched *loggia* (1696) used as a grandstand by the Knights.

Ramla Tal-Bir Bay

East of terminus of main coast road to the north, near the Marfa landing place.

Small sandy bay suitable for families. No amenities are available on the public beach, but the *Ramla Bay Hotel* with its private beach can be used by visitors. The adjoining bay of *Ramla Tal-Qortin* lies to the east.

Ramla Tat-Torri Bay

North coast 2.5 km east of junction with Marfa road 1½ m north of Mellieha.

A sandy beach at present marred by seaweed. No amenities.

Red Tower

(St Agatha's Tower) Knights' fortification on Marfa Ridge, west of the main coast road above Mellieha Bay.

This fortification, although designated a tower, was a strong coastal fort with five cannon and a garrison of 40 men. Standing on high ground overlooking the South Comino Channel, it also served as a signalling station between Malta and Gozo. Its one floor, 30 yds square with a double barrel-vaulted ceiling, stands on a base 12 ft high. Small windows are cut in the walls and a spiral staircase leads to the roof. A 2 ft parapet surmounts the roof with four corner towers rising a further 10 ft. The entrance is approached by a flight of stone steps probably originally separated from the doorway by a drawbridge. The many watchtowers round the coast were expected to defend themselves against single pirate vessels but were to be abandoned in the face of a major landing of the enemy. Fort St Lucian, Fort St Thomas and the Red Tower were to be held. The tower last saw action in 1798 when French troops landed in Mellieha Bay.

Above: Red Tower
Right: St Paul's Bay

St Julian's with Paceville (pop. 7600) Part of the Sliema conurbation, 3½ m north-west of Valletta. For bus services, see p. 20. For details of accommodation, see p. 22.

St Julian's, once a fishing village on St Julian's Bay, has developed so rapidly in recent years that together with its extension Paceville it has become the most fashionable tourist area on the island. There are hotels of all categories, with a Casino and swimming pools at Dragonara Point. Many lovely 18th c. houses can still be found in this modern resort. The entrance to St Julian's Bay is guarded by one of Grand Master Pinto's defensive towers.

St Paul's Bay

Resort 10 m north-west of Valletta on the main coast road. For details of accommodation see p. 23.

Before the building boom of the 60's—and the inevitable abuse of its perfect setting—this was just another Maltese fishing village. Now it is the most popular summer resort in Malta. Its villas, apartments and hotels stretch for nearly 2 m along the southern shore of the bay from Xemxija beach to **Bugibba**. The northern shore, too, has its quota of villas and flats. It is a centre for water sports and sailing, with good rock bathing.

Parish Church of St Paul On the side road leading from the main road to Bugibba (signpost). This 16th c. church was much embellished by Grand Master Alof de Wignacourt, who added porticoes to the front and sides. It was almost entirely wrecked by one of the few bombs to fall on St Paul's Bay, but has been carefully restored.

Traditionally, the church stands on the site of one of the most famous of St Paul's miracles: the episode of the viper and the fire (Acts 28).

Beyond the nearby shore lies a reef which has been suggested as an alternative site for the saint's shipwreck (see *St Paul's Islands*, below). This reef, just visible, would be a hazard for any ship caught in a *gregale* and blown on to the shore.

Close by is the *Wignacourt Tower* (1610). The work of Vittorio Cassar, this was the prototype for Fort St Lucian and Fort St Thomas. It is built on two floors, but unlike the larger forts it has only one rectangular chamber on each floor. The *Din L'Art Helwa* (the Maltese National Trust) has restored the tower, which will become a museum.

At the far end of Bugibba there is an unfortunate example of the developer's disregard for Malta's archaeological heritage. This is the *Bugibba Temple*, now engulfed by the *Dolmen Hotel*. Sited near the sea and only 20 ft above it, this little trefoil was apparently a fishermen's temple. Decorated blocks with relief carvings of fish were found here, an example of which can be seen in the National Museum. The dolmen-like appearance of the surviving trilithon entrance was the inspiration for the name of the hotel.

St Paul's Islands

At the northern entrance to St Paul's Bay.

This is the traditional site of the shipwreck of St Paul in 60 AD. The larger islet, *Selmunett*, can easily be reached by small boat. It is crowned by a statue of St Paul, erected in 1845.

St Thomas' Bay

On the east coast, reached by road south from Marsaskala ($\frac{1}{2}$ m) or east from Zejtun (1$\frac{1}{2}$ m).

The north shore of this large bay has recently been developed, with a promenade and access to the water made easy. It is not really suitable for small children, but adult non-swimmers can find shallow water.

Salina Bay

On the main coast road 1 m south-east of St Paul's Bay. The road skirts the eastern shore, which offers some rock bathing.

Salina is named after the salt pans at the head of the bay. Salt pans can be found in many areas of Malta and Gozo, but those at Salina are the largest group and still in use commercially. During the Roman and Arab periods the main salt pans were at Mellieha (meaning 'salt pond' or 'pan'). As piratical incursions increased in the Middle Ages the population retreated inland, mainly to Naxxar, and the salt pans were abandoned. The Salina pans were dug during the time of Grand Master La Vallette. During the 17th and 18th c. salt was exported, chiefly to the Adriatic coast for distribution to the interior. After the expulsion of the Order from Malta until about 1850 the salt pans fell into disuse, but were then repaired by the British. Near the salt pans, at the junction of the coast road and the road to Naxxar, stands the 16th c. *Annunziata Chapel*.

Tal-Lunzjata Catacombs These are located beyond the chapel to the right, separated from the side road by fields. Care must be taken to go round the fields, which are under cultivation.

The westernmost group has four separate catacombs showing good examples of canopied tombs. 20 yds to the east lies a further catacomb of greater interest. The pilasters and tympanum of the doorway are carved out of the rock. Inside, to the left, is an *agape* table, and nearby three impressive canopy tombs. These have fine carved pilasters and spiral decoration. Another interesting carv-

ing is that of the stag near the entrance. It is thought that this was the last resting place of a wealthy family, the main members occupying the central tombs and the more distant relatives the simpler tombs in the side passages. The date of these burial chambers is uncertain, possibly the 6th c. AD.

Salina Bay was well fortified by the Knights. The *Ghallis* and *Qawra Towers* guarding the entrance to the bay were erected at the personal expense of Grand Master de Redin (1657–1660). Each tower was equipped with two guns and four men. On each shore was a redoubt and a *fougasse*. The *fougasse* on the eastern shore where the salt plans begin is in a good state of preservation.

A *fougasse* is an excavation in the rock about 12 ft deep and 7 ft in diameter, slanting away from the beach. The hole was loaded with a barrel of gunpowder to which a fuse was attached. The barrel was covered with a piece of wood closing the circumference of the hole. On it were placed an assortment of cannon-balls and rocks. When the enemy landed the fuse would be ignited and the landing party showered with missiles. A number of these rock cannon were constructed in the 17th c. to protect the bays of Malta and Gozo.

San Anton Palace see **Attard**

San Pawl Milqghi
Ancient site near Bur Marrad on St Paul's Bay—Mosta road, 1 m from St Paul's Bay. The high-walled enclosure lies 500 yds along a rough side road leading out of the village to the west. Keys from the National Museum.

San Pawl Milqghi ('St Paul Welcomed') is the traditional meeting place of the shipwrecked Apostle and the Roman Governor Publius. Excavations of the Italian *Missione Archaeologica* have brought to light the remains of an agricultural establishment of the 2nd c. BC. Pippers and settling tanks indicate that it was founded for the extraction of olive oil. The original establishment was destroyed by fire in the 1st c. AD, but was refounded by the 4th c.

The church of *San Pawl Milqghi* (1616–22) was built on earlier foundations. Records

show that there was a chapel here in 1488, and it is possible that there was an even earlier one, for this is a much venerated place. A tradition that the church stands on the site of the villa in which Publius entertained the Apostle has been supported by excavations, which have revealed a Roman dwelling.

San Pawl Tat-Targa see **Naxxar**

Santa Venera
Suburb of Hamrun on the Valletta–Hamrun–Rabat road, 2 m west of Valletta.

On the right-hand side of the road approaching the Fleur de Lys roundabout is the *Casa Leoni* or *Dar il-Ljuni*—the House of the Lions. It was built in 1730 by Grand Master Manoel de Vilhena as his country house, and was the official residence of the British Lieutenant-Governor. It has a beautiful formal 18th c. garden. (Not at present open to the public.)

Selmun Palace
Approached by turning (signposted) off the main coast road, 1 m north of St Paul's Bay.

This 18th c. palace stands on the high ground overlooking St Paul's Bay from the north. Designed by Domenico Cachia (the Maltese architect who remodelled the Auberge de Castile et Leon) it is a Baroque version of Verdala Palace. Although more ornate with its encircling balcony, moulded windows and bell tower, it lacks the gracefulness of Gerolamo Cassar's 16th c. palace (the angled corners, however, have an undeniable subtlety).

Selmun Palace was the most important property of the *Monte di Redenzione*, a pious foundation set up in 1607 for the redemption of Christian slaves in the Barbary States.

The foundation was the inspiration of a Maltese Capuchin, Father Raphael. While preaching in St John's Conventual Church Father Raphael gave such a harrowing account of the sufferings of these unfortunates that the congregation was moved to contribute to the setting up of the foundation, under the patronage of Grand Master Alof de Wignacourt. Other bequests followed (including Selmun Palace) and the foundation was able to ransom many slaves, both Maltese and Knights of the Order. When raids from North Africa ceased and there were no longer slaves to be ransomed, the properties of the *Monte di Redenzione* were combined with the *Monte di Pietà*. This was a pawnbroking institution set up by the Order in the 16th c. to help the needy. The funds from these properties, used for charitable purposes, together with the *Monte di Pietà*, are administered by the Maltese Government. All 17th and 18th c. buildings belonging to the *Redenzione* are adorned with a shield bearing three cones surmounted with the letter 'R'.

Adjoining the palace is the little chapel of

Selmun Palace

Our Lady of Ransom. The interesting altarpiece shows a benefactress of the *Redenzione* freeing a slave. Graffiti of ships are near the church door.

Senglea (L'Isola) (pop. 4500) Town $3\frac{1}{2}$ m south of Valletta built on peninsula in Grand Harbour. Can be reached from Valletta by bus (see p. 20) or *dghaisa* from the Customs House (see p. 21).

One of the original Three Cities of the Knights, Senglea is now a post-war town, risen from the rubble of the bombing raids. In the mid-16th c. it served as a retreat for Grand Master Juan de Homedes who created pleasure gardens, a park and a zoo on the little promontory. Grand Master de la Sengle, who succeeded him, built the fortifications and founded the town in 1554.

Senglea was still largely uninhabited with two windmills, a church and a scattering of dwellings when it was attacked by the Turks in 1565. Bearing the brunt of the attack was Fort St Michael, which has since been demolished (1922) to make way for a school. In 1941–42 Senglea suffered badly from the air attacks on Grand Harbour and has since been largely rebuilt.

Although the old town has virtually disappeared, Senglea uniquely links the past with the present. On one side of the little peninsula the pleasant marina looks across to Fort St Angelo and St Lawrence, the Knights' first Conventual Church in Vittoriosa. On the other, the great *St Michael's Bastion* towers over the modern dockyard. The town, laid out in a grid pattern, is bisected

by Victory Street. At the beginning is the new square and parish church (see below). At the far end is the old church of *St Philip*, designed by Carlo Vella in 1662, which miraculously escaped destruction. Behind the church a little garden affords magnificent views of the harbour and Valletta. The *vedette*, or sentry post, a reconstruction of the original, was removed to safety during the war. It has an amusing feature: the carved eyes and ears symbolically watching and listening for the enemy fleet.

Half-way along Victory Street, St Julian Street (near civic centre and buses) leads down to the little church of *St Julian*, founded in 1411 and rebuilt in 1539 and 1696.

Parish Church of Our Lady of Victory The original church (1682) was destroyed in 1941. The church's most valued possession is a wooden statue of the *Virgin* which is kept in the last chapel on the left of the nave encased in silver. Legend describes how centuries ago the statue was being carried in a small ship from Spain to the East when storms drove the vessel towards Malta and on to the shore at Senglea. The ship made several attempts to leave, but each time a storm blew up and forced her back. Not until the image was taken ashore did calm weather prevail, enabling the ship to put to sea. In 1921 the statue was given a crown of gold, and to celebrate the occasion the parish church was granted certain privileges. The altar is of the basilica form, covered by a canopy, and the priest is allowed to celebrate Mass facing the congregation. The clergy are also allowed to preach in the open air, a privilege which is indicated by the large umbrella carried in the procession on 8 September, the day of the church's *festa*. This is one of the most colourful *festas* on the island. The procession, with the beautiful statue of the young Virgin adorned in silver and jewels and a crown of gold being carried down to the waterfront, makes an unforgettable sight.

Siggiewi (pop. 4700) Village $5\frac{1}{2}$ m south-west of Valletta.

Originally a small farming community established in the 15th c., Siggiewi is now a prosperous agricultural centre. The old part of the village retains some good 16th c. houses with carved window frames: many examples may be seen in Old Church Street and Old Main Street, both of which run into the main square.

Parish Church of St Nicholas (1675) At the summit of the broad street leading up from the main square, this is one of Malta's most imposing churches. It was designed by Lorenzo Gafà, who was also responsible for the Cathedral at Mdina and the Church of St Lawrence, Vittoriosa. In viewing his exterior, however, one must exclude the modern additions: the fine west portico and huge dome on its high drum, both from the 19th c.

Vedette, Senglea

It is the superlative richness of Gafà's *interior* which singles him out as a master of the Baroque. The ornate chancel, painted vaults and detailed modelling of the arches are essential details in his grand design, while the use of an attic course serves to enlarge the space and increase the impact of the view along the nave.

The little 17th c. *Palace of the Secretary of the Inquisition* survives in St Margaret Street (reached by bearing right from the south side of St Nicholas' Church.

Tal-Providenza (Our Lady of Providence) 1 m south of Siggiewi on the road to Ghar Lapsi is one of the most beautiful little churches in Malta. The ornate dome and lofty portico confirm the delicacy of the late Baroque (1750).

Skorba see **Zebbieh**

Sliema (pop. 20,000) Town and resort 2½ m north of Valletta. For details of accommodation, see p. 22.

This is the largest residential and tourist area in Malta, with hotels, night clubs, restaurants, bars and shops. There is a good bus service to Valletta (see p. 20). At 'Ferry' bus terminus on Sliema Creek (there is no longer a ferry) boats can be boarded for harbour tours or trips to Comino. For details see p. 21. The origin of the name 'Sliema' is of some curiosity. It is from the first word of the Maltese '*Sliem Ghalik Marija*' ('Hail Holy Mary'), the salutation given by returning fishermen to a statue of the Virgin. The town is a wholly modern development, dedicated to tourism. Its most attractive feature is the promenade running beside the sea from

Qui-si-Sana on Dragut Point to Paceville. Rock bathing is possible for most of its length, but only in a calm sea.

One of the outer defences of Valletta, *Fort Tigné*, stands on Dragut Point. It was commissioned by Grand Master Manoel Pinto in 1761 but not built until 1793—which makes it the last significant defence-work to be built by the Knights before their departure from the island. It was designed by a French engineer, Cavalier Tigné. It is a simple fort, constructed to support Fort St Elmo in preventing the entrance of enemy vessels into Marsamxett Harbour, but unlike Fort St Elmo, unable to withstand siege. It is not open to the public.

Ta'Hammut Dolmens Ancient site 6 m north of Valletta off main coast road from Sliema. A secondary road leads from the head of Qalet Marku Bay (with a Knights' tower on the south shore) to Burmarrad and Naxxar. Just north of this road, about 200 yds from the main road, one can see the dolmens, forming a line about 20 yds apart. The furthest inland is ruined, but the central one is in a good state of preservation: a natural step in the rock raises its height. The third dolmen was excavated by Prof. J. D. Evans in 1955, and the pottery found clearly places them in the Bronze Age (see p. 31).

Ta'Kaccatura see **Ghar Dalam**

Tal-Hlas see **Zebbug**

Tal-Lunzjata Catacombs see **Salina Bay**

Tarxien Village adjoining Paola, 3 m south of Valletta.

Megalithic temples The superb temple complex on the outskirts of the village has made Tarxien of primary interest for students of Malta's prehistory. The temples are often included in a tour embracing the Hypogeum in the adjoining town of Paola. They are in fact only 400 yds to the east of the Hypogeum and can be reached by heading back to the main square of Paola and turning right at the first intersection (Tarxien Road), which is signposted to the temples. (Those approaching Tarxien direct from Valletta are also recommended to go via the square, following the signs.) For opening hours, see p. 29.

The entrance to the site is through a small *museum* containing a collection of decorated blocks and artifacts. Others are in the National Museum in Valletta. Those on the site are exact copies of originals found *in situ*.

The complex consists of three temples with a few scattered blocks of a small *early temple* off to the east. The South and East Temples, both 4-apsed, are the earliest of the main group (c. 2400 BC). The Central Temple, of a slightly later date, is the only surviving 6-apse temple in the Islands.

Church of St Nicholas, Siggiewi

South Temple The first to be entered, this temple has a large forecourt with a cistern at the centre. The stone balls scattered about were used as rollers to transport the blocks of stone (an example of this will be seen in the Central Temple). The main entrance is a modern restoration.

Further restoration will be seen on the site, particularly where cracked blocks have been capped with concrete to prevent rainwater from destroying the stone. Where the original height is unknown these have been left with a wavy edge. Restoration work can be clearly distinguished from the original.

Before entering the modern doorway two *libation holes* should be noted in the block in front of the threshold slab. To the right of the paved inner court stands the remains of a *statue* (**A**) calculated to have been more than 9 ft high : that of the cult goddess herself. All that remains is her pleated skirt, two fat legs and two tiny feet (the original is in the National Museum). To either side and beneath her are decorated blocks with curvilinear patterns in relief (copies).

This right-hand apse had a further treasure to offer. To the right of the entrance to the inner passageway is a copy of a fine *altar block* with carved spirals (**B**). This has an altar niche above, with a porthole slab framed within a trilithon. This was perhaps the most exciting discovery of the excavators, for the space behind was filled with animal bones and the altar itself (which has a close-fitting plug in front) contained a goat horn and what must have been a sacrificial flint knife. (The original altar is in the National Museum.)

The left-hand apse is also rich in decorated blocks, two with *animal friezes* (**C**). Note, too, the stone *bowl* (**D**) with pitted decoration.

The inner passageway and the next court are paved. The uprights of the inner door (**E**) have V-perforations and bar-holes, showing that the entrance could be closed (the door would be hung on leather thongs or ropes). Facing this door is the *central niche* (**F**) with a great slab decorated with a spiral separating it from the court. The niche has semicircular benches. The left apse is regular, but the right apse has been adapted to lead into the later Central Temple.

The entry passage to the **Central Temple** (**G**) also has loop and bar holes. The *central court* (**H**) is impressive, with massive paving and well-fitted wall slabs. In the centre is a large flat bowl, and on the left an even larger stone bowl (**I**). In the left-hand wall of the entrance (within the left apse) is a fine trilithon opening leading to a chamber within the thickness of the wall (**J**) with more niches. A corresponding doorway on the right of the entrance in the right apse leads into the most interesting of the temples' smaller chambers (**K**)—again within the thickness of the wall. Two of the innermost wall slabs of this chamber bear *engravings*, one of a bull and one of a sow and piglets, while the third has a square 'oracle hole' at floor level opening into another very small chamber within the walls. In this same right apse is an opening (**L**) leading to the outside and the Eastern Temple. One of the paving stones beside the opening has been prized up to show a stone roller still in place under the threshold slab, and to demonstrate that the temples were not paved with flags but with huge stone blocks. Entry to the second pair of apses is dramatically barred by a deep decorated *sill-stone* (**M**) on an enormous threshold slab. This has a spiral motif (suggesting eyes) with a V carved between (perhaps a brow or nose) which may be taken to symbolize a forbidding goddess guarding the sanctum. Two

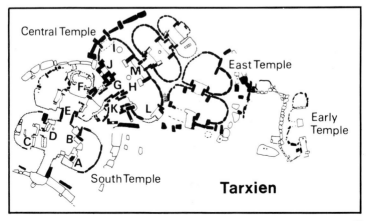

Central Temple

East Temple

Early Temple

South Temple

Tarxien

finely decorated slabs screen the apses on either side. The orthostats lining these apses are amazingly well fitted. The passage leading to the final pair of apses has another massive threshold slab. The left-hand apse has a little cupboard in one corner. The right-hand apse was destroyed by the construction of a Roman cellar. Part of the Roman wall remains in the centre, the rest is modern reconstruction.

The visitor will by now have seen the best of this fine temple complex. The remaining **Eastern Temple** is of lesser interest but has features worth noting.

The left-hand apses of this 4-apse temple have been considerably altered and the façade damaged in the building of the Central Temple. The precise fitting of the orthostats in the two right apses is remarkable,

but their chief interest lies in the building techniques they reveal. At the top of the face of some of the blocks there is a semicircular notch designed, it is thought, to take the tip of a wooden lever. The blocks would have been brought to the site on rollers, erected and then adjusted for a perfect fit with the aid of the lever.

Tas-Silg

Ancient site 1 m east of Marsaxlokk off road to Delimara (not open to public). Large-scale excavations conducted by the Italian *Missione Archaeologica* revealed four distinct phases of occupation at this site —Temple culture, Punic, Roman and Christian. Bronze Age sherds scattered around the hilltop also suggested occupation during this period.

So far these excavations show that the ruins of a *temple* of the Tarxien period (2000 BC) were adapted to form part of a Punic *sanctuary* (c. 6th c. BC). This was probably dedicated to Melkart, a principal deity in Phoenician mythology, the guide and protector of merchants and mariners. The site was still a sacred place in the 1st c. AD when there was a temple dedicated to Astarte/Hera. Inscriptions to the goddess under both her Phoenician and Greek names have been found. By the 4th c. AD the temple appears to have been adapted as a monastery.

Marsaxlokk Cippi It is probable that the two famous stone columns discovered in 1697 at Marsaxlokk came from this site. One was sent by Grand Master de Rohan to Louis XVI of France as a gift and is in the Louvre; the other is in the National Museum in Valletta (see p. 112). The bilingual inscription—Phoenician and Greek—on the *cippi* gave the key to the Phoenician alphabet.

The little church of *Santa Marija Tas-Silg* (St Mary of the Snows) is $\frac{1}{2}$ m from Marsaxlokk en route to the site. It was founded in 1650 and rebuilt in 1832. It is interesting as an example of small church architecture in the early 19th c.

Sacred altar (top) and entrance to Central Temple, Tarxien

Valletta (pop. 14,500) Capital of Malta. For details of accommodation, see p. 22.

History When the Knights of the Order of St John landed in Malta in 1530 it soon became apparent that to hold the harbour (and thus the island), defensive works must be built on the peninsula of Sceberras, where the city of Valletta now stands. At that time the harbour entrance was guarded only by St Elmo, then a small fort, and with the threat of an imminent Turkish attack it was agreed that work on new defences should be rapidly advanced. Efforts were concentrated on the strengthening of three positions: the Fort of St Elmo, the Fort of St Angelo which defended the Knights' stronghold at Birgu, and the promontory of L'Isola (Senglea).

These defences were heavily damaged in the Great Siege of 1565, and their repair made substantial demands on the Knights' exchequer. But the lesson of the siege had been learned: never again must the high ground of Mt Sceberras be taken over by the enemy. Immediately after the siege Grand Master La Vallette decided to build a fortified city on the strategic peninsula. In this he was supported by Pope Pius IV, who at the end of the year sent his military engineer Francesco Laparelli to Malta to inspect the fortifications. Within three days Laparelli prepared a report for the Council of the Order with plans for a 'gridiron' city laid out within a massive defence system. The first stone of this new city was laid on 28 March 1566; within five years two miles of ramparts had been raised and the domestic buildings so far advanced that the Convent was able to move from Birgu to Valletta.

It was originally proposed to level the ground for the foundations of the city, but this proved too costly. (This accounts for the 'humpbacked' conformation of the city, in which the streets between Merchants' and Republic Street are on the level and the others step down to the bastions.) Another idea was to dig stone for the buildings from the Manderaggio on the north side of the peninsula (below the modern Anglican Cathedral) thus forming a creek for the galleys, but at a certain depth the stone was found to be unsuitable and the project abandoned. It also proved difficult to move men and materials from one bastion to another, so a perimeter road was added to the original plan.

The city is an object lesson in town planning. Stringent rules were applied to the erection of houses on the main streets, one restriction being that steps should not project into the streets. Archways were opened into the ground floors of many buildings, providing entrances to shops (most of them now sacrificed for modern shopfronts) and squares laid out for recreation. Unlike the arrangement of the Knights' other cities the Langues' auberges were not confined within a *collachio* (walled area). Each was located near

the ramparts allocated to their defence, with the Magisterial Palace in the centre of the city midway between the Gate of St George (City Gate) and Fort St Elmo.

Laparelli went on leave from Malta in 1568, and had the misfortune to die of the plague shortly thereafter. The task of building the city was inherited by his assistant, Gerolamo Cassar, architect to the Order. The Valletta that survives from the 16th c. is largely the work of this man, who built the seven auberges, the Magisterial Palace, the Conventual Church of St John (now the Co-Cathedral) seven other churches in Valletta and some private palaces. A number of these churches and palaces have later Baroque additions, but the solidity and grandeur of the buildings lying within Laparelli's fortifications are uniquely the inspiration of Gerolamo Cassar.

The scale of Valletta, which is little more than $\frac{1}{2}$ m long from City Gate to Fort St Elmo, makes it a walker's city. Restrictions on traffic (no unauthorized parking is permitted in the city) make sightseeing much easier, and those approaching the city by car are recommended to leave it in one of the spacious car parks outside the City Gate. The main shopping street (formerly Kingsway, now Republic Street) is closed to traffic except between 1pm–4pm. Later on the street comes to life as the Maltese throng it for the evening promenade. This is a very Mediterranean occupation—the young people strolling arm-in-arm, the older ones window-shopping or sitting at coffee tables. With its narrow, stepped streets offering glimpses of the sunlit harbours on either side, Valletta invites—and rewards—a

Aerial view of Valletta and its harbours

Church of St Catherine of Italy

ventual chaplain. The façade was altered in the late 17th c. The bust above the central window of *Pope Innocent XI* was put up by Grand Master Ramón Perellos, as a thank-offering for a decision made in his favour by the Pope during a dispute between the eccle-siastical authorities and the Magisterial Court. In 1752 the church was enlarged and the campanile added. The interior has a rect-angular nave with a painted barrel vault (in need of restoration) and semi-circular apse. Opposite, on the corner of Merchants' Street, is the church of **St Catherine of Italy**, which was once the church of the Langue and is now the parish church of the Italian commu-nity in Malta. It was designed by Cassar in 1576, with the fine *portico*, attributed to the Italian Vittorio Carapecchia, added in 1713. The interior is octagonal, making it the first of the centrally planned churches. The main altar is contained in a rectangular recess and is surmounted by a small dome. The central dome is spacious, the lantern effectively illu-minating the interior. The church contains two noteworthy works of art. The altarpiece *The Martyrdom of St Catherine* is one of Mattia Preti's finest works, presented by the artist c. 1659. Above the altar to the right of the main entrance is *Our Lady of Sorrows* by Benedetto Luti (1666–1724).

Entering Castile Place, one sees to the right the massive tower of the **St James' Cavalier**, covering the St James' Bastion in front of it. Within its walls is a *gift shop* selling Maltese products.

Auberge de Castile et Leon Once the auberge of the Spanish and Portuguese knights, this is now the Prime Minister's office. The origi-nal building, the work of Gerolamo Cassar (1574) was remodelled and given a new façade by Domenico Cachia in 1774, during the reign of Grand Master Pinto. Built around a galleried courtyard it is a fine example of 18th c. Maltese Baroque. The ornately carved windows of the façade achieve a splendid

leisurely exploration. Curio and souvenir shops, flower stalls, coffee shops and bars offer endless points of interest (and refresh-ment) *en route*.

Walking tour 1: the city (see map) Starting point: **City Gate**. Inside the gate, turn right along the arcade and then cross by the bombed shell of the Opera House into Victory square.

Here are two historic churches. The first, on the right, is the oldest in Valletta, **Our Lady of Victory** (1566). This was the first building to be erected in La Vallette's new city, to commemorate the victory over the Turks. It was here that the Grand Master's body was entombed prior to the building of the Cathe-dral, in which it now rests.

At one time this was the parish church of the Order in Valletta, under the care of a Con-

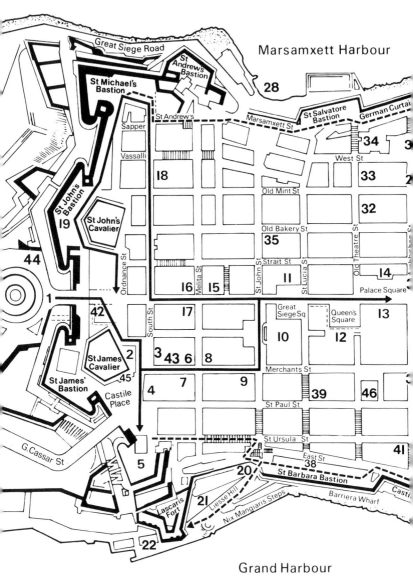

Marsamxett Harbour

Great Siege Road

St Andrew's Bastion

St Michael's Bastion

28

St Andrew's

Marsamxett St

St Salvatore Bastion

German Curtain

Sapper

34

3

Vassalli

West St

33

2

18

Old Mint St

32

St John's Bastion

St John's Cavalier

Old Bakery St

35

19

Strait St

44

Ordnance St

Melita St

St John's St

St Lucia St

Old Theatre St

11

14

16

15

Palace Square

1

17

South St

Great Siege Sq

Queen's Square

13

42

10

12

St James Cavalier

2

3 43 6

8

45

St James' Bastion

Merchants St

4

7

9

Castile Place

39

46

St Paul St

G. Cassar St

St Ursula St

41

5

38

20

St Barbara Bastion

East St

Castile

Lascaris Fort

21

Liesse Hill

Nix Mangiaris Steps

Barriera Wharf

22

Grand Harbour

Valletta

Walking tour 1: the city

1 City Gate
2 Our Lady of Victory
3 St Catherine of Italy
4 Auberge de Castile et Leon
5 Upper Barracca Gardens
6 Auberge d'Italie
7 Palazzo Parisio
8 St James
9 Castellania
10 Co-Cathedral and Museum of St John
11 Law Courts
12 Bibliotheca (National Library)
13 Magisterial Palace and Armoury
14 Chancery
15 Auberge de Provence (National Museum of Archaeology)
16 St Francis
17 St Barbara
18 Admiralty House (Fine Arts Museum)
19 Hastings Gardens

St Sebastian Bastion
English Curtain
St Sebastian St

27

St Christopher St

French Curtain

St Gregory Bastion

26

Ball's Bastion

Republic St

St Dominic St
St Nicholas St
Old Hospital St
North St

Fort St Elmo

36

Abercrombie's Curtain

Mediterranean St

25

St Lazarus Curtain

24 23

Walking tour 2: the fortifications

20 Victoria Gate
21 Our Lady of Liesse
22 Old Customs House
23 Lower Barracca
24 Nevaio and Fish Market
25 Hospital of the Order
26 War Relics Museum
27 Auberge de Baviere
28 Manderaggio

29 Archbishop's Palace
30 Auberge d'Aragon
31 Hostel de Verdelin
32 Manoel Theatre
33 Carmelite Church
34 St Paul's Anglican Cathedral
35 St Augustine
36 St Dominic
37 Gesù Church and Old University
38 St Lucia
39 St Paul Shipwrecked
40 St Roch
41 St Ursula

42 Tourist Office
43 Post Office
44 Bus Terminus
45 Maltese Handicrafts
46 Market

symmetry, while the doorway makes a superb centrepiece with its elaborate portal and staircase flanked by 18th c. bronze cannon. Above the portal is a bust of *Grand Master Pinto*, surrounded by banners, weapons, armour and trophies. The central window is framed by similar carving and topped by the coat-of-arms of Pinto. The arms of the Langue of Castile and Leon surmount the cornice.

From Castile Place continue east to the **Upper Barracca Gardens**, from which one can enjoy a superb view of the Grand Harbour. These arcaded gardens, part of the fortifications defended by the Italian Langue, were built in 1661 by Flamino Balbiana, Grand Prior of the Langue, as a recreation ground for the Knights. They were then known as 'Il Belvedere d'Italia'. The roofing was removed from the arcades in 1771 by the Council of the Order after a conspiracy had been hatched within their shelter by the Italian knights. There are a number of monuments and statues in the gardens, among them the bronze group *Les Gavroches* by the Maltese sculptor Antonio Sciortino. (Other works by Sciortino are in the Museum of Fine Arts.) Lascaris Wharf can be reached by a steep road behind the entrance to the gardens or by a longer route down Gerolamo Cassar Street off Castile Place.

Leaving the gardens, return to Castile Place and turn right down Merchant's Street. The first building on the left, adjacent to the church of St Catherine, is the **Auberge d'Italie**, now the General Post Office. As with Gerolamo Cassar's other auberges, the massive rusticated quoins at the corners mark the limits of the building, showing that it occupied the same site in 1574. During the reign of the Italian Grand Master Carafa (1683) the auberge was enlarged, and his bust, surrounded by an elaborate sculpture of military paraphernalia, is above the entrance. The building follows the traditional plan, with a central courtyard (in it stands a reconstructed *arch* bearing the arms of Carafa). Some of the rooms retain the old arches and ceiling slabs, the more important ones (including the entrance hall) their vaulted ceilings.

Opposite is the *Palazzo Parisio* (c. 1725), a gloomy building with a symmetrical façade, originally of two storeys. It also is built around a courtyard. It was here that Napoleon lodged in 1798 during the French occupation of Malta.

The church of **St James** on the corner of Melita Street dates back to 1612, but was virtually rebuilt by Giovanni Barbara in 1710. It served the Langue of Castile and Leon. The exterior is highly ornate with grouped pilasters, carved doorway and windows, with a winged cartouche above the central window supporting the coat-of-arms of the Langue. The *interior* is based on an oval,

Auberge de Castile et Leon

with the altar in a deep niche. The internal architecture, like the external, makes the most of the contrast between light and shade. An angel motif is predominant in the rich carving. The main altarpiece, depicting *St James* (for whom the knights of Castile had a special devotion), is by Filippo Paladini (1544-1614). Of historical interest is the much venerated little painting of *Our Lady of Sorrows* on the altar. It was brought to Malta in 1646 by a priest of the Order who had saved it from being destroyed by drunken soldiers (sword marks are still visible).

Further down on the right at the corner of St John Street is the **Castellania**, which at the time of the Order housed the civil and criminal courts and prisons. Started in 1748 by Francesco Zerafa it was completed 10 years later by Giuseppe Bonici. The lavish carving on the façade with the figures of *Justice* and *Truth* is the work of the Sicilian Maestro Gian. Prominent are the crescent moons, heraldic device of the Grand Master Pinto in whose reign the building was constructed. Ground floor shops with living accommodation on the mezzanine floor were an integral part of the design. The hook at the corner of the building is believed to have been used to suspend convicts sentenced to confinement in a cage.

From here turn left into St John's Street to reach St John's Square in front of the Cathedral.

Co-Cathedral of St John The great Conventual Church of the Order of St John was built between 1573-77 to serve the members of the Order in Malta and Europe. It was not part of the diocese of Malta but came under the jurisdiction of the Grand Prior of the Conventual Church.

The architect was Gerolamo Cassar and the benefactor Grand Master La Cassière, who not only paid for the construction but also provided an endowment for its upkeep. The church was consecrated by the Bishop of Monreale, Sicily. (For opening hours, see p. 29.)

The stark simplicity of the exterior reflects the militant calling of the Knights, as the sumptuousness of the interior mirrors their love of the arts. Two bell towers flank the façade, the one on the right with an interesting treble clock showing the time, day of the week and date of the month. These towers were crowned with spires which were removed in 1941 after bombing had made them unstable. The wings were added after Cassar's death.

Cannon In front of the cathedral are two bronze cannon. That on the right was brought over to Malta by the German knight Langreve von Hessen, the Captain-General of the Fleet in 1619. Made in 1600, it bears the Battenberg coast-of-arms. That on the left with the coat-of-arms of Grand Master Manoel de Vilhena was made in 1726.

Interior The internal dimensions of the cathedral, which is rectangular, are 189×118 ft.
The great barrel vault of the nave and apse leads the eye towards the high altar. The dramatic tunnel-like effect is emphasised by the lack of entablature between the pilasters and the springing of the arches; the slightly pointed ribs are only 64 ft above the floor. The fifth rib (and the pilaster supporting it) are thickened to stress the division between nave and choir. The nave has six bays on either side, separated by huge walled buttresses. These bays, which contain the chapels of the Langues, are connected by arched openings forming aisles running parallel to the nave.

The interior is a mass of colour and intricate carving. The *vault* was painted between 1622 and 1666 by Mattia Preti, who first designed most of the sculptured stonework, thus creating a harmonious whole. The paintings depict 18 scenes from the *Life of St John*, painted in oils directly on to the primed stone. The seated figures at the sides of the 12 windows of the nave represent saints, martyrs and heroes of the Order. (The 'shadows' of these figures, painted on the adjacent ribs of the vault, create a clever three-dimensional effect.)

The mosaic *pavement* of the nave, side chapels, sacristy and oratory is composed of multi-coloured inlaid marble tombstones emblazoned with coats-of-arms and symbols, commemorating the flower of the European aristocracy who lived in Malta in the 16th–18th c.

During the month of June the walls of the nave are hung with the magnificent Flemish tapestries housed in the church museum (see below) in honour of the Festival of St John.

The first bay to the right of the entrance (**A**) leads to the Oratory of St John. The visitors' entrance is via the third bay (**C**) (see below). The next bay (**B**) contains the *Chapel of St James* of the Langue of **Castile, Leon and Portugal**. The altarpiece and the two lunettes are by Mattia Preti. There are two monuments to Grand Masters. That of *Manoel de Vilhena* in black marble and bronze is by the Florentine Massimiliano de Soldani. The relief shows Vilhena examining the plan of Fort Manoel. The monument to Grand Master *Manoel Pinto* was executed by the Roman sculptor Vincenzo Pacetti. (Note the fine mosaic portrait of Pinto.)

The third bay (**C**) leads to a flanking passage and the south wing of the cathedral. On the right is the visitors' entrance to the oratory.

Oratory of St John Erected during the reign of Grand Master Alof de Wignacourt (1603), this oratory was altered in later years. The series of *Saints of the Order* and the three panels in the ceiling are by Mattia Preti (1662). Behind the altar, overshadowing all else, is the *Beheading of St John*, one of Caravaggio's last works and the most important painting in Malta. Caravaggio came to Malta in 1608 and after executing several paintings (including a portrait of Grand Master de Wignacourt which hangs in the Louvre) he was received into the Order.

Within a year, however, he was unfrocked for an unknown crime and left the island. His turbulent life ended in 1610.

Stairs lead up to the **church museum**, which houses the cathedral's priceless collection of *Flemish tapestries*. These tapestries, which are hung in the nave of the cathedral every June, were presented in 1697 by Grand Master Ramón Perellos. They were executed by Judocus de Vos, the subjects being taken from paintings by Rubens and Poussin. Besides the tapestries there is a magnificent collection of 17th and 18th c. vestments, and Caravaggio's beautiful painting *St Jerome*.

Campo Santo This courtyard cemetery is accessible from the museum. It contains the remains of some of the victims of the Great Siege, brought from Fort St Angelo.

In the fourth bay of the cathedral (**D**) is the *Chapel of St George* of the Langue of **Aragon**. All the paintings are by Mattia Preti. The altar was embellished by Grand Master *Ramón Despuig* who is commemorated by a bronze medallion. There is an exceptionally fine monument to Grand Master *Ramón Perellos* in this chapel, with charming figures of Justice and Charity, sculpted by Giuseppe Mazzuoli of Volterra. The lavishly sculptured monument, with two slaves supporting a profusion of arms and banners and a bust of Grand Master *Nicolas Cotoner*, whom he commemorates, is by G. B. Foggini. There are also monuments to the Grand Masters *Martin de Redin* and *Rafael Cotoner*.

Next (**E**) is the *Chapel of St Sebastian* of the Langue of **Auvergne**. The lunettes, scenes from the life of the Saint, are by Giuseppe d'Arena. The altarpiece is now ascribed to Cassarini, a painter of the Caravaggesque circle. The monument is to Grand Master *Clermont Gessan* who reigned for less than a year in 1660.

The last chapel on this side of the church (**F**) is that of the *Chapel of the Blessed Sacrament*. It is enclosed by a screen. The *silver gates*, presented to the church in 1752 by the Chevalier de la Salle and the Bailiff de Guarena, are said to have been blackened to save them from being looted by Napoleon. The large 15th c. wooden *crucifix* on the right wall, painted in tempera, was brought from Rhodes. The *keys* hanging beside the gates are from the Turkish fortresses of Mahometta, Lepanto and Passava, captured by the galleys of the Order in 1601. The painting of the *Blessed Virgin* over the altar was bequeathed to the church in 1617 and replaces the much venerated painting of Our Lady of Phileremos brought from Rhodes and subsequently given to Paul I of Russia by Grand Master Hompesch.

The **chancel** is enclosed by a marble balustrade. The *high altar* of lapis-lazuli was designed by Lorenzo Gafà and made in Rome in 1686. The choir stalls, pulpit and wooden lectern decorated with reliefs from the *Life of St John* are Neapolitan, late 16th c., a gift from Grand Master Garzes. The two bronze *lecterns* (1577) are French, while the 17th c. silver *sanctuary lamp* is from Rome. The colossal group *The Baptism of Christ* (c. 1667), dominating the choir, is by Giuseppe Mazzuoli.

At the top of the left aisle (**G**) is the *Chapel of St Charles* or the *Chapel of the Holy Relics*. This was given to the **Anglo-Bavarian** Langue revived in 1784. The wooden figure of *John the Baptist* came from the poop of the Grand Carrack in which the Knights sailed from Rhodes.

Next (**H**) is the *Chapel of St Michael* of the Langue of **Provence**. Here are monuments to the Grand Masters *Antoine de Paule* and *Jean Paul de Lascaris*. The imperial eagle from the arms of Lascaris is sculpted on the walls, while his tomb shows the coats-of-arms of members of his family. In this chapel are steps leading to the **crypt** (open on application to the sacristan 10.00–12.00). The first 11 Grand Masters, Grand Master Ximenes and Sir Oliver Starkey, La Vallette's English secretary, are buried here. The ceiling and wall decorations are by Niccolò Nasini. On the altar is an early 16th c. group of the *Crucifixion*.

In the next bay (**I**) is the *Chapel of St Paul* of the Langue of **France**. Unfortunately this chapel was 'restored' in the 1840's and most of Preti's embellishments lost. His *altarpiece* survives. The lunettes are by the German artist Lucas Killian. There are monuments to the Grand Masters *Emmanuel de*

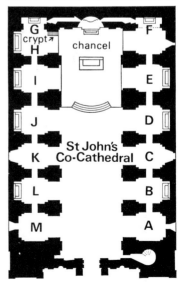

Rohan, *Adrian de Wignacourt* and to *Jacques de Wignacourt*, the Grand Master's brother. The fine tomb of the *Prince of Orleans*, brother of King Louis-Philippe, is by Jean-Jacques Pradier.

The *Chapel of St Catherine* of the Langue of **Italy** in the next bay (**J**) is one of the finest. It has a richly decorated altar and the altarpiece *The Mystic Marriage of St Catharine* is one of Preti's most striking works. There is an imposing monument commemorating Grand Master *Gregorio Carafa*; his bust is by Algardi.

From the next bay (**K**) the north door of the cathedral leads to Great Siege Square. The last chapel of the left aisle (**L**) is the *Chapel of the Magi* of the Langue of **Germany**. The sculptures are 17th c., the white marble altar 1730. The altarpiece *The Adoration of the Magi* and the lunettes are by the Maltese Stefano Erardi (late 17th c.).

In the last bay (**M**) a slab at the foot of a pillar marks the tomb of Mattia Preti (d. 1699) the Italian artist who came to Malta in 1662 and spent most of his working life here, embellishing the island's churches. His work in the cathedral must, of course, be his greatest memorial. A further painting by him will be found in the adjacent *Sacristy*. This is *Saints Cosmas and Damian*. In addition there are a number of other noteworthy paintings here, including a *Baptism of Christ* by Perez d'Aleccio and a portrait of *Grand Master Pinto* by Antoine de Favray.

At the west end of the church, to the left of the main entrance, is the last of the monuments to the Grand Masters, that of *Marc'Antonio Zondadori* by Massimiliano de Soldani of Florence, dated 1725.

After leaving the cathedral turn right. At Republic Street, turn right again. In Great

Monument to Grand Master Nicolas Cotoner with detail, St John's Co-Cathedral

Siege Square is Antonio Sciortino's *monument* to the dead of 1565; facing are the modern *Law Courts* built on the bombed site of the Auberge d'Auvergne. Further along on the right is the arcaded Queen's Square with a statue of *Queen Victoria* by Giuseppe Valenti of Messina.

Bibliotheca (The National Library) On the south side of the square stands the 18th c. building of Malta's Public Library. The arcaded front has a central balcony supported on columns; a restrained and rhythmical design. (For opening hours, see p. 29.)

The Order founded a library in 1555, but it was not firmly established until 1612 when Grand Master Alof de Wignacourt forbade the sale of a deceased knight's books, which then became the property of the Order. From this time onwards all books were housed in a hall adjoining the Conventual Church. A considerable number were amassed through bequests and legacies, and it finally became imperative to rehouse the library in a larger building. However, it was not until 1776 when Grand Master de Rohan sent for the Italian architect Stefano Ittar that work was started on the new building, which was completed in 1786.

The library contains more than 300,000 volumes, many of great rarity, a rich collection of manuscripts including illuminated works of the 14th and 15th c., and a number of *incunabula* (books produced before 1501). Above all, it contains the Archives of the Order of St John from the 12th c. to the end of the 18th c., including the Charter of King Baldwin I of Jerusalem granting land to the Knights (1107), and the Papal Bull of Paschal II instituting the Order in 1113. A varied collection of manuscripts is always on display.

Magisterial Palace Adjoining Queen's Square and facing Republic Street and Palace Square is Gerolamo Cassar's great Palace of the Grand Masters. Originally the Council of the Order had planned to build the palace on the high ground at the entrance to the city (site of the present Auberge of Castile and Leon), but when Grand Master del Monte decided to move the Order from Birgu in 1571 he persuaded the Council to buy a house erected by his nephew Eustachio in the centre of the city.

This property formed the nucleus of the new palace. The plan was not altogether a success, for the severe façade lacks symmetry. The windows of Eustachio's private dwelling, the north-west corner, are more closely spaced and the building is too long for its height. The two Baroque *gateways*, an improvement on the original design (previously there had been only one gateway), were added by Grand Master Pinto in 1745. The palace remained the official residence of the Grand Master until the departure of the Order in 1798: it was then used by the British Governors.

The palace is built round two courtyards. The *upper courtyard* (with an archway into Queen's Square) has Pinto's *clock* (1745) with Moorish figures striking the hours. The *lower courtyard* has a bronze statue of *Neptune* which once stood in the centre of the old fish-market by the harbour.

Armoury Entered from the lower courtyard. This collection, which has yet to be finally arranged, comprises about 5700 pieces from all over Europe, from the 16th to mid-18th c. Outstanding are Grand Master Alof de Wignacourt's gold-damascened suit of armour made by Geronimo Spacini of Milan c. 1615, and his sapping suit weighing 110 lbs. There

Magisterial Palace

are also suits of armour belonging to two other Grand Masters: La Vallette and Garzes and to the Grand Commander de Verdelin.

In the north-west corner of the lower court-yard (or to the right of the main entrance from Palace Square) is the beautiful oval staircase now closed to the public which gives access to the State Apartments. (Note the width and shallowness of the steps, to allow the passage of knights in armour.)

State Apartments The present access to these is from the upper courtyard (north corner). (Resident guide. For hours, see p. 28.)

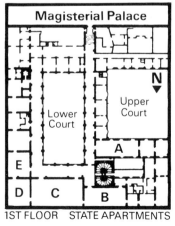

1ST FLOOR   STATE APARTMENTS

Tapestry Chamber (**A**) This was formerly the Council Chamber of the Order. It is hung with the dazzling **Gobelin tapestries** donated to the Order by Grand Master Perellos, the only surviving complete set of the series *Les Teintures des Indes* made from designs presented to Louis XIV by Prince John Maurice of Nassau. The panels depict lush scenes from tropical South America and the Caribbean, with fine portrayals of herdsmen, savages and wild beasts. The arms of the donor, Perellos, may be seen in each of the paintings over the six side doors. Above the tapestries is a frieze of oil paintings illustrating *Naval Battles of the Order*, and above the paintings are the coats-of-arms of the Order and of Grand Master Lascaris. There is a very beautiful Renaissance *ceiling*.

After this feast of colour the *State Dining Room* (**B**) with its portraits of past sovereigns is an anti-climax, but beyond is the splendid *Hall of St Michael and St George* (**C**). This was the Chapter Hall of the Knights, acquiring its name from the first investiture here of the British order in 1818. It has a coffered ceiling and, at the end of the room opposite the throne, the *musicians' gallery* from the Grand Carrack which brought the Knights from Rhodes. Most interesting is the frieze of the *Twelve Episodes from the Great Siege* painted with great verve by the Spanish artist Matteo Perez d'Alesio c. 1580. The sequence commences on the wall to the left of the throne with the arrival of the Turkish fleet on 18 May 1565 and continues in a clockwise direction to the final scene of their flight and departure on 13 September.

Gobelin tapestry, State Apartments
Magisterial Palace

Through the Hall of St Michael and St George is the *Ambassadors' Room* (*Red Room*) the audience chamber of the Grand Master (**D**). The frieze here, also painted by d'Alesio, depicts the *History of the Knights of St John, 1309–1524*, covering their period in Rhodes. There are also portraits of the German knight *Frederik Langreve von Hessen*, Captain-General of the Galleys, by Andrea Generoli, of *Louis XV* by J. B. van Loo, of *Louis XVI* by François Callet, of *Catharine the Great* by Levitzky and of *Grand Master Alof de Wignacourt* by Cassarino.

The last of the state rooms is the *Yellow Room* (**E**), formerly the pages' waiting room, with a continuation of the historical frieze representing the period prior to the departure of the Knights from the Holy Land. Here there are two early 17th c. *paintings* of biblical subjects by Ribera. The majolica vases are Urbino ware and the furniture 17th and 18th c. Maltese.

Opposite the palace in Palace Square stands the old **Chancery** of the Order (1602) where the Grand Master's bodyguard was quartered. The Doric portico was added by the British after their formal acquisition of the island in 1814, and the building, which continued its function as a guard-room for the palace, was known as the *Main Guard*. It is now the offices of the Libyan Cultural Institute.

Leaving Palace Square and proceeding up Republic Street in the direction of City Gate, the next important building on the right, occupying an entire block, is the **Auberge de Provence** (1571) designed by Gerolamo Cassar. Its balanced façade is contained within massive quoins of alternating narrow and wide bands of stone. The portico and the central first floor window are framed by columns, Doric below and Ionic above. The use of both segmental and triangular pedi-ments on the first floor windows provides further contrast. The central window is surmounted by the arms of the Langue. Although the façade has been much altered by modern shopfronts it is interesting to recall that the building was originally designed to incorporate shops.

The *entrance hall* is vaulted and painted, while the *great hall* running along the front of the upper floor has a wooden ceiling and richly painted walls. It is one of the most resplendent rooms in the city.

National Museum of Archaeology This is housed on two floors of the auberge, and has a representative collection of Malta's prehistoric finds. (For opening hours, see p.28.) To the right of the ticket desk are Roman anchors recovered from the seabed round the Maltese islands. Next is the main *Prehistoric Gallery*. Here are table models of the temple sites, a relief map of Malta showing the prehistoric sites, and a chart of the prehistoric sequence. The showcases are in chronological order starting with the right-hand wall. Dates are approximate.

Case 1 (Ghar Dalam and Grey Skorba Phases, 3800–3400 BC). Impressed and incised ware from the Ghar Dalam cave related to the Stentinello culture in Sicily, the earliest type to be found in Malta. Slingstones, animal heads.

Case 2 (Red Skorba Phase, 3400–3200 BC). Curious forked-handled ladles and female figurines from the Skorba site.

Case 3 (Zebbug Phase, 3200–2800 BC). Head of statue *menhir*, incised pottery.

Case 4 (Ta'Hagrat temple, Mgarr, 2800–2400 BC). Contemporary model of megalithic building, incised and painted pottery.

Cases 5–7 (Xemxija Tombs, 2800 BC). Pottery, greenstone axe amulets and personal ornaments.

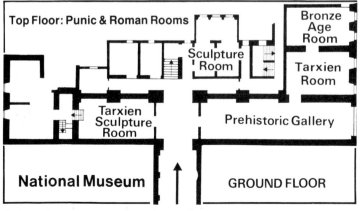

Top Floor: Punic & Roman Rooms

Bronze Age Room

Sculpture Room

Tarxien Room

Tarxien Sculpture Room

Prehistoric Gallery

National Museum

GROUND FLOOR

Case 8 (Ggantija temples, Gozo, 2800–2400 BC). Arrowheads. Casts of limestone heads. The bulk of the finds from these temples is in the Gozo Museum.

Cases 9–11 (Hypogeum of Hal Saflieni, 2400 BC). A selection from the rich collection unearthed at the Hypogeum includes hardstone axe pendants, personal ornaments and a plate decorated with bulls and goats. Facing are two *centre cases* with objects from the Hypogeum, including the famous little terracotta figurine the *Sleeping Lady* and other small statuettes.

Case 12–13 (Hagar Qim, 2400–2000 BC). The tiny, exquisitely modelled headless statuette of a female figure; limestone 'fat lady' statuettes. In the facing *centre case*, statuettes from the same temple. Perforations suggest that the heads were made separately.

Case 14 (Kordin, 2800–2400 BC). Collection of tunnel-handled pots.

Case 15 (Mnajdra, 2400–2000 BC). Pottery and statuettes.

Leading out of the gallery is the *Tarxien Room* with a fine collection of pottery recovered from the temple site. Note the amphorae with tunnel-handles and the large decorated pithos (storage jar). The right-hand wall shows casts of the bull and sow with piglets which are engraved on an inner chamber wall of the Central Temple. In a case to the left of the entrance doorway are interesting hammerstones. One *centre case* contains symbols connected with the fertility cult, another flint and bone tools and an obsidian knife. The obsidian, a natural glass, probably came from Lipari.

With the exception of the four cases to the left of the entrance, the exhibits in the *Bronze Age Room* adjoining come from the Tarxien temple site. After the collapse of the Temple Civilization (c. 2000 BC) the temple became a Bronze Age cemetery (2000–1400 BC). The vessels displayed contained the ashes of the dead. The bronze axes and daggers and personal ornaments (*centre case*) were buried with the dead. The pottery does not show the sophistication of the Temple period. Pottery in *Cases 1 & 2* to the left of the door comes from the Bahrija site (800 BC). The anchor-shaped pottery probably belonged to

a loom. Pottery in *Cases 3 & 4* is from the Borg-in-Nadur site near Birzebbuga (1400–900 BC). Note the pedestalled bowl. In *Case 4*, note the fragment of Mycenaean pottery (13th c. BC) imported into Malta. A reconstruction relates this to a typical 'Kamares' pot of the period with a painting of a squid. Returning to the entrance hall, ascend to the *Punic and Roman Rooms* on the top floor. In showcases on the landing are jewellery and other objects from Phoenician-Punic tombs (7th-6th c. BC) and terracotta masks for the 6th-5th c. BC.

To the left of the stairs is a gallery containing objects from Punic rock-cut tombs at Rabat, Siggiewi and other sites. In the centre is a terracotta *sarcophagus* (5th c. BC) found near Rabat. A small room leading off this gallery contains Punic architectural fragments, 7th c. BC pottery and Attic red and black-figure ware found in local sites.

The gallery on the opposite side of the landing has further objects from the late Punic and early Roman periods, including an interment in a clay amphora. Also in this gallery is a votive *cippus* with Phoenician and Greek inscriptions found near Marsaxlokk. The inscription, which records a vow made to the god Melkart, gave many clues in the decipherment of the Phoenician alphabet.

The corridor and small rooms immediately to the right of the stairs show objects imported from Mediterranean countries.

Cult figures in National Museum: Sleeping Lady (left) and Fat Lady (right)

On the other side of Melita Street is the church of *St Francis* (1681) with the arms of Grand Master Carafa above the entrance. There are four *altarpieces* by Mattia Preti and paintings by Filippo Paladini and Pietro Gagliardi. The ceiling painting just inside the door was the work of Giuseppe Cali. Across Republic Street is the church of *St Barbara*

(1739) by Giuseppe Bonici, the church of the Langue of Provence. It now serves the English, French and German Catholic communities. The interior of the church is based on an elongated oval, and the *altarpiece* is by Antoine de Favray.

Turning to the right down South Street and past the junction with Old Mint Street one reaches the palace which houses the Museum of Fine Arts. The original building here was one of the earliest in Valletta, erected on a site acquired in 1569 by Chev. Fra Jean de Soubiran. His palace later became the property of the Order, who leased it to various knights. It was restored by the Treasury c. 1762 and in 1785 became the residence of Bailli Pierre Suffren de Saint Tropez, Captain-General of the Galleys. After the Knights left Malta the premises were leased to the Naval authorities and it became **Admiralty House**, once more the official residence of the commander-in-chief of a navy. It was handed over to the Maltese Government in 1961. The palace has been beautifully restored and was opened as a museum in 1974.

Museum of Fine Arts The museum is attractively laid out with paintings mainly from the 17th, 18th and 19th c., mostly bequests from the Knights. The galleries should be toured in chronological order, starting from the first floor. (For opening hours, see p. 28).

First floor (14th-17th c.)

Room 1: 14th c. *Room 2*: 15th c. There is a particularly fine *Madonna and Child with Saints* by Domenico di Michelino (1417-91) and *Nativity* by Maestro Alberto (15th-16th c.). *Room 3*: 16th c. *Room 4*: Venetian, including *A Man in Armour* by Domenico Tintoretto (1560-1635). *Room 5*: Dutch. The *Portrait of a Lady* was once attributed to Holbein, but comes from the circle of Jan van Scorel (1495-1562). *Room 6*: Venetian. *Room 7*: 17th c. *Room 7a*: Antonio Sciortino Room. *Room 8*: 17th c. *Judith* by Le Valentin (1594-1632), a painter much influenced by Caravaggio, and *Christ Holding the Cross* by Guido

Reni (1575-1642), which once hung in the Grand Master's bedroom in the Magisterial Palace. *Rooms 9-10*: 17th c. Here are four robust canvases by Matthias Stomer (1600-50). In a case is the terracotta model by Melchior Gafà (1630-67) for his *St Thomas* in Sant'Agostino, Rome. *Room 11*: 17th c. *Rooms 12-13*: 17th c., Mattia Preti.

Ground floor (18th-20th c.) Note the furniture, which is 17th and 18th c. Maltese and Sicilian.

Room 14 (with a vaulted painted ceiling) contains works by Antoine de Favray. A short description of this important painter is hung in the doorway. *Room 15*: 18th c. French. There is a striking canvas *Fire on the Tiber* by Claude Joseph Vernet (1714-89). *Rooms 16-17*: 18th c. Italian. *Room 18*: 19th and 20th c. Italian. *Room 19*: 18th-19th c. Louis de Cros paintings of historic Malta. *Room 20*: 17th-19th c. Maltese, including works by Stefano Erardi (1630-1716). *Room 21*: Edward Caruana Dingli (1876-1950) Bequest. *Room 22*: 18th-19th c. Maltese, including works by Francesco Zahra (1680-1760). *Room 23*: 20th c. Maltese (note ceiling). *Room 24*: Contemporary Maltese art (note ceiling).

Basement (History of the Order of St John) *Room 25*: Religion. *Room 26*: Hospital, including silverware and jars from Santo Spirito Hospital. *Room 27*: Army. *Room 28*: Navy, including shipyard's model of 18th c. man-of-war. *Room 29*: Insignia and Administration. *Room 30*: Minor arts.

In a room beneath the courtyard is a fine newly-mounted collection of *Gold Coins of the Order*.

To complete the tour continue down South Street to the car park, then turn left on to **St Michael's Bastion** (see *Walking tour 2*) for a superb view of Marsamxett Harbour. From here continue along the defences to **St John's Bastion**. Within the bastion lie the **Hastings Gardens**. The monument is to *General the Marquis of Hastings*, Governor of Malta 1824-26, who died at sea near Naples. His remains were brought back to Malta and are buried beneath the monument. The view, which takes in Mosta and Mdina, can best be enjoyed from the sentry-post at the point of the bastion, from where one can also appreciate the colossal thickness of the walls with their broad, sloping parapets.

Leave the gardens by the road running down beside **St John's Cavalier**. St John's and St James' Cavaliers were built on either side of St George's Gate (the present City Gate) to defend the approaches to the city. Their ramparts overlook the two harbours: St James' the Grand Harbour and St John's Marsamxett. St John's Cavalier is once more in the hands of the Knights of St John: in use now as the Embassy of the Sovereign Order. From the cavalier walk right along Ordnance Street and so out to City Gate.

Admiralty House

Walking tour 2: the fortifications

The bulk of Laparelli's fortifications stand as they did when the city of Valletta was first built, part of the greatest complex of fortifications handed down from the 16th and 17th c.

The city lay within a defensive ring, the strong land front approximately 1600 yds from Fort St Elmo at the tip of the peninsula. The four bastions of St Michael, St John, St James and St Peter with curtain walls between and a deep ditch in front guarded the land front. The curtain wall between the two central bastions of St John and St James was pierced by a gate, while behind these bastions were two great cavaliers. Four further bastions were constructed on the Marsamxett shore and three facing Grand Harbour, all with curtain walls, which with Fort St Elmo made the city the most heavily defended *enceinte* in Europe.

Starting point: **Upper Barracca**. From the Upper Barracca (see *Walking tour 1*) with its view of the southern shoreline and fortifications of Valletta, turn right into St Ursula Street. Turn right again at the bottom of the steps (noting *en route* the splendid entablature of the East Street façade, with the arms of Cotoner) and down the short flight to the lower street level. Passing through the *Victoria Gate*, descend Liesse Hill.

On the right is the church of **Our Lady of Liesse** (1620). This elegant little church was rebuilt in 1740 to the designs of Francesco Zammit at the expense of the Langue of France, to whom it belonged. It was bombed in 1940 but has been restored. The façade is unusual, splayed back so that the single bell tower is set at an angle. The low dome, customary in centrally planned churches (see p. 35) is barely visible behind the raised centrepiece of the façade. The interior of the church is circular, with three main altars. The terracotta statue of the *Madonna and Child* was brought from Rhodes and once stood in the old chapel at Fort St Elmo.

The site of the *Old Fish Market* (1615) with the statue of Neptune now in the Magisterial Palace, was opposite this church. In its place is a semi-circle of shops, rebuilt after the war, which have now abandoned the tradition of selling fish. (This is done further along the quay.) From here continue through the tunnel (1642) under the *Fort of Lascaris*.

Old Customs House (1744) Immediately on the left on the waterfront. The architect of this building, Giuseppe Bonici, was originally an engineer, and his talents were fully employed by the demands of the site, on the seafront overlooking Grand Harbour.

The building's foundations had to be sunk beneath the waters of the harbour and the walls, 12 ft thick in places, built of coralline masonry up to the first floor level to resist erosion by salt water. The upper part is of the softer globigerina limestone, and an interesting comparison may be made of the weathering qualities of the different types of stone.

View of fortifications from Upper Barracca

The classical formality of the façade, with its superimposed Doric pilasters and massive entablature, is also seen in the plan of the building. A wide hall cuts through the centre, and the rooms are symmetrically placed on either side. The lower floor is vaulted.

Returning through the Victoria Gate, ascend the steps and cross the wooden bridge to *St Barbara Bastion*. This leads to *Castile Curtain* and the **Lower Barracca**. In the time of the Order this was the St Christopher Bastion, the responsibility of the Langue of Castile.

During the French occupation the Barracca was used to grow vegetables for the French garrison, and with the coming of the British it was turned into an ornamental garden. The pseudo-Greek temple is a monument to *Sir Alexander Ball RN*, who did so much to aid the Maltese in their uprising against the French. He was the first Civil Commissioner of Malta, and his popularity was such that this monument was erected through public subscription.

The long low building to the west beneath the curtain is the *Nevaio*. It was built by Grand Master de Vilhena in the early 18th c., and used for the storage of ice brought from Sicily during the winter. The ice was on sale to the general public. The smaller buildings, near the water's edge, now the Department of Fisheries and *Fish Market*, were the quarantine quarters for ships' crews.

A block of flats to the north of the Barracca occupies the site of Grand Master Verdala's slave prisons (1585) which were demolished during the war. Continue down Mediterranean Street (St Lazarus' Curtain) to the **Hospital of the Order** (1575) which after the Conventual Church was the Knights' most important building. It was badly blitzed but has now been restored as the Mediterranean Conference Centre (see p.29). The *Great Ward*, more than 500 ft long, runs along the side of the street overlooking Grand Harbour. The whole complex consisted of three quadrangles with subsidiary wards, offices and quarters for the medical staff. In its time this hospital was amongst the foremost in Europe as a centre of medical teaching and research. It was probably also the richest, for the Order, true to the designation of 'Knights Hospitaller', lavished

large sums on the upkeep and running of its *Sacra Infirmeria*. The hospital did not serve the members of the Order alone but cared for the sick, insane and destitute of all races and creeds. The Great Ward had 300 canopied beds—wool canopies for winter and netting for summer. The walls were hung with tapestries and paintings, and the patients—who fed from silver dishes—were served by the Knights themselves. The hospital was in effect a sanctuary, where all were considered equal.

The Grand Hospitaller was the Pilier or head of the French Langue, and the Knights shared equally the responsibility of caring for the sick. Here in their hospital the Knights put aside their arms and trappings of nobility and humbled themselves in the common service of humanity.

Fort St Elmo At the point of the Sceberras peninsula stands the historic fortress which played such a vital part in the Knights' defences during the Great Siege of 1565 (see p. 15). At this time it was the only fortification on the Sceberras peninsula, and became the primary target of the Turkish guns: only when it fell could they carry their attack to the other Knights' strongholds. The fort is now garrisoned by the Malta Armed Forces and not accessible to the public.

The fort had its origins as a watchtower. Close by was a chapel dedicated to St Elmo, patron saint of seamen. After the Moslem invasion of 1488 the tower was converted into a small fort, with the chapel within its walls. Soon after the arrival of the Order in Malta plans were made for the construction of a new and larger fort, but these were not carried out until 1552, the decision no doubt hastened by a Turkish landing in Marsamxett Harbour the year before. The need to have a strong fort guarding the entrance to this harbour was obvious: without it the Turks would be able to anchor their fleet here with impunity while preparing their attack on Birgu. (The fort had an equal significance, of course, in the defence of Grand Harbour.) The designer of the fort was the Spanish military engineer Pietro Pardo. The plan was a four-pointed star, with the bastions at the points. There was a seaward cavalier, and a ravelin facing Marsamxett Harbour. Destroyed by the Turks during the siege, the fort was rebuilt by La Vallette on a larger scale, with massive bastions on the landward front. In 1687 Grand Master Carafa, on the advice of the engineer Grunenberg, considerably strengthened the fort by enclosing the entire point with bastions and curtain walls. Grand Master Perellos made further improvements, and a treble row of casemates was added by the engineer Tigné during the reign of Grand Master Pinto. The British further strengthened the fortifications in the early 19th c. with the addition of the outer bastions. Within the walls of the fort are two chapels. The historic little chapel of *St Elmo*, just inside the main seaward gate, has a coffered vaulted roof and intricate stone carving round the altar niche. It was first restored in 1649. Above the altar are the arms of Nicolas Cotoner. The *second chapel* nearby was built in 1729 and has the arms of Perellos above the door.

The remains of General Sir Ralph Abercrombie and of Sir Alexander Ball RN are interred in the outer bastions which bear their name.

In front of the main landward entrance to the fort at the point of the peninsula are the circular slabs which cover the *underground granaries.*

Within the St Gregory Bastion, further on, is a *War Relics Museum*, with a collection of various weapons and vehicles (including one of the three famous naval aircraft, the Gloster Gladiators) which played their part in the heroic defence of the island in World War 2. (For opening hours, see p.28.)

Rounding the point, one reaches the *French Curtain*. Here are the first views of Marsamxett Harbour. Following the *English Curtain*, one passes the *Auberge de Baviere* (1696) which served the Anglo-Bavarian Langue during the short period of its existence (1783–98). It is now a school.

Turning south-west at the *St Sebastian Curtain*, one reaches the *German Curtain*. At the top of the steps of Archbishop's Street, to the left, is the *Auberge d'Aragon*, and further on the dominating spire of the *Anglican Cathedral* (St Paul's) which was built in 1838 on the site of the Auberge d'Allemagne, demolished for the purpose (for descriptions of the Auberge d'Aragon and Anglican Cathedral see *Other places of interest in Valletta*, p. 118).

From *St Salvatore Bastion*, note the recessed area below which marks the site of the proposed *Manderaggio*—a miniature harbour which the Knights had planned to excavate from the rock to protect their galleys from storms. The work was started, but never completed.

Marsamxett Street leads up to the steps of St Andrew's Street (with *St Andrew's Bastion* below on the right). From here one climbs to Melita Street and then up further steps to rejoin the road. The route ascends, via Sappers Street, to **St Michael's Bastion**. From here one can enjoy excellent views of the creeks of Marsamxett Harbour, Manoel Island with its fortress and the fortified Dragut Point. Those interested in the architecture of the fortifications will also enjoy visually aligning the gun embrasures of the left-hand flank of the bastion with the angled wall of the next bastion (St John's) to see how effectively the defenders could cover both this and the curtain wall with enfilading fire. The tour of the fortifications may be concluded by following *Walking tour 1* from this point back to City Gate.

from Sliema Ferry bus terminal are available. For bus services, see p. 20. *Dghajjes* (water taxis) can be hired for trips to the Three Cities from Valletta Old Customs House steps (no fixed charges).

Grand Harbour, the prize at the heart of the Mediterranean, was the main reason for Malta's history of foreign domination. But the harbour has also been the source of her prosperity. It reconciled the seafaring Knights of the Order of St John to their sojourn in what at first seemed an inhospitable land. It enabled Britain to use the island as a naval base and port on the route to India, bringing trade and employment to the Maltese. Now, with the expansion of the docks, it is becoming an important part of the economy of the new Republic. The visitor is probably less aware, however, of its present significance than of its stirring history as a battleground, the scene of heroic resistance in two grim sieges.

Dramatic views of the harbour can be enjoyed from the Upper Barracca or similar vantage points on the fortifications. But the reverse view—from the water level looking up at the fortifications—is equally impressive

The harbour is two miles long, the main channel running for 6000 yds from the northeast with a depth of 12 fathoms for nearly the whole length. In addition to this huge inlet a series of rocky promontories jut out from the south shore to form deep-water creeks, providing safe anchorage for a large number of ships. Until 1903, when the British built a substantial breakwater across the harbour entrance, the only threat to this remarkable haven was the dreaded *gregale*, the fierce north-east wind which springs up in the winter months with little warning.

At the southern arm of the entrance lies *Fort Ricasoli* like a huge stone ship facing *Fort St Elmo* to the north. Alongside Fort Ricasoli in *Rinella Creek* is the tank-cleaning depot of the Malta Drydocks. On the foreshore of *Bighi Peninsula* bounding Rinella Creek can be seen concrete air-raid shelters with the old Royal Naval Hospital (now a school) on the heights above. On the west side of Bighi is picturesque *Kalkara Creek* with the pink Villa Portelli (c. 1675) formerly residence of the Flag Officer, Malta, on the Bighi shore. The bastions of *Vittoriosa* (the Knights' first city) rise above the other shore. This is the site for the proposed new Yacht Marina. The creek is wide and deep, capable of providing

safe anchorage for the world's largest vessels (The *Ark Royal* once anchored here.)

At the point of the Vittoriosa promontory the massive bulk of *Fort St Angelo* towers above the water. On the other side of the promontory is St Angelo Wharf and then St Lawrence Wharf running alongside *Dockyard Creek*, once the galley creek of the Knights. Although only 500ft wide it is deep enough to take large cruise ships.

Across the creek is the marina of *Senglea*, the second of the Knights' Three Cities. Round Senglea Point, with its bastion and little *vedette*, is *French Creek*. The square promontory is surrounded by wharves, and the whole area is being rapidly developed. Behind Kordin is *Marsa Creek* the commercial port, also under development. The industrial complex here reaches round to the great hornworks of the Floriana Lines, with warehouses lining the waterfront. The dredged deep-water quay along the northern shore of the harbour can provide berths for ocean-going liners.

From the demi-bastion of the Upper Barracca (above the Old Customs House) to the outer bastion of Fort St Elmo at the point of the Sceberras peninsula, Valletta's massive fortress wall stretches in a continuous line.

Other places of interest in Valletta

Archbishop's Palace Bottom of Archbishop Street.

Designed by Tommaso Dingli in 1622, with a second storey added in 1952. The doorway is framed by four Ionic columns supporting a concave entablature and above is a statue of *St John the Baptist*.

Auberge d'Aragon Independence Square, at the bottom of Archbishop Street. Now the Ministry of Education.

Built in 1571, this is the smallest and least altered of Cassar's auberges. It is a flat-roofed, single-storied building, simple and beautifully proportioned. Melitan 'fat' mouldings adorn the three windows on either side of the entrance, while the façade is framed by Cassar's rusticated corners and a cornice running all the way round the building. The doorway with its semi-circular heading (restored) is in the 16thc. Maltese style. The portico was added in 1842. The entrance hall, barrel vaulted, leads to an arcade surrounding a central courtyard. The arcade was filled in when the portico was built and now forms a passage.

Built on to the back of the auberge with its entrance in West Street is the church of *Our Lady of Pilar* (1670). This was the church of the Langue of Aragon. It was improved and decorated in 1718 at the expense of the Grand Master Ramon Perellos and Fra Raymondo Soller, Bailiff of Majorca. It was restored in 1864. The façade, raised on a plinth to compensate for the slope of the street, is cleverly adapted to the narrow site. The interior is similarly confined, with a short nave and octagonal area beneath the dome. The high altar is impressive, with a titular *altarpiece* by Stefano Erardi.

Hostel de Verdelin Archbishop Street, facing Palace Square.

This charming 17thc. building, with its elaborate and fanciful façade reminiscent of Sici-

lian Baroque, makes a striking contrast with the austere exterior of the earlier Magisterial Palace across the square. The pigeons which form part of the decoration over the windows have a special significance. The owners, according to tradition, were obliged in the time of the Knights to feed the pigeons in the city squares.

Manoel Theatre (1731) Old Theatre Street.

This delightful theatre is one of the oldest still in use in Europe. It was built through the munificence of Grand Master Manoel de Vilhena. The plain front belies the intimate charm of the interior, where four tiers of boxes encircling the oval auditorium look down on a deep-set stage. The richness of the decoration recalls the glittering days of the Knights, when the theatre first opened its doors to the Grand Master and his retinue for the opera 'Merope' given by the Italian Langue. It served as a ballroom as well as a theatre, both in the Knights' period and in the early days of British rule. Unfortunately it suffered from neglect in this century and was used as a cinema, but has now been refurbished and is a worthy National Theatre for the new Republic of Malta.

Carmelite Church (1573) Old Theatre Street.

Originally built by Gerolamo Cassar, this church has been much altered and is now engulfed by a vast new dome. This unfortunately has meant the destruction of the barrel vault of the nave, although the cross-barrel vaults of the side chapels remain.

St Paul's Anglican Cathedral (1839) Independence Square. Open to visitors from 08.00–12.00 on weekdays.

The Anglican Cathedral is the only significant non-military building to have been constructed by the British during their occupation of Malta. It was commissioned by Queen Adelaide, aunt of Queen Victoria, to serve the British population who at that time had no place of worship other than the chapels of the garrison. It was built at her own expense on the site of the Auberge d'Allemagne, which had been pulled down to make way for it.

The Admiralty architect, William Scamp, chose the neo-classical style with spire in the Wren tradition. This spire has made the cathedral the major landmark of a seaward approach to Valletta—but it should be remembered that spires may also be seen on some Maltese Baroque churches (those on the twin towers of St John's Co-Cathedral in Valletta were removed during the last war). An adaptation imposed on Scamp was the resiting of the Ionic portico originally intended for the main (western) entrance. This was switched to the eastern end to provide a façade for Independence Square, facing the Auberge d'Aragon. The entrance to the cathedral is now from West Street.

Anglican Cathedral from Marsamxett Harbour

Church of St Augustine Corner of Old Bakery and St John Streets. Recently designated the third of Valletta's three parish churches.

Originally constructed in 1572 by Gerolamo Cassar, but rebuilt in 1764 by Domenico Cachia in the Baroque style. It was extensively damaged in the war, and has since been restored and a second belfry added. The interior is in the form of a Greek Cross, the vault richly decorated.

Church of St Dominic Corner of Merchants and St Dominic Streets. The first of Valletta's three parish churches (1571).

This site was acquired by the Dominican fathers in 1571 for their church and convent in place of St Lucia. By a decree of Pope Pius V the new church became the first parish church of Valletta, and hence the mother church of the city. It was rebuilt in 1804 and elevated to the status of Basilica in 1816.

Gesù Church (1592-1600) Corner of Merchants and Archbishop Streets.

This church belongs to the University and forms part of the same block. Its façade is typical of Jesuit churches of the period, with a raised centrepiece and two superimposed orders. The interior is rectangular, the transepts the same depth as the side chapels.

Some fine paintings are all but lost in the gloomy and austere interior. Behind the high altar is Filippo Paladini's *Circumcision*. In the second chapel on the left the altarpiece *St Peter Freed by the Angel* and two lunettes are by Mattia Preti. The altarpiece in the next chapel is *The Return from the Flight* by Giovanni Carracciolo (1570-1637).

A vestibule entered from the fourth bay on the right (or from Archbishop's Street) leads to the *Oratory of the Onorati* (1600). This has beautifully carved and decorated walls and paintings of Biblical subjects by the Maltese artist Stefano Erardi. Opposite is a second oratory, *St Philip*, with fine carving.

Adjoining the church is the *Old University*, now in use as a Junior College (the modern university is at Msida). The University was founded in 1592 by the Jesuits, with the aid of a grant from the King of Spain, as a college for the teaching of Letters, Philosophy and Theology. When Grand Master Pinto expelled the Jesuits from the island in 1768 their property, with the consent of Pope Clement XIV, was turned into a public university (1769) with an additional faculty for medicine and surgery.

Church of St Lucia (1570) East Street facing St Lucia Street.

This elegant little church is one of the earliest in Valletta. It was first used by the Dominican Fathers from Birgu (the first friars to establish themselves in the new city) who lived in a nearby house and tended the spiritual needs of the workmen and earliest inhabitants.

The façade is crowned by a bell tower with four bells. The tower has a statue of *St Lucia* on one side, *St Chiara* on the other and one of *St Paul* on top. There is a side door on to St Barbara Bastion. The interior is barrel vaulted, and the original organ of the church is in the gallery above the main entrance.

Church of St Paul Shipwrecked St Paul Street below St Lucia Street. The second of Valletta's three parish churches (1577).

Designed and started by Gerolamo Cassar, this church is thought to have been finished by the architect and painter Garagona in the late 16th c.

The *interior* is a Latin cross with an unusually wide nave. The side chapels are richly decorated. The *Chapel of the Blessed Sacrament* halfway up the left aisle was designed in 1680 by Lorenzo Gafà. It has a multi-coloured marble floor and fine communion rails; the paintings are by Antoine de Favray. The striking main *altarpiece* of *St Paul's Shipwreck* is by Filippo Paladini. The ceiling frescoes (c. 1900) are by Attilio Palombi of Rome. The beautiful polychrome statue of *St Paul* to the left of the main entrance was created by the Maltese sculptor Melchior Gafà (brother of Lorenzo) in 1657. It is carried in solemn procession on 10 February, when thousands gather in Valletta to commemorate St Paul's shipwreck on the island. The treasures of the church are also displayed on this occasion: a collection of gold and silver artifacts unsurpassed by any other church in Malta.

Church of St Roch (1681) St Ursula Street between St Christopher and Archbishop Streets.

Throughout Malta St Roch (or Roque) was revered as the protector of the plague-afflicted, and the history of any church bearing his name is bound up with the epidemics which so often ravaged the island. After the plague of 1591 the Jurats of the Università vowed that a church dedicated to St Roch would be built in the city of Valletta. The resulting church was enlarged following a second plague in 1675. The benefactor was the Grand Master Carafa and the architect unknown. His church, however, is one of the most ingeniously designed in the city.

The entrance is set in a niche, to avoid an atrium and conserve space. Inside, four barrel vaults support the low dome. The main *altarpiece* is by Stefano Erardi.

Church of St Ursula (1583) Corner of St Ursula and Archbishop Streets.

Reduced to a shell by bombing, this little church has been reconstructed to the original design. It has an unusual façade, showing the Mannerist tendencies which preceded the Baroque. Traditional Maltese elements are the two small windows on either side of the door and the circular 'eye' above.

Verdala Palace $1\frac{1}{2}$m south of Rabat (Saqqajja Square) on the Buskett Road.
Part palace, part castle, Grand Master de Verdalle's summer residence towers four-square above the orange groves of the Buskett Valley. This stately building was designed as a safe summer retreat for the Grand Master, to protect him from the surprise raids of corsairs and Turks. It is a romantic spot: the palace encircled by formal gardens and terraces and beyond them pinewoods thickly carpeted in spring with freesias, asphodels and irises.
Designed by Gerolamo Cassar (the Maltese architect of St John's Conventual Church and the Magisterial Palace in Valletta) Verdala was begun in 1586, the year of the architect's death. Its first three storeys rise to a height of 77ft from the dry moat (from which the building stone was quarried), with bastioned corner towers making a further storey. A bridge over the moat and a flight of steps leads to the *main (first) floor*. The doorway bears a Latin inscription expressing the hope that dew and rain might fall on Mount Verdala —a reminder that the site of the palace, in one of the highest parts of the island, was chosen for its exposure to the cooler elements. The building's only other entrance is from the terrace at the back.

The interior plan is almost symmetrical. The entrance lobby has an ante-room on one side with a beautifully-proportioned oval *staircase* on the other. This striking staircase, with its broad shallow steps (designed for knights in armour) is similar to Cassar's other great staircase in the Magisterial Palace.
The entrance lobby leads to a high barrel-vaulted *hall*, the lunettes at either end showing episodes from de Verdalle's career, painted by the Florentine artist Paladini. Opening out of the hall are four square rooms, two on each side, decorated with frescoes from the time of Grand Master de Vilhena and early British Governors.
The *upper (second) floor* follows the same plan. The French prisoners-of-war detained in 1812 were housed in the great hall on this floor (a chess board carved on one of the stone flags is believed to be their work). The towers are divided into five low storeys containing some small ill-lit cells—for corsairs or deviant knights?
The chapel of *St Anthony the Abbot* in the palace grounds is traditionally attributed to Gerolamo Cassar, although the coat-of-arms of Grand Master Nicolas Cotoner is carved on the main façade and above the altar reredos. The beautiful *Madonna and Saints* is by Mattia Preti.
It is hoped that the palace, now a guest house for foreign dignitaries, will eventually be opened to the public.

Victoria Lines 19th c. fortifications.
Constructed by the British in the 1880s, the line of fortifications runs along the escarpment of the Great Fault. This ridge of high ground, from *Fomm ir-Rih* in the west to the coast below *Bahar-ic-Caghaq* in the east, is a natural defensive line protecting the harbours and heavily populated areas of the south-east from enemy landings in the open bays of the north. The Lines consisted of a series of strong points and forts—*Fort Bingemma*, *Fort Mosta* and *Fort Madliena*—with a continuous breastwork about 5ft high. The forts were armed with large guns brought from England, 38- and 25-tonners. The forts are still among the best preserved of the period, although the breastworks have been damaged by erosion.

Vittoriosa Town on peninsula on east side of Grand Harbour, 3m south of Valletta.
History Vittoriosa (Birgu), one of the 'Three Cities' of the Knights, is Malta's most historic town. Here the Phoenicians found shelter for their trading ships, and built a temple to Astarte on the tip of the promontory. When the Romans followed they rededicated the temple to Juno.
The point was later fortified by the Arabs, who conquered the island in 870 AD. The Normans in turn made their conquest (1090)

Verdala Palace

and made *Birgu* their coastal headquarters. Count Roger built a small church (dedicated to St Lawrence) on the waterfront and Birgu became, with Mdina, one of the two parishes in the island. Throughout the Middle Ages Birgu's fortress—known first as *Castello a Mare* and then as *St Angelo*—was given to a succession of feudal overlords.

In 1430 the fort and governorship of Birgu passed to the de Nava family who remained as governors, or *castellani*, until 1530, when the Order of St John arrived in Malta and set up their Convent here. The Knights built palaces, churches and auberges, and strengthened the fortifications.

After the heroic part played by the citizens of Birgu in the Great Siege of 1565 the town was renamed Vittoriosa. Although the Knights moved their Convent to the new city of Valletta in 1571, Vittoriosa remained their naval centre and enjoyed their patronage. Then for more than 200 years, until the last Inquisitor left in 1798, Vittoriosa became the seat of the Inquisition in Malta.

When Malta passed into the hands of the British in 1800 Vittoriosa continued in its naval tradition. Fort St Angelo became a Royal Navy Establishment and was renamed *HMS St Angelo*. The little peninsula received a tremendous battering in 1942—its second siege—when 69 direct hits were scored on the fortress alone. Fortunately, enough remains or has been restored to give the visitor a picture of Vittoriosa as it was in the days of the Knights.

The fortifications When the Order arrived in Birgu in 1530 Grand Master de L'Isle Adam immediately set about strengthening Fort St Angelo, and in 1532 ordered the construction of landward walls to the town. A few years later Grand Master de Homedes, convinced of the need for further defences, set up a Commission of Engineers to study the problem. The Commission submitted a plan for improving the landward defences. They advised the addition of two posts (Auvergne and Provence) protected by ravelins and joined by a curtain wall (French Curtain). The two posts would be covered by the two most dominant fortifications, the Cavaliers of St James and St John. Two further posts were to be built at the ends of these fortifications: the Post of Castile on the Kalkara side and the Post of Aragon overlooking the galley creek (now Dockyard Creek). A ditch would be built on the landward side, and a line of bastions along Kalkara Creek from the Post of Castile through the Posts of Allemagne and Angleterre to Fort St Angelo. A part of the latter post was pulled down in 1904 to make way for a tennis court, and much of the Post of Aragon destroyed in 1816 by the explosion of an ammunition magazine. No bastions were built on the western shore of Birgu, which was used for the berthing and repairing of galleys.

Walking tour of the fortifications and old city (see map) Starting point: **Advanced Gate** (by Vittoriosa bus stop). This splendidly carved gate, restored in 1722 by Grand Master Manoel de Vilhena (note date and carved relief over gateway) is part of the old *Post of Aragon*, from which one crosses the moat through the *Couvre Porte* to the *Post of France* (the two posts were originally connected by a drawbridge). The next gate is the *Main Gate* of the old city, also restored by de Vilhena.

Entering Main Gate Street (with the *Gate* and *Post of Provence* on the right) one turns left and then right at the rear of *St John's Cavalier*. St John's Tower Street leads along the *French Curtain* to *St James' Cavalier*. Steps lead down beside the cavalier to the *Posts of Genoa and Auvergne*, where the *Gate of Auvergne* leads out to a bridge over the ditch and steps down to Kalkara boatyard. The ditch is planted with olive trees, and air-raid shelters can be seen cut into the walls. The *outer ravelin* beside the Kalkara steps was built by slaves while Fort St Elmo was under siege. (*Note on the Post of Genoa* Unlike the other posts, which were manned by the Langues by which they were named, the Post of Genoa was manned by sailors from a Genoese ship which happened to be in the harbour at the time of the siege.)

Post of Castile The easternmost strongpoint of the Knights' defences (beyond the Post of Genoa) played a vital role in the Great Siege. It was here that the Turks almost broke through and conquered the city. With its hornworks and four lines of defence rising in steps, this is a magnificent *enceinte*, which proved itself in the most desperate hour of the siege. A *plaque* commemorates the wounding of the Grand Master Jean de la Vallette, when he rushed to rally the defenders after the Turks had mined and breached the position.

Advanced Gate, Vittoriosa

It is possible to walk right along the bastions overlooking the creek to the *Post of Angleterre*. At the end of the *Post of Allemagne*, opposite the back of the large Benedictine convent (once the hospital of the Order, see below) steps lead down to the *Infirmary Sally Port* where the wounded from Fort St Elmo were landed during darkness. This is a good starting point for a tour of the historic sites of the old city. (The only buildings open to the public are the churches and the Inquisitor's Palace.)

Hospital of the Order (1531) This was the first *Sacra Infirmeria* of the Knights in Malta. (The front may be seen from St Scholastica Street, reached from Observer Street.) It was enlarged by an additional storey by Grand Master de Homedes in 1538 and the accommodation improved by La Vallette. The wounded of the siege were cared for in this hospital. When the new Infirmary was erected in Valletta the building was transferred (in 1650) to the Benedictine nuns. The adjoining church (1679) dedicated to *St Anne* was designed by Lorenzo Gafà.

St Scholastica Street leads to T Sopran Street and thence to **Vittoriosa Square**. This historic square was La Vallette's Headquarters throughout the siege. Here he encouraged the townsfolk and reviewed his troops. The famous clocktower used as a vedette was destroyed during the war. The *Victory Monument* was erected by Grand Master Perellos. The iron railing is of particular interest: the sword and cross are shown holding down the crescent. On the west of the square, on the pavement, a stone bollard marks the entrance to the Order's *collachio*, or precinct.

Auberge d'Allemagne (1532) On the east side of the square. The building was damaged in the war and a new façade built in 1956. The greater part of the interior survived. The building was used by the German knights until 1571, when the Order transferred officially to Valletta.

Auberge d'Auvergne et Provence (1532) in T Sopran Street, leading off the square, stands this small auberge considerably altered since the 16th c. Part of the façade was rebuilt in 1926, and the whole building is divided into separate private residences. The main door can be seen at No. 17. It was in use until 1571.

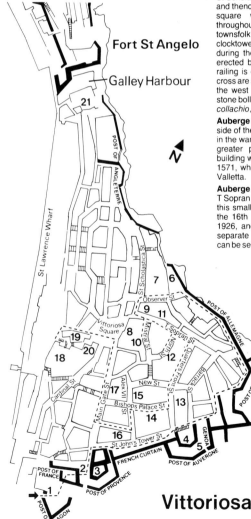

Fort St Angelo

Galley Harbour

St Lawrence Wharf

POST OF ANGLETERRE

St Scholastica St

Observer St

POST OF ALLEMAGNE

Vittoriosa Square

T Sopran St

Mistral St

Quarter St

Barrack St

POST OF CASTILE

Main Gate St

Cardinal St

Alex VII St

New St

Bishops Palace St

St John's Tower St

FRENCH CURTAIN

POST OF PROVENCE

POST OF FRANCE

POST OF ARAGON

GENOA

POST OF AUVERGNE

Vittoriosa

Walking tour
1 Advanced Gate
2 Main Gate
3 St John's Cavalier
4 St James' Cavalier
5 Gate of Auvergne
6 Infirmary Sally Port
7 Hospital of the Order
8 Auberge d'Allemagne
9 Auberge d'Auvergne
   et Provence
10 Auberge d'Angleterre
11 Auberge de France
12 Norman House
13 Armoury
14 Bishop's Palace
15 Residence of the
   Order's Chaplains
16 Palace of the
   Università
17 Inquisitor's Palace
18 St Lawrence
19 Oratory of the
   Holy Crucifix
20 Oratory of St Joseph
21 Auberge d'Italie

Turning up Quarters Front Street, cross New Street and continue towards the fortifications. The big building on the left is the *Armoury*. Built before the Great Siege, it was used for the storage of military equipment before the Knights moved to Valletta (ground floor only). It was subsequently enlarged and used for different purposes. In 1800 it served as the first British Naval Hospital in Malta, and later as a barracks.

In Bishop's Palace Street, leading off Quarters Front Street, is the former *Bishop's Palace*, (Nos 26/29). Erected in 1542 by Bishop Cubelles it was later enlarged. The prisons attached to the palace were destroyed in the early years of this century.

Continuing along Bishop's Palace Street, turn right into Pope Alexander VII Street. At No. 9 is the *Residence of the Order's Chaplains*. This attractive house was bought for the Order's chaplains soon after they arrived in Birgu.

In the reverse direction Pope Alexander VII Street leads to Convent Front Street, where stands the *Palace of the Università*. This palace was built in 1538 by Grand Master de Homedes for the Civil Administration, or Università, of Birgu. It served as the seat of the Università until the latter was abolished by Sir Thomas Maitland in 1818. In 1867 it became the Lyceum of Malta and later, in 1880, it was converted into the first Arts and Technical School. It is now a private residence.

The tour now leads back to the main street by which the town is entered, Main Gate Street. Turn right, in the direction of the square.

Auberge d'Angleterre Halfway up Mistral Street, to the right, is this elegant house, acquired in 1534 by Sir Clement Weston from Catherine Abela. It retains much of its original character. It has five main windows, with a balcony and door under the second from the left. The circular window over the doorway is a Maltese characteristic. The upper windows display the Melitan 'fat' mouldings. The adjoining house belonged to Sir Oliver Starkey, La Vallette's English secretary and Turcopilier of the Order. (The Turcopilier was the head of the cavalry and the coastal defences, an office held by the Prior of the English Langue.)

Auberge de France (1533). Returning to T Sopran Street, one sees at No.24 the most impressive of these modest auberges—an appropriate dwelling, perhaps, for the Langue which had supremacy in the Order. On two floors, its windows are decorated with the heavy roll mouldings (the Melitan 'fat' mouldings) common in Malta after the arrival of the Knights. This building has been recently restored and now houses a museum of political history.

A diversion up North Street, to the right, offers a tantalising glimpse of the island's early domestic architecture. The first houses, on the left, have the 16thc. Maltese windows, and at No. 10/11 is the *Norman House*, an interesting if considerably restored survival.

Inquisitor's Palace This late 16thc. palace was built around the old Castellania (Civil Court) of the Knights. (For hours, see p. 28.) The Inquisition in Malta was unlike that of other European countries. The Inquisitor was a Vatican Delegate sent to deal with disputes between the Grand Master and the Bishop. As the Grand Master, although a sovereign, was also the head of a religious body, differences between the two ecclesiastical dignitaries had to be settled by the Vatican. The impartiality of the Inquisitor had to be maintained, and for this reason his palace was located in Vittoriosa, away from the Order established on the new city of Valletta.

The Inquisitor, like the Grand Master and the Bishop, had his court and his prisons. The prisoners of all three were harshly treated (as were the Knights when they transgressed their code of conduct), but the sombre palace in Vittoriosa was not the scene of the grim tortures practised by the hated Inquisition on the mainland.

The palace is a rambling old building enlarged and altered by successive Inquisitors to accommodate their courts in greater comfort. The severe but imposing façade dates from the mid-17thc. In the *entrance hall*,

Victory Monument, Vittoriosa

remnants of a painted ceiling recall the bomb blast which wrecked the doorway. The great Dominican church and monastery opposite, also destroyed, have since been rebuilt.

The palace is built round a garden and three small courtyards. The *Courtyard of the Castellania* lies to the left of the entrance hall. It was built in 1530 by Niccolò Flavari, who was one of the Knights' architects in Rhodes. (The Gothic arcade is typical of the architecture of the Knights in that island.) To the left are the *kitchens* and ahead a passage leading to a second small courtyard with a garden. Returning to the entrance hall, a passage to the right leads to some of the prisons and a third small courtyard, probably used by the prisoners. Two Arabic inscriptions are engraved on the facing wall: translated they read 'Truly God is with those who patiently persevere' and 'There is no religion except Islam'.

The main *staircase* facing the entrance leads to the Inquisitor's public apartments. The staircase was rebuilt in 1733 by the Inquisitor Stuppanus with the financial help of Pope Clement XII. This is recorded in an inscription at the top of the staircase. The same inscription commemorates the two Inquisitors of Malta who eventually became Popes. They were Fabio Chigi (elected Pope Alexander VII in 1655) and Antonius Pignatelli (elected Pope Innocent XII in 1691). Other inscriptions commemorate the Inquisitor Jacob Carracciolo who between 1706–10 enlarged the palace at his own expense, Inquisitor Frederico Borromeo who restored the façade in 1660, and Inquisitor Tommaso Ruffo who also enlarged the palace between 1694–98. Note the black and white cross on the ceiling, the coat-of-arms of the Inquisition.

From a door on the left of the staircase landing visitors can reach further cells and descend to the garden.

Public apartments At the top of the stairs is the door into the audience and reception rooms. The ceiling of the splendid *main hall* is of carved wood. Beneath are the coats-of-arms of the 62 Inquisitors who lived in the palace. 25 of these became Cardinals: the Cardinal's red hat is depicted above their insignia. On the right of this hall is the *Inquisitor's private chapel* (1700) which contains an interesting folding altar, probably 18th c. The next apartment off the end of the main hall is decorated with the arms of Stuppanus and Pope Clement XII. Beyond are three more halls with decorative friezes. Returning to the main hall, the hall beyond has another painted frieze and a painted wall. At the end is a gallery. A small door to the left of the gallery leads into the *Courtroom of the Inquisition*. There is a second, lower doorway through which the prisoners were obliged to pass, forcing them to bow down before the Inquisitor as they entered.

The *Inquisitor's private quarters* are on the far side of the courtroom, up steps. The palace is furnished with period furniture (mainly 18th c.) and paintings.

The top floor has three other spacious halls embellished with friezes. A covered loggia overlooks the garden. This floor is being restored and at present is not open to the public.

Leaving the Inquisitor's Palace, continue to Vittoriosa Square and then turn left to descend to the waterfront (St Lawrence Landing Place).

Collegiate Church of St Lawrence Although the present building dates only from 1691 this church is steeped in history. It was the island's first parish church, the *San Lorenzo-a-Mare* of Count Roger the Norman. It was later the first Conventual Church of the Order of St John in their new homeland, and then the church of the Inquisitors. In it the survivors of two great sieges gave thanks for their deliverance.

The original church was founded in 1090 and rebuilt on a larger scale in 1505. In 1530 Grand Master de L'Isle Adam and the Council of the Order adopted St Lawrence as their Conventual Church. Unfortunately it was extensively damaged by fire in 1532 and the beautiful tapestries brought by the Order from Rhodes were destroyed. It was in the restored church that Grand Master La Vallette, the Knights and the people of Birgu gathered on 18 May 1565—the day the Turkish fleet was sighted—and it was to this church that they returned in their hour of victory.

In 1571 the Knights of St John left Vittoriosa for Valletta. Their last act before embarking at the wharf was to attend a Pontifical High Mass held by the Grand Prior of the church. Then, no longer the church of the Knights, St Lawrence became the church of the Apostolic Delegates and Inquisitors. For over 200 years the Inquisitors resided in Vittoriosa, proving themselves generous benefactors to the church. The church achieved Collegiate status in 1820.

The present church was built in 1691 to the design of Lorenzo Gafà. With the cathedral in Mdina it stands as the architect's greatest monument. Unhappily it was bombed in the last war and the Chapter Hall, Museum, Sacristy, dome and Chapel of the Blessed Sacrament were destroyed.

The rebuilt church recreates the splendour of the original. The austere and powerful façade is enhanced by the church's setting, high on a plinth looking out on the waterfront and the *Freedom Statue*, commemorating the end of the British military base in 1979. On either side of the main (west) doorway are statues of *St Paul*, patron saint of the island, and *St Lawrence*, patron saint of the city. On the left of the doorway is a tablet with

a Latin inscription by Canon A. Zammit Gabarretta, which translated reads:

'In this principal temple of Vittoriosa, the illustrious City, dedicated to St Lawrence, the Grand Master of the Order of St John, Jean de la Vallette, accompanied by a large multitude of Knights and people of Malta, gave thanks to God, after obtaining victory over the Turks in the year of grace 1565. Ever mindful of that important day, the Chapter and People of this City, known for piety and famed in arms, happily placed this monument in the year of grace 1965.'

The richly decorated *interior* is in the form of a Latin cross. The paintings on the vaults of the nave, choir and transepts depicting scenes from the *Life of St Lawrence* are copies on canvas by Raphael Bonnici Cali (the originals painted directly on to the vault by Ignazio Cortis were too badly bomb-damaged to be restored). The portraits of the Grand Masters of the Order of St John with their coats-of-arms, and the four coats-of-arms of Popes (at the crossing) remind us of the church's past. The four Popes are especially significant: Urban II under whose pontificate St Lawrence was raised to the status of a parish in 1090, Pius VII who made it a Collegiate church in 1890, and Alexander VII and Innocent XII, the former Inquisitors.

The altarpiece *The Martyrdom of St Lawrence* was donated to the church in 1689. Noteworthy is the fine pulpit made from walnut wood from Constantinople, executed in 1889 by Vittoriosa craftsmen, and the wooden pedestal of the statue of *St Lawrence* in the south aisle. The pedestal, made in Vittoriosa in 1903, was shattered in the bombing, but

the pieces were retrieved and put together again.

A side door in the north aisle leads into a little square. To the north is the *Oratory of the Holy Crucifix* (1770). These precincts were the burial ground of those killed in the Turkish incursions of 1551 and during the Great Siege of 1565. The grounds are blessed every year on the morning of 7 September after a Holy Mass for the repose of the dead. Another square, up two flights of steps, is enclosed by the *Oratory of St Joseph* and the *Chapel of Our Lady of Damascus* (c. 1500). The chapel was used by the Greek community who had accompanied the Knights from Rhodes to Malta. In the chapel are preserved the hat and sword of La Vallette, traditionally said to have been placed there when the Grand Master was about to enter the church of St Lawrence for the thanksgiving service at the end of the siege.

Between the chapel and the church is the old Chapter Hall housing a small *museum* containing, among other treasures, relics donated by the Knights and the Inquisitors. These include a small silver cross on which the Grand Masters used to take their oath of office, and a silver altar cross of Byzantine design, both from Rhodes. Also from Rhodes is the set of green velvet sacred vestments donated by Grand Master d'Aubusson in 1476 to the Conventual Church of the Order. A 17th c. white brocaded chasuble was donated by Pope Alexander VII, who resided in Vittoriosa as the Inquisitor Chigi.

If the outer entrance is closed, the museum may be entered via the choir of the church, going through the vestry and up the stairs.

St Lawrence Wharf and Church of St Lawrence (right), Vittoriosa

Auberge d'Italie At the end of St Lawrence Street (see map). This is some distance from the other auberges of Vittoriosa at the end of the peninsula opposite Fort St Angelo. It is now a modern dwelling house (the original was destroyed in the war) and not worth visiting. The reason for the isolated site of this auberge was its necessary access to the wharf (traditionally the post of Admiral of the Navy was held by the Pilier of the Italian Langue).

St Lawrence Wharf This was the headquarters of the Order's Navy. It is reached from the square in front of St Lawrence Church, where stands the 1979 *Freedom Monument*, commemorating Maltese independence.

Passing through the gate, note on the right the *Naval Bakery* (1842). This was built on the site of the slipways for the repair of the Order's galleys. Next is the old palace (1545) built to house the Order's *Treasury*. The ground floor was used as a bakery and when the Treasury was moved to Valletta in 1578 the upper floor became a sail loft for the galleys. The adjoining church, dedicated to *Our Lady of Mount Carmel* (1652), was built from contributions made by the galley crews. It was severely damaged in 1942 but has been restored. Next to the church is a convent and further on the building (1680) which was the *Residence of the Captain-General* of the Order's Fleet. It was bombed and is only partially restored. The two palaces with a modern colonnade in front (now the new Customs House) were the private *Residences of the Captains of the Galleys*. Other buildings on the wharf belonging to the Order's arsenal and fleet were destroyed by the heavy bombing in 1942.

Galley Harbour This boat chamber or moat, separating the fort from Birgu, sheltered the Order's flagship. There was in fact room for two galleys, which could be repaired here in safety. The eastern end of the moat was left solid for defence and to provide protection from the heavy winds of the winter months. The *boat stores* on the right are those originally used by the Knights for refitting their galleys.

Fort St Angelo Although at present closed to the public, it is hoped that this historic monument will soon be made accessible.

This great octagonal fortress dominating Grand Harbour was only a small fort with two guns when the Order of St John arrived in Malta. It was totally inadequate for the defence of the Knights' new home, and Grand Master de L'Isle Adam immediately set about strengthening it. In 1541 Grand Master de Homedes, on the advice of the engineer Ferramolino, built a cavalier and dug a ditch between the fort and Birgu which could be flooded with seawater. The Grand Master who would finally put the defences to the test, Jean de la Vallette (1557–68), built a three-line defence system of batteries at different levels. During the Great Siege of 1565 St Angelo was the key to the Knights' defence, and would have been their last stronghold if Birgu had fallen.

A century later the threat of a Turkish invasion was still present and Grand Master Gregorio Carafa (1680–90) engaged Don Carlos de Grunenberg, engineer to the King of Spain, to advise on the fortifications. At his own expense Grunenberg constructed three great batteries, completing under Grand Master de Wignacourt the great fortress we see today. As the flagship *HMS St Angelo* the fort later became headquarters of the C-in-C Mediterranean, until the departure of the British forces in 1979.

Tour The fort may be approached either by crossing the Grand Harbour by ferry from the Customs House, Valletta, or from the St Lawrence Wharf, Vittoriosa. From the parade ground in front of the fort a steep ramp leads up to the *Main Gateway*.

Before entering the fort it is possible to make a preliminary exploration of the great **Homedes Bastion** to the right. This is entered by a small door at the foot of the bastion (*High Gate*). The thickness of the walls, which can be best appreciated here, reaches 50–60 ft in places. By a labyrinth of passages one reaches the far side of the bastion, adjacent to the moat or Galley Harbour. The *Water Gate* gives access to the moat and from the narrow landing stage one can look up at the old wall of the Arab fort, built of coralline. (For a description of the Galley Harbour, see under *St Lawrence Wharf* above.)

Returning to the *Main Gateway* of the fort, note the inscription above bearing testimony to the works of Grunenberg. Inside the gate, note the groove for the portcullis.

To the right of the gate are the *Slaves' Quarters*, which could hold up to 1000 slaves. (The artist Caravaggio, who fell from favour with the Knights, was imprisoned here.) To the left of the gate, a ramp leads to the upper level of the fort (note on either side the shallow steps, for knights in armour). At the top of the ramp is a *granary*, $32\frac{1}{2}$ ft deep, which could hold 45 tons of wheat.

Galley Harbour, Fort St Angelo

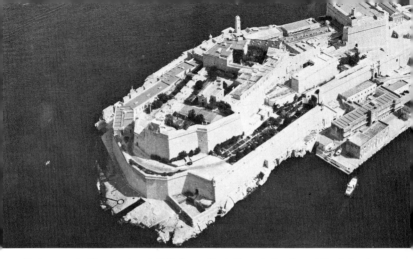

Having ascended the ramp, turn right. On the left is the *Chapel of the Nativity*. This is one of the oldest places of worship in Malta. Hewn out of the rock in the pre-Saracenic period, it was re-dedicated by Count Roger the Norman after his conquest of Malta in 1090. Originally it was the only church in this part of the island, a dependency of the Norman cathedral at Mdina. Under the Knights, after the building of St Lawrence, Vittoriosa, it became the chapel for the fort. In the Second World War it suffered extensive bomb damage, but has been successfully restored.

Opposite the chapel is an *oubliette* discovered in 1903. This is a deep hole, cut out of the solid rock, which served as a prison for the knights who had infringed the rules of the Order. Although the term of their confinement was never more than a few weeks pending their trial, the conditions of their imprisonment can be imagined by those visitors who are able to steel themselves for a brief descent into this tomb of the living. The 24 hours of darkness were relieved by a single hour of daylight when the slab covering the hole was removed for the feeding of the prisoners. Scratched on the walls of the dungeon are various inscriptions and coats-of-arms which bear witness to the fate of these unhappy knights, whose ultimate execution (often by drowning in a weighted sack dropped from the battlements) must have been a happy release.

To the right, a passage and flight of steps lead up to the **cavalier** built by Ferramolino, now used as the saluting base. From here one can enjoy magnificent views of Vittoriosa, Valletta, the creeks of Grand Harbour and the surrounding countryside. On the ramparts is an old *bell* (1716) once used to raise the alarm and now rung on 8 September to commemorate the victorious ending of the

Great Siege. In the days of the Order the cavalier was the flag-tower proudly flying the Order's banner; in this century the guns on the cavalier fired the only salute ever given to a merchant ship, as the gallant crippled *Ohio* finally entered Grand Harbour in August 1942.

Descending from the cavalier, one finds beneath its walls the little *cemetery* used for the victims of the Great Siege. The bodies were deposited in what was originally a water cistern (note the well-head to the right) as there was nowhere else to bury the defenders of the fort who were killed. In 1676 the cemetery was reopened for the victims of the great plague of that year.

Going towards the seaward end of the fort there are two places of interest. The *Captain's House* was built by the de Nava family and altered in 1555 for use as the Magisterial Palace by Grand Master de la Sengle. When the Convent moved to Valletta the palace became the residence of the Governor of the Fort. The interior is not on view.

Chapel of St Anne This attractive little chapel, opposite, was also originally built by the de Nava in the 15th c. It was altered by Grand Master de L'Isle Adam in 1531 when the narrow bays were opened out and the new structure roofed with Gothic vaulting. The chapel is reputed to be built on the site of the Temple of Juno, and the Egyptian granite pillar in the centre is supposed to be from that temple.

In 1935 the chapel (used as a store since the departure of the Knights in 1798) was re-dedicated as the chapel of *HMS St Angelo*. Its association with the Royal Navy is maintained in the roll of honour of British ships lost at sea as a result of enemy action between 1940–45, and the book recording the names of the naval personnel killed in action who are buried in Malta.

Fort St Angelo

Wied-iz-Zurrieq Harbour 7 m south-west of Valletta, approached via Zurrieq or Qrendi. This tiny harbour, tucked beneath the cliff in a narrow inlet, has been here for many centuries. (The police station was once a Knights' tower.) It is the starting point for trips to the **Blue Grotto**, a series of natural caverns in the rock which can be reached by hired boat (charges displayed by the boats). The caves are best seen early in the day, but only when the sun is shining and the water calm. There are two small restaurants.

Wignacourt Aqueduct On the main Valletta–Rabat road running from Fleur-de-Lys roundabout at Santa Venera to Attard.

(The roundabout takes its name from the arch, bearing the French royal *fleur-de-lys* of the Wignacourt arms, which formerly spanned the road at this point. The arch was demolished during the war to allow the passage of military vehicles.)

By the end of the 16th c., the lack of a fresh water supply for the new and rapidly growing city of Valletta was causing considerable concern to the Order of St John. Rainwater in the underground storage tanks and wells was insufficient for the citizens in times of drought, and a water famine was not infrequent. After the exceptionally dry years of 1608–9 the Grand Master Alof de Wignacourt commissioned the building of an aqueduct to carry water to the city from the springs beyond Rabat, 9½ m away. Parts of the aqueduct, completed in 1615, may still be seen on its route (Rabat–Attard–Hamrun–Valletta).

Xemxija Ancient site on north side of St Paul's Bay on road to Mellieha.
Neolithic tombs On the highest point of the Bajda ridge above the village is one of the most interesting of recent archaeological discoveries. The best approach to the site is

to alight from the bus (or leave the car) at Xemxija church. A road to the left leads up to the modern village of *Mistra*. Crossing the field beyond the village (note cart ruts) the visitor should ascend to the knoll above the ridge, the site of the tombs.

The six shaft and chamber tombs were excavated by Prof. J. D. Evans in 1956. Material found dates back to 2800 BC: a few later pieces show that the tombs were in use in the Middle Ages.

As the tombs are not separately identified on the site, a general description will be given of the most important, which is covered by a grille.

A round vertical shaft opens into a small chamber with a domed roof. This chamber has been extended by the addition of small lobed chambers with pillars of rock left between the lobes as roof supports. It is thought that this type of tomb may have been the model for the earliest temples built above ground.

The dead were placed in these tombs on their sides in a crouched position, knees drawn up to the chest. They were entombed with pottery and other objects.

Zabbar (pop. 9700) Town 4 m south-east of Valletta.
½ m to the south of Cospicua, Zabbar is linked to the Three Cities by history. It was here that the Turkish armies encamped after disembarking at Marsaxlokk in 1565, prior to the Great Siege. The growth of the harbour settlements after the siege was shared by that of Zabbar, whose population increased further in the 17th c. when the construction of the Cottonera Lines ensured the inhabitants' future safety.

In the last years of the 18th c. Zabbar came under the patronage of the Grand Master Ferdinand de Hompesch, who raised it to the

Skorba's importance lies in three revelations. First was its identification as a Neolithic village—the first to be discovered in Malta. Second was the retrieval of materials of different prehistoric phases, from Ghar Dalam to Tarxien, which gave the first clear picture of the time-scale of Maltese prehistory. Finally two new phases, earlier than that of the Temple Culture (see p. 32), were discovered. These are indicated by the names *Grey Skorba* and *Red Skorba*, given to hitherto unknown pottery styles dating from 3600 BC and 3400 BC respectively.

The excavations were carried out by Dr D. H. Trump between 1960–63.

Tour At the centre of the site are the remains of a *trefoil temple* of the Ggantija phase, with a tall megalith standing on the inside of the entrance passage. The façade and first two apses have disappeared, but the stone paving of the entrance passage with its five libation holes can be clearly seen. The *torba* floors of the apses also remain (*torba* is a cement-like substance made from crushed globigerina limestone). Fragmentary north walls still stand to a few feet. The temple was modified in the Tarxien phase, when the third (inner) apse was walled off from the internal courtyard with a trilithon and porthole slab entrance with altars set in the corners. Later still, in the Bronze Age, this inner apse was adapted for use as a hut.

To the east of the trefoil temple is a *second temple* built in the Tarxien phase with four apses and a niche, of which little remains but the foundation stones.

By far the most interesting aspect of Skorba was the discovery here of the remains of a **village**, the only prehistoric village site in Malta. This existed on the site of the temples, before the latter were built. Traces of huts of various phases were found, from Grey Skorba (3600 BC) to Ggantija (2400 BC). These would have been of mud brick on stone foundations.

To the west of the trefoil temple, the foundations of a *wall* some 36 ft long were found. This had much valuable material deposited against it, the evidence of the first human occupation of the island c. 4000 BC.

Zebbug (pop. 7800) Village 4 m south-west of Valletta.

In 1777 this old agricultural village was elevated to the status of a city by Grand Master Emmanuel de Rohan. The *De Rohan Arch* commemorating this event is at the entrance to the village on the Valletta road. The village should be entered by the road to the right of this arch, which leads to the main square.

The domestic architecture of Zebbug dates back to the 16th c. Houses of this period, with windows showing the typical Melitan 'fat' mouldings, can be seen in St Anthony Street and in Hospital Square (both approached by the east end of St Philip's Church).

status of a city. It was one of the last acts of Malta's last Grand Master, whose weakness as a ruler was balanced by his regard for the Maltese people. Their response was the construction of a *triumphal arch* dedicated to Hompesch in 1798—the year of his surrender to Napoleon. The arch stands at the junction of the Zabbar–Paola and Zabbar–Zejtun roads.

In 1800 Zabbar (used as a headquarters by the Maltese insurgents) suffered heavy damage from the guns of the French garrison in Vittoriosa.

Parish Church of Our Lady of Grace Standing on the site of an earlier church, this building was designed by Tommaso Dingli and built in 1641. Little of Dingli's work remains. The omission of bell towers from his design displeased the parishioners, and the façade was replaced between 1738–42. Dingli's dome, damaged by the French guns and subsequent earthquake, was replaced in 1928. The architect's work is now mainly seen in the exterior of the chancel and transepts and in the beautiful barrel vault of the nave.

Sanctuary Museum Adjoining the church, this museum was set up in 1954 on the initiative of the then parish priest the Rev. Fr. Joseph Zarb. An ecclesiastical historian, Fr. Zarb has devoted years to the salvage of the church treasures now on display in the museum. He has made a special study of the connection between the Order of St John and the church, demonstrated by the fine collection of maritime votive paintings.

Zebbieh Hamlet 7½ m north-west of Valletta on the Mgarr road. Signposted from Mosta church.

Skorba This important prehistoric site is to the north of the hamlet, reached by the second turning to the left off the Ghajn Tuffieha road. Key at the National Museum.

Church of Our Lady of Grace, Zabbar

Parish Church of St Philip Built in 1599, this church bears the imprint of Gerolamo Cassar, the architect of the Conventual Church (Co-Cathedral) in Valletta, and is probably the work of his son Vittorio. In particular the main doorway with its semi-circular heading, Doric columns and balustrade is almost a replica of that of the Co-Cathedral. The dome, supported on a high octagonal drum with eight rectangular windows, is also in the tradition of the master. The interior of the church is of great richness, with a finely decorated coffered vault.

The oldest church in Zebbug is **St Roque** (1593) in old Main Street to the north of the church. It is typical of the little churches of the period with its bell-cot, plain doorway with circular window above and *zuntier*, or forecourt, in front.

A more ornate church is the lovely little Baroque *Tal l'Abbandunati* (1758). Here the giant corner pilasters of the façade are reminiscent of a classical temple, but the central window above the beautifully carved doorway and the little low side windows are in the tradition of the early Maltese chapels. To find the church from St Philip's Square (5 min. walk) take the road down the right-hand side of the police station on the south side of St Philip's Church (Angel Street), bear right then left at *Our Lady of Angels* church (18th c.). Tal l'Abbandunati stands on the left of the tree-lined road ahead.

Tal Hlas Small church reached by turning off Qormi–Zebbug road short distance west of Siggiewi turning.

This attractive country church was designed by the Maltese architect Lorenzo Gafà, who was responsible for many of the island's most important churches. Tal Hlas has some

interesting features which make it worth a detour. Most unusual is the raised atrium, with porticoes on either side, and the single order on the façade which is not continued on the sides where a string course divides the two stories. A detail common to many of the isolated country churches is the placing of the windows, protected by grilles, on either side of the door. These enabled the priest to say Mass to the people without unlocking the door: a necessary precaution during a time of persistent pirate raids.

Zejtun (pop. 9700) Town 4 m south of Valletta.

The history of this old town reaches back into antiquity. Punic and earlier remains have been found in the locality, and its proximity to Tas Silg, on a height to the north of this important site suggests the area was inhabited in prehistoric times.

Evidence of a flourishing Roman settlement is in the remains of a *Roman villa*, recently discovered in the grounds of the Girls' Secondary School and still under excavation. Built in the early 3rd c. AD, the villa was well equipped with presses for extracting oil. (The name of the town is derived from the Semitic *zejt* meaning 'oil', so it is likely that the oil industry continued during the Arab domination.)

Documents in the Cathedral at Mdina show that as early as 1090 the district was known as 'St Catherine', and in 1436 the parish of St Catherine was established from the villages of Zejtun, Zabbar and Ghaxaq. Among other fine buildings, Zejtun possesses two of the most important ecclesiastical monuments in Malta: its present and former parish churches.

Church of St Roque, Zebbug
Right: Church of St Gregory, Zejtun

Parish Church of St Catherine (1692). This magnificent church is considered by many to be Lorenzo Gafà's finest work. Gregory Bonnici, a nobleman who had property at Zejtun, bought the site in the centre of the village and financed the building of the church for thirty years. The labour was voluntary. The interior was completed in 1720, when the church was opened to the public. The exterior of the church, with its two super-imposed orders and arcaded side walls (serving as a screen for the buttressing) has a classical elegance. Few architects could rival Gafà in his creation of powerful domes, and that of St Catherine is no exception. The distinctive double ribbing, tall lantern and strong octagonal drum are typical of his work. The splendour of the richly painted *interior* is enhanced by Gafà's use of the attic course, seen in many of his other churches.

Old Parish Church of St Gregory This fascinating medieval church, one of the oldest in the island, is situated near the south-east exit of the town. (To reach it from St Catherine's Church, follow St Gregory Street.) Regrettably the church is kept closed (see below), but visitors may apply to the priest of St Catherine's parish church for admission.

The church was built in 1436 on the site of an earlier building. Of this building the nave and façade survive, the latter with a typical low gable and bell-cot. The Renaissance doorway, added by the Knights in the mid-16th c., is an interesting stylistic contradiction to their other modifications.

These entailed the addition of large transepts to the original medieval nave. The transepts are strangely out of proportion to the rest of the building, particularly when viewed from

the outside. Internally they have Gothic vaults which continued the architectural tradition established in Rhodes. The low saucer dome was added at the same time and is the earliest example of a dome in Malta. The drum is solid and the only light source is an opening at the centre of the dome.

The imposing military style of the Knights' architecture, so typical of their buildings in Rhodes, is seen in the massive external walls of the transepts and the narrow windows. One should also note at the east end of the church the sloping base of the external wall, in the style of the Knights' fortifications.

Secret passages In 1969 Mr G. M. Debono, the parish verger, made a strange discovery. While repairing the roof near the dome he noticed a stone slab which was raised a few inches above the surrounding level. The slab was lifted to reveal the entrance to three narrow passages about $2\frac{1}{2}$ ft wide and 6 ft high, with lengths of 30 ft, 41 ft and 31 ft. They lie within the southern transept with their ceiling about 2 ft below the roof. (Their existence explains the disproportionate height of the transepts seen from the outside.)

The first passage, facing east, has three loop-holes overlooking Fort St Thomas at Marsaskala. The second, facing south, has two loop-holes overlooking Fort St Lucian at Marsaxlokk. The third passage along the west wall is blind. In this passage, behind a blocking wall, were found the ancient remains of some fifty persons.

The presence of the remains was a complete mystery, and at present no documentary evidence has been found to account for the fate of these people. The only explanation lies in an examination of the function of the passages. It is assumed that they were incor-

porated in the church by the Knights as a fortified refuge for the parishioners at the time of the corsair raids, and it may be that these people were the victims of a siege.

Permission to view the passages may be obtained from the verger, and a contribution to church funds is suggested. *Important note*: As it no longer serves as the parish church, St Gregory's is invariably closed. The time at which it is most certain to be open is during the Feast of St Catherine in November.

Every year, on the first Wednesday after Easter, St Gregory's is the scene of a great annual pilgrimage from the parish church of Tarxien, commemorating the deliverance of the islands from the Arabs in 1090. The Archbishop, Cathedral Chapter and other notables take part.

Zurrieq (pop. 6500) Village 5 m south-west of Valletta.

Much of this village, one of the original ten parishes of Malta, has survived the time of the Knights. Most interesting is the 17th c. palace known as the *Armeria*, reached by Britannic Street which leads out to the main square of the bus terminus. Towards the end of the Knights' rule it was used as an armoury, supplying arms to the surrounding villages. Its plain façade has a central flight of steps with a balcony over the doorway. The top of a crenellated watch-tower in the garden can be seen from the street. The palace, which is privately owned, contains a collection of furniture and antiques.

The parish church of *St Catherine*, designed by an unknown architect and altered many times, is remarkable only for some very fine paintings by Mattia Preti, who lived for a time in the village. At the back of the house of the parish priest nearby are the considerable remains of a *Punic tower*.

Hal Millieri Location of two historic churches (built between 14th–16th c.) between Zurrieq and Qrendi, to serve a village of this name that has since disappeared. To reach them, turn right off the Qrendi–Mqabba road just outside Qrendi or left outside Zurrieq. (Go up country lane following signs and look out for two churches, one on the right approached through a gate in a walled garden, one isolated on the left further on.)

Church of the Assumption The first of the two churches (enclosed by wall) has an arched vault and contains some remarkable recently restored *murals*, the best examples of their kind in Malta.

St John the Evangelist This little building, now abandoned, has the typical features of a Maltese country chapel, with its low gable, bell-cot, Renaissance door and waterspouts. In the forecourt or *zuntier* stands an interesting survival: a stone *olive crusher* of the Roman period which has been converted into a baptismal font.

Xarolla Windmill North-east of Zurrieq on the road to Safi. The only corn-grinding mill in Malta still in working order, this was one of several erected during the time of Grand Master Manoel de Vilhena. Up to the beginning of the 20th c., windmills were a characteristic feature of the Maltese landscape. They still stand as round towers without sails in the country areas.

Before the time of the Knights animal-driven mills (*centimoli*) were used to grind corn. The wind-driven type was introduced by Grand Master de Homedes, who erected the first in his estate at Senglea. The Order of St John thereafter had a monopoly on the erection and ownership of windmills.

Close by the windmill is the tiny primitive 16th c. church of *St Andrew*.

Church of St John the Evangelist, Hal Millieri

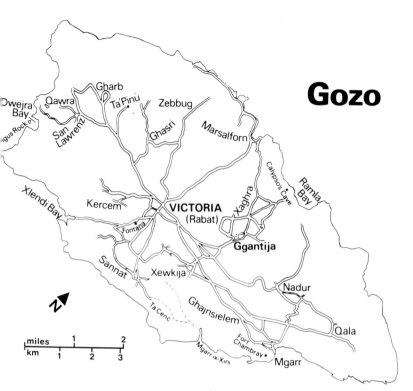

Gozo

The Island Malta's sister island lies four miles to the north across the Fliegu Channel. Between Malta and Gozo is the little island of Comino and the uninhabited islet of Cominotto, part of the diocese of Gozo. The island is 9 miles long and 4½ miles wide, with an area of 26 square miles.

The name by which the Gozitans know their island, 'Ghawdex' (pronounced 'Owdesh'), is a memento of the Arab occupation of the Maltese Islands. Its other name 'Calypso's Isle' springs from a legend surrounding a cave on the north coast. This, it is said, was the dwelling place of Calypso, the nymph who offered Ulysses immortality if he would stay with her forever. In the event the charms of Calypso and her island detained the hero for seven years before his release, at Zeus' command, reminded him of other obligations.

Linking Malta and Gozo is a regular car ferry service which in good weather conditions offers a short 20-minute crossing. The visitor lands at Mgarr harbour, from which there are bus and taxi services to Victoria, the island's capital, a good centre for excursions. (For details of car ferry and bus services, see p. 21.)

The geological structure of Gozo is similar to that of Malta with one important difference—the greater preponderance of blue clay which makes excellent soil. With the large number of springs, this makes Gozo a more fertile and noticeably greener island, with plentiful fruit trees and vines. Fodder is grown in abundance, creating a variety of additional hues. The pale yellow of the indigenous winter sorrel gives way to the springtime fields of silla, the bright crimson clover, and later on, under the summer sun, the tall fennel's brilliant yellow dazzles the eye.

A feature similar to the north of Malta are the steep-sided luxuriant valleys, a continuation of the faults which fractured Malta into a series of limestone ridges. These extend up through the Fliegu Channel (itself a fault depression filled by the sea) into Gozo. The smaller island is generally more hilly, and the flat table-shaped hills are a feature of the landscape. The coastline is jagged with steep cliffs and few inlets. The western cliffs, again like Malta, drop precipitously to the sea, from a maximum altitude of 500 ft.

Gozo's close relationship to Malta goes back to prehistoric times. The similarity of the megalithic temples of Ggantija to those of Tarxien, Mnajdra and others in Malta is evidence of a common culture. Under the Romans, both islands were given the status of a *municipium*, and both were granted local self-government in the Middle Ages under the council known as the Università. The head of

Gozo's Università—the Captain of the Rod—was known as the Hakem.

The subservience of the island to Malta stems from the time of the Knights, when the fear of a takeover of the island by the Turks compelled the Grand Master to abolish the office of Hakem and appoint a governor.

The settlement pattern in Gozo is very different to that in Malta. This is largely due to one catastrophic event: the devastating raid by the Turks in 1551 when almost the entire population was either slaughtered or carried off into slavery. Records, too, were destroyed, but it can be assumed that in the Middle Ages Gozo had its hamlets with the main concentration of population in the Castello and Rabat (Victoria). After the raid recovery was slow, and although some of the slaves were redeemed and the island resettled from Malta, it was not until the Knights built their defensive towers in the mid-17th century that a scattering

Xewkija viewed from Ta Cenc

harbour might be seen as a liability. For most travellers to this peaceful island (even those who must wait for a calm sea) it is seen as its greatest asset.

The economy The Maltese Islands are divided into ten constituencies with Gozo (including Comino) forming the Tenth Electoral Division. Gozo is thus governed as an integral part of the Maltese Islands, with the executive functions of the central government carried out by and through the Head of the Office for Gozo Affairs.

Gozo is predominantly a farming country, and as such plays an important part in the general economy of the islands. Without fruit, vegetables and milk from Gozo, Malta would be more dependent on imported foodstuffs.

The island is noted for its exquisite hand-made lace, while handspun sheep and goat's wool is made up into knitted and crocheted garments. These ancient skills are a great asset to the fast-growing Maltese tourist industry.

of Gozitans left the shelter of the Castello for the countryside. Even so, the villages did not grow to any size until the late 18th and early 19th centuries, when the threat of raids had passed. This explains the straggling layout of Gozitan villages, unlike those of Malta (developed at an earlier date) which have a nucleus of narrow, easily defended streets. The shape of the villages, too, conforms to that of the hills on which they are usually built to conserve the fertile land below.

The landscape may be greener in Gozo, the skyline more uneven than in Malta, but unmistakeably they are sister islands. The images are the same: the Baroque churches soaring above the huddled villages, the honey-coloured stone, the cubic farmhouses and chapels, the brightly-painted fishing boats in the harbours, the ancient pattern of rural life.

In this age of high-speed travel Gozo's lack of an airport or large

Gozitan women

The people The majority of the population of over 24,000 are employed in farming, fishing or lace-making. Animal husbandry is part of their way of life. Like the Maltese, the Gozitans are an extremely hospitable people, though less volatile and more reserved. Like most country-folk they are thrifty and hardworking.

The population is, on the whole, older than in Malta, for many of the young people 'emigrate' to the larger island where there are more opportunities. They invariably do well, and some achieve careers of distinction.

Maltese is spoken, but—as in the rural districts of the larger island—it is more strongly Semitic than urban Maltese.

For information about hotels, restaurants, beaches etc. see Practical Information Section.

Calypso's Cave see **Ramla Bay**

Dwejra Bay West coast, 3½ m west of Victoria, reached from San Lawrenz (½ m).
At the entrance to this rocky U-shaped bay stands the massive *Fungus Rock*, otherwise known as *Il-Gebla tal-General* (The General's Rock). The story behind the two names was the discovery here (by a general in command of the Knights' galleys) of a fungus effective against dysentery and haemorrhages. The fungus was considered by the Order to be so valuable medicinally that Grand Master Pinto forbade the climbing of the rock without his permission. The sides were made vertical, a watchman installed in a cave, and the only access was by a box drawn by pulleys along a rope stretching from the rock to the cliff edge.
The road here also gives access to **Qawra**, otherwise known as the Inland Sea.
This crater-like depression, caused by the collapse of the roof of a large subterranean cave, is now a landlocked fisherman's harbour, the sea entering through a natural tunnel lying under 170 ft of rock. A minute's walk away an impressive rock formation—the *Azure Window*—forms an archway over the sea. It is an area of fossils, mostly shells, embedded in the rocks. The inland sea is good for swimming, and there is a car park and snack bar.

Fontana Architectural monument on outskirts of Victoria ½ m along Victoria–Xlendi road. In the valley on the left-hand side of the road is an arched *public washhouse* built by the Knights. The spring here was a source of water for the people of the town.

Fort Chambray see **Mgarr**

Ggantija Megalithic temples (2800–2400 BC) 1½ m east of Victoria. Approached by right fork ¾ m from the junction of the Xaghra road with the Victoria–Mgarr road.
This magnificent temple complex—a 5-apse temple, a 4-apse temple and a large forecourt—is aptly named 'The Giant's Tower'. The temple block, roughly D-shaped with the adjoining temples sharing a common frontage facing south-east, has a *perimeter wall* of massive coralline boulders (one 18 ft x 20 ft) placed alternately vertically and horizontally. Although these temples have few interior fittings their sheer size and the height of the standing walls makes them the most impressive in the Maltese Islands.
5-apse temple This is the earlier and larger of the two temples. Part of its unrestored façade retains a height of 18 ft. The massive *threshold slab* (**A**) is the largest of its kind in the Maltese islands. In both temples the passages and surviving altar blocks are of globigerina, while the inner walls are of rough coralline boulders. The crevices between the blocks contain fragments which show these walls were once plastered and painted with red ochre.
This temple differs from those in neighbouring Malta in one special feature: the outer apses are smaller than the inner. In the right-hand outer apse (**B**) are *altar blocks* with traces of spiral reliefs similar to those of Tarxien, and a fire-reddened circular *hearth*. The inner passage has the usual bar-holes for securing the door and libation holes in the floor slabs.
The inner apses are majestic in size. That on

Azure Window, Dwejra Bay
Right: Ggantija

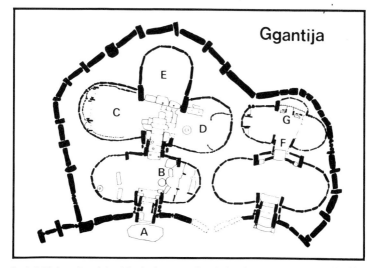

Ggantija

the left (**C**) has altar slabs at the back supported by modern blocks. It was here that the block engraved with a snake (in the Gozo Museum, Victoria) was found. The right apse (**D**) has the remains of an altar niche (with a porthole opening) in the left-hand corner and another hearth towards the centre.

Below the modern boundary wall of the forecourt is a *megalithic wall*.

The central apse (**E**) is raised. Below the pitted step is an *inscription* in Phoenician found when the temple was cleared in 1827. It says 'In the Name of Our God Jehovah' and its origin is a mystery.

4-apse temple This lies to the north and conforms to the usual plan of two large outer apses, two parallel smaller inner apses, and a central niche. The two free-standing *upright slabs* tapering to a narrow base which flank the inner passage (**F**) should be noted. There are traces of an altar in the central niche (**G**).

Ghajnsielem
Village 2½ m south-east of Victoria.

Just to the north of this village is the *Santa Cecilja Tower* (c. 1530) built to overlook the approaches to the bays of Ramla and Mgarr. It now stands empty, the lower floor a sheep pen.

Behind the tower is a *chapel* of unknown antiquity which can be entered by scrambling over a stone wall. Condemned in 1575, it was later re-used. The building is partly carved in the rock. The roof, outer walls and inner rubble walls (with no signs of mortar or plaster) are original. The large lintel over the south door is a Punic block.

Gharb
Village 1 m north-west of Victoria.

Here are some of the oldest houses in the island, many with beautifully carved balconies.

At the entrance to the village from Victoria (on the left) is the house of *Carmela Grima* (see Ta'Pinu). It is distinguished by a plaque. It is occasionally open to the public, and shows how a farmer's house was furnished in the 19th c.

Parish Church of the Immaculate Conception (1732). Dominating the little village from every viewpoint, this is one of the most interesting churches in Gozo. The graceful façade is concave, with a statue of *Faith* over the main door and to the right and left statues of *Hope* and *Charity*. Balustrades encircle the church and adorn the bell towers. The dome, which has no drum, is in proportion to the modest size of the church, and the towers, seen from the front, are an unusually dominant feature.

The *interior* has a circular plan. The main altarpiece, by Gio Nicolo Buhagiar, is of the *Visitation of Our Lady to St Elizabeth*, a gift from Grand Master de Vilhena. The side paintings are by Francesco Zahra.

The old parish church of *Taz-Zejt* (1675–78) with a small cemetery, is about 500 yds to the north-east of the parish church.

Ghasri
Village 1½ m north-west of Victoria.

This village lies at the head of the Ghasri Valley leading down to the *Wied il-Ghasri* (1 m) a scenic spot with rugged cliffs and a deep gorge, a natural fishermen's haven reminiscent of Wied-iz-Zurrieq in Malta. A road from Marsalforn to the *wied* is under construction. In the meantime it can be reached by a country road north from Ghasri along the valley.

The *Gordon Lighthouse* (1856) is reached by the Ghasri Valley road. (The last ¼ m uphill must be done on foot.) The lighthouse, which is open to the public, commands a wonderful view of the Maltese Islands. The light is visible for 45 miles.

Kercem
Village ½ m west of Victoria.

To reach this village by car or on foot from Victoria, go to St Augustine's Square (see map of Victoria). With your back to the monastery, turn left and first left. Continue through Kercem, bearing left, to the *Tal-Lunzjata Valley*. This is the greenest place in Gozo, reserved as a hunting ground for the Grand Masters (some of the towers which they used for shooting can still be seen).

An arched entrance (leave car outside) with a guardhouse and stables leads through to the little *Chapel of the Annunciation* under the cliff, one of the most ancient in Gozo. It dates from 1347 and was rebuilt in 1629. The coat-of-arms in the small sacristy (added in 1700) is that of the Testaferrata family. The altarpiece, the *Annunciation of Our Lady*, is by Fra Luca Garnier, Knight of the Order.

Further along on the opposite side of the valley is a medieval *public washplace*, from which the water was once carried in casks to Victoria. The arch was rebuilt by Grand Master Perellos.

Marsalforn
Village 2 m north-east of Victoria. For details of accommodation, see p. 23.

With its new hotels and villas this fishing village is rapidly growing into a popular seaside resort. Its tiny inner harbour, *Il-Menqa*, shelters the colourful *luzzus* of the local fishermen.

A road leading left out of Marsalforn passes the two little bays of *Qbajjar* and *Xwieni* with a Knights' *redoubt* on the point between and salt pans on the shore. It continues to the Ghasri Valley, from which one has access to the villages of Ghasri and Zebbug.

Mgarr
Village and harbour 3 m south-east of Victoria.

Gozo's only port offers a picture postcard setting, with the steep hill topped by its Gothic church rising above the harbour. Here one can see the gaily-painted Gozo fishing boats, their design unchanged for 500 years. They now operate as cargo boats between Grand Harbour and Mgarr.

Church of the Immaculate Conception, Gharb
Right: Harbour Mgarr

On the heights is the pseudo-Gothic church of *Our Lady of Lourdes* (1888). To the west lie the ramparts of **Fort Chambray**. Designed by the military engineer de Tigné in 1723 as a citadel, it was not until 1749 that work was commenced at the personal expense of the Bailiff Jacques François de Chambray, sometime Commander of the Galleys, who was later to become Governor of Gozo. It was the last of the great fortifications of the Knights, the only one to put up a strong resistance to the French in 1798. The intention to establish a township here on the lines of Valletta was, however, never realised. The inhabitants of Fort Chambray in the next century were chiefly the British garrison and their families, whose presence here is marked by the graves of those of their number who died of fever. There is no admission to the fort, which at present is being developed as a tourist complex.

Mgarr-ix-Xini Inlet on south coast 1 m from Xewkija. Reached by country road along the Xini Valley from Xewkija.
During the period of the Knights this attractive inlet was used as a galley harbour. In earlier days it was a landing place for corsairs in their attacks on the island. The tower was built in 1658.

Nadur Village 3 m west of Victoria.
This village, situated on the heights above the fertile valleys of Ramla, San Blas and Dahlet Qorrot is the largest in the island, centre of a fruit-growing district which was once the game preserve of Grand Master de Wignacourt.
The parish church of *SS Peter and Paul*, designed in 1760 by Giuseppe Bonici, has a monumental grandeur, with a 19th c. façade and dome—strongly neo-classical—added to the Baroque original. The interior decoration is lavish, the walls and pillars faced in multi-coloured marble as at Xaghra. The *ceiling paintings* depict scenes from the lives of the two saints, and their fine *processional statue*, made in France in 1885, is in the right aisle. The skeleton of *St Coronatus*, the best preserved relic in the two islands, lies over the altar of Our Lady of Carmel in the right transept.

Qala Village 4 m west of Victoria.
To the north of the village is an 18th c. *windmill*.
Sanctuary of the Immaculate Conception (17th c.) 1 m east of the parish church along Immaculate Conception Street. The sanctuary has been a place of pilgrimage for many centuries. The original chapel was erected in the time of the Normans. Inside the entrance, to the left, steps lead down to a grave said to be that of the 15th c. hermit *St Kerrew*. It is a place of devotion, particularly for mothers with sick children. The *altarpiece*, the work of the Italian Frederico Barocci (1535–1612) was presented to the church by Bishop Cagliares in 1615.
On the outside of the walls are numerous graffiti of ships of the 17th and 18th c.

Qawra see **Dwejra Bay**

Rabat see **Victoria**

Ramla Bay 2 m north-west of Victoria.
Reached by turning left off the Victoria–Mgarr road 1 m from Victoria, or via Nadur. A clear expanse of red-tinted sand sheltered by shallow cliffs makes this the best sandy beach in the Maltese Islands. Apart from a new restaurant tucked into the cliff under Calypso's cave, this beach has no tourist facilities: a situation which one hopes for the sake of the view will be preserved.
At the western end of the bay the ground plan of a Roman villa could once be seen: it is now covered by sand. Artifacts found during excavation are in the Gozo Museum, Victoria. Above the villa site are the remains of a Knights' *redoubt*, and a few feet under the

sea, spanning the bay, is a *wall* built by the Knights to deter enemy landings.

High on the western arm of the bay is *Calypso's Cave*. Traditionally this is the cave where the shipwrecked Ulysses dwelt for seven years with the nymph Calypso, daughter of Atlas. The cave, with a marvellous view of the bay and valley below, is said once to have reached down to the sea, but the passages have now been blocked by rock falls. This is one of the many legends woven into the story of Gozo, 'Calypso's Isle'.

San Lawrenz Village 2½ m north-west of Victoria.

One of the older villages, although the present parish church is of recent construction. From here one can reach *Dwejra Bay* and *Qawra* (see entries).

Sannat Village 1 m south of Victoria.

Gozo's principal lace-making village. At the entrance from Victoria stands a Knights' *tower*.

Ta Cenc Beauty spot reached via Sannat. From the left-hand side of Sannat church, follow signs, keeping left at last fork before hotel. (The hotel is signposted 'Ta Cenc', but should be avoided as there is no through road from it.)

This rocky plateau has awe-inspiring cliffs dropping vertically 470ft to the sea. It is a place of solitude, of birds and lizards and dolmens. A track, difficult for cars, leads down to *Mgarr-ix-Xini* (see entry).

Ta Pinu Basilica situated ½ m along side road turning right at junction on Victoria–Gharb road, 1½ m west of Victoria.

This imposing church, built 1920–36, stands in the open country in isolated splendour. The exterior is neo-Romanesque, with a 154ft high detached campanile. It encloses a much venerated 16thc. barrel-vaulted

chapel, now found behind the apse in the form of a Lady Chapel. The history of the modern basilica begins with this little chapel of *Ta Pinu*, which takes its name from a certain Pinu Gauci who was entrusted with its care in the middle of the 17thc.

On the morning of 22 June 1883 a peasant woman, Carmela Grima, was passing Ta Pinu on her way home to Gharb when she heard a voice calling her to the chapel. As she knelt in prayer the voice again spoke to her, commanding her to say her *Ave Maria* three times 'in memory of the three days My Body lay in the Sepulchre'. It was then revealed that on six occasions Francesco Portelli, another villager from Gharb, had also heard the voice. In 1887, amid intense excitement, the two were interviewed by Bishop Pietro Pace. Numerous cures and acts of grace were then attributed to the intercession of Our Lady of Pinu, and the shrine became a place of pilgrimage.

Victoria (Rabat) (pop. 5000) Capital of Gozo. For details of accommodation, see p. 23.

The Diamond Jubilee of Queen Victoria is commemorated in the name of this town. The Maltese, however, know it as 'Rabat': a more appropriate name when one compares it with the Rabat in Malta. Both towns feature a citadel and adjoining suburb and are located some distance inland. The citadel hill which dominates the town (*Il Kastell*, or the *Gran Castello*) was first occupied by the Arabs. The Normans extended it to the slopes below the hill to the south, the site of the present old town which belongs mainly to the period of the Knights (see below).

It Tokk This is the main tree-lined square separating the old town from the citadel. On the west of the square stands Grand Master de Vilhena's Baroque *Banca Giuratale* (1733) now the Department of Information.

Ramla Bay Opposite: Cathedral, Victoria

Old Town With its maze of narrow streets, this part of Gozo is well worth exploring for the architectural details of previous centuries. Like Gharb it has many beautiful old carved balconies.

In Market Street, leading off It Tokk, is the *Basilica of St George* (1678) designed by Vittorio Cassar. The church was originally composed only of the nave. Of recent construction are the aisles (1935), the dome (1939) and the transepts (1945). The finished composition is, however, satisfying. The church has a rich interior, glowing with light from the stained glass windows. Prominent is the marble and bronze *canopy* over the high altar, a copy in miniature of Bernini's canopy in St Peter's, Rome. The vault paintings depicting episodes from the *Life of St George* are by the Italian Gian Battista Conti. The main altarpiece, *St George and the Dragon*, and the altarpiece in the left transept are by Mattia Preti. The statue of *St George* is the work of a local artist, Paola Azzopardi, and was carved out of a tree trunk.

Rundle Gardens East of It Tokk, down Republic St, these gardens were planted in 1914–15 and named after Sir Leslie Rundle, Governor of Malta 1909–15.

Citadel Approached from the north-west corner of It Tokk by Castle Hill. A recent archway gives direct access to the square in front of the cathedral. The original gate is to the right. Embedded in the wall is a Roman *inscription* commemorating the erection of a statue to a certain Marco Vallio by the people of Gozo during the reign of the Emperor Antoninus Pius (138–161 AD) when the island was a Roman *municipium*.

Cathedral (1697–1711) This impressive building was designed by Lorenzo Gafà (architect of the Cathedral of Mdina, Malta) to replace a Collegiate church badly damaged in the earthquake of 1693.

The site is arresting. The restrained Baroque façade is splendidly set off by the flights of steps leading up from the little square. There is a single bell tower. Although Gafà was noted for his domes, the feature is missing from this building. Instead, the illusion of one is created in the interior by the use of a *trompe l'oeil panel* over the crossing painted by Antonio Manuele of Messina. The effect is enhanced by the height of the vault, raised by Gafà's use of tall pilasters and an attic course.

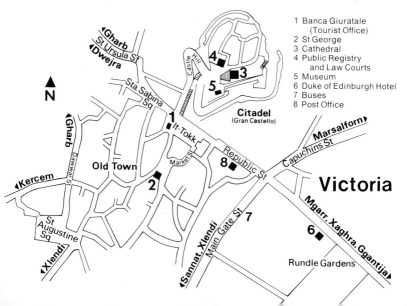

1 Banca Giuratale (Tourist Office)
2 St George
3 Cathedral
4 Public Registry and Law Courts
5 Museum
6 Duke of Edinburgh Hotel
7 Buses
8 Post Office

The *high altar* (the green is malachite) is the work of Vincenzo Belli and was brought from Rome in 1885. The *baptismal fonts* (1742) are of marble from the Zebbug area.

On the north side of the square is the *Public Registry*, which before 1551 was the residence of the Hakem of Gozo. (The Hakem was the Captain of the Rod of the Gozo Università.) Melitan 'fat' mouldings seen on early buildings decorate the upper windows. Adjoining are the *Law Courts* built by Grand Master de Wignacourt in the 17th c.

A small arch on the south side of the cathedral leads to the *Casa Bondi* (17th c.) restored by Sir Harry Luke in 1937. This now houses Gozo's Museum.

Museum With one exception the exhibits here are of material discovered in the island of Gozo.

Ground floor
Room on left Contains three Roman inscriptions and a Punic inscription. The alabaster statuette of *Romulus and Remus* was found in 1720 and was the property of Grand Master Pinto. The 1st c. AD *oscillum*, carved in low relief, was found in Ramla Bay.

Room on right To the right, tombstone (1270 AD) from St Augustine cemetery. *Inscriptions* of the period of the Knights, including one (1579) to the noble Sicilian Bernardo Dopuo who died fighting the Turks in 1551 after killing his wife and daughters to save them from slavery.

Outside Two passages winding through the walls were tunnelled as an escape route after

the siege of 1551. The inscribed blocks of stone are from the *Gorgion Tower* (17th c.), built to defend Xewkija, which was pulled down in 1943 to make way for an airstrip.

First floor
Top of stairs and room on right Amphorae and anchors from a Roman wreck discovered on the seabed off Xlendi.

Room on left A small numismatic collection. *Saracenic tombstone* (1173 AD). The pathetic inscription laments the death of Majmuna who died at the age of 12.

Main room Go anti-clockwise. To the right of the door, *Case 1*: contains pottery from Ghar Dalam to Tarxien phases (Santa Verna Temple). Beside it, a *block* with relief of snake and phallic emblem from Ggantija. *Case 2*: Relics from Roman villa at Ramla and Punic amphora and contents found at Santa Marija Bay, Comino. The contents were under the split amphora, weighed down with stones

Top: Citadel, Victoria
Above: Restored balcony on Casa Bondi, Victoria

In the village square stands the parish church of *Our Lady of Victory* (18th c.). This fine church has an unusual interior, with wide aisles and massive columns faced with inlaid marble. There are ten side chapels. The main altarpiece is of the *Nativity of Our Lady* and the paintings in the transepts are of the *Victory of the Great Siege* and the *Victory of the Christians over the Turkish Fleet at Lepanto in 1571*. The charming statue of the *Bambina* (Our Lady as a Girl) is in the third chapel of the right aisle. It was made in Marseilles in 1873.

In the village are two caves of prehistoric interest. The first, *Xerri's Grotto*, is reached by taking Church Street out of the square, then Bullara and Xerri's Grotto Street. *Ninu's Grotto* is in January Street to the north of the church. Both lie under private houses (open to the public) and have stalagmite and stalactite formations.

Xewkija
Village 1½ m south-east of Victoria.

Rotunda Xewkija's new parish church, dedicated to St John the Baptist, has been largely built by voluntary village labour and subscriptions. The foundation stone was laid in 1952, and the church completed in 1971.

Inspired by the church of Santa Maria della Salute in Venice, this building was designed by Giuseppe Damato, who built the new parish church of Christ the King at Paola. Beneath the huge dome, the feeling of space is tremendous. This dome is said to rival that of Mosta, but in fact is smaller with an external diameter of 90 ft (Mosta is 118 ft) and a height of 245 ft. It can seat a congregation of 4000. It was built over the old parish church, which acted as a core for the new building. (A similar technique was used at Mosta, the old church being dismantled when the new one was complete.)

Xlendi Bay
1½ m south-west of Victoria. For details of accommodation see p. 23.

Lying at the foot of a fertile valley, this is one of the prettiest bays in the Maltese Islands, but in danger of being ruined by overdevelopment. Nevertheless with its row of small houses on the waterfront and benches under the tamarisk trees, the character of the fishing village is retained. A *tower* (1658) guards the bay.

Zebbug
Village 1½ m north of Victoria.

This straggling village is one of the highest in Gozo and is surrounded by fertile agricultural land. Fine quality marble was once quarried from the outskirts of the village and used for many of the Maltese church altars, including the altar of St George's Chapel in the Co-Cathedral, Valletta.

The parish church dedicated to the *Assumption of Our Lady* was built in 1736 and enlarged in 1938.

and buried in sand. *Case 3*: Local Punic and Roman pottery. *Case 4*: Contents of local Punic tombs. Cinerary urn (glass) 2nd c. AD. *Case 5*: Tarxien cemetery phase pottery from Xaghra and Victoria. *Case 6*: Ggantija phase pottery from Xaghra. *Case 7*: Material from Ggantija temples.

To the left of the cathedral, Fosse Street leads up to the *Cathedral Museum*. Off this street to the left is Milite Bernardo Street, with the *Folk Art Museum* in a medieval building with Siculo-Norman windows. The medieval *citadel* is sadly ruined, but a tour of the ramparts (start from Quarters Street off the square by the Law Courts) gives wonderful views of the surrounding countryside.

Xaghra
Village 2 m east of Victoria.

The village straggles across a plateau rich in archaeology, with its main feature the dramatic temples of *Ggantija* (see entry).

Top: Citadel fortifications
Above: Xlendi Bay

BOOKS ON MALTA

Archaeology

Evans, J. D. *The Prehistoric Antiquities of the Maltese Islands* (Athlone Press, 1971)

Ridley, Michael *The Megalithic Art of the Maltese Islands* (The Dolphin Press, 1971)

Trump, D. H. *Malta: An Archaeological Guide* (Faber & Faber, 1972)

History

Bradford, Ernle *The Great Siege of Malta, 1565* (Hodder & Stoughton, 1961 and Penguin Books)
The Shield and the Sword: The Knights of Malta (Hodder & Stoughton 1972 and Fontana)

Evans, J. D. *Malta* (Ancient Peoples & Places Series, Thames & Hudson, 1959)

Perowne, Stewart *The Siege Within the Walls: Malta 1940–43* (Hodder & Stoughton 1970)

Schermerhorn, E. *Malta of the Knights* (Heinemann, 1929)

Scicluna, Sir Hannibal P. *The Church of St John in Valletta* (Malta, M. Danesi, 1955)
A Short History of the Knights Hospitallers of St John of Jerusalem, Rhodes & Malta (Malta, Empire Press, 1970)

Architecture

Braun, Hugh *Introduction to Maltese Architecture* (Malta, Progress Press, 1957)

Denaro, Victor F. *The Houses of Valletta* (Malta, Progress Press, 1967)

Hughes, Quentin *The Building of Malta 1530–1795* (Alex Tiranti, 1956)

Fortress: Architecture and Military History in Malta (Lund Humphries, 1969)

Natural History

Borg, John *Descriptive Flora of the Maltese Islands including the Ferns and Flowering Plants* (Malta, 1927)

Folklore

Cassar-Pullicino, Joseph *Studies in Maltese Folklore* (University of Malta, 1976)

General

Blouet, Brian *The Story of Malta* (Faber & Faber, 1967)

Boissevain, Jeremy *Saints and Fireworks* (Athlone Press, 1965)

Bryans, Robin *Malta and Gozo* (Faber & Faber, 1966)

Hogg, Garry *Malta: Blue Water Island* (Allen & Unwin, 1967)

Kummerly, Walter *Malta, Isles of the Middle Sea* (Harrap, 1965)

Luke, Sir Harry *Malta: An Account and Appreciation* (Harrap, 1960)

Monsarrat, Nicholas *The Kappillan of Malta* (Novel) (Cassell & Co 1973 and Pan Books)

Owen, Charles *The Maltese Islands* (David & Charles, 1969)